Michael W. Kirst

The New Accountability

The New Accountability
High Schools and
High-Stakes Testing

Edited by
Martin Carnoy, Richard Elmore,
and **Leslie Santee Siskin**

RoutledgeFalmer
NEW YORK AND LONDON

Published in 2003 by
RoutledgeFalmer
29 West 35th Street
New York, NY 10001
www.routledge-ny.com

Published in Great Britain by
RoutledgeFalmer
11 New Fetter Lane
London EC4P 4EE
www.routledge.co.uk

RoutledgeFalmer is an imprint of the Taylor and Francis Group.

Printed in the United Stated of America on acid-free paper.

10 9 8 7 6 5 4 3 2 1

Library of Congress Cataloging-in-Publication Data

The new accountability : high schools and high-stakes testing /
edited by Martin Carnoy, Richard Elmore, and Leslie Santee Siskin.
     p. cm.
Includes bibliographical references and index.
   ISBN 0-415-94704-9 (hardcover : alk. paper) — ISBN 0-415-94705-7
(pbk. : alk. paper)
   1. Educational accountability—United States—Case studies. 2. High schools—
Standards—United States—Case studies. 3. School improvement programs—United
States—Case studies. I. Carnoy, Martin. II. Elmore, Richard F. III. Siskin, Leslie Santee.
   LB2806.22.H54 2003
   379.1'58—dc21
                                                                    2003001504

Contents

Introduction

This book is about the encounter between an established but troubled institution—the American high school—and a deep-seated impulse in our society to make things better. Underlying this encounter are two seemingly incompatible movements in American education: the inexorable increase in the number of years that young people stay in school and the reforms to improve how much students learn at each level of schooling. In today's global economy and increasingly unequal society, the two movements meet their greatest challenge in America's high schools.

High school is where low-income young people—many of them African Americans and Latinos—who now make-up a higher fraction of students than in the past, make it or break it educationally. High school determines how they will be incorporated into the work world and other social structures. High school is also where educational reformers' efforts to improve how much students learn face the acid test. If students do not finish high school with their cohort, they are likely to be marginalized from the mainstream, and to become a social liability. So, reforms aiming to improve educational quality must ultimately be evaluated in terms of improving high school completion rates. And our understanding of whether educational reforms as a whole are succeeding or failing is to be found most clearly in America's high schools.

High schools are established institutions with established structures and established ways of doing things. They have been changed in the past fifty years, but mainly in ways to accommodate an increasingly diverse population. If we assume that their charge was to graduate this youth population, they have had mixed success. The bad news is that the absolute number of high school completers was about the same in 2000 as in 1970, but the proportion of seventeen year olds who completed fell from 76 to 71 percent (National Center of Education Statistics 2001, table 103). The good news is that the percentage of high school graduates who go on to college rose from about one-half to almost two-thirds (NCES 2001, table 185). The percentage of students in high school taking higher level math and science courses in high school has also risen steadily since the early 1980s (NCES 2001, table 142), and the percentage of high school graduates taking the SAT college entrance tests has risen from 32 percent to 45 percent since 1978, with almost no decline in the average math score and only modest decline in the average verbal score (National Center of Education Statistics, 1979, p. 67; 2001, table 137). These generally positive results on the SAT occurred despite massive immigration of non-English speakers into American schools. The percent taking the ACT test also rose, from 26 percent of graduates in 1978 to 38 percent in 2000. Average scores on the ACT rose in this period (NCES, 2001, table 138). So, although it is widely argued that the quality of a high school degree has fallen in the past thirty years, the main problem in high school is that the percentage of young people *getting* a degree with their high school class hit a wall at 75 percent of the age cohort, and has since declined.

Many of the earlier criticisms of high schools were based on how poorly prepared high school *graduates* were. Ernest Boyer produced a set of damning reports about the failure of high schools and of graduates (Boyer 1983). *A Nation at Risk* also criticized the low standards and skills of graduates (National Commission on Excellence in Education 1983). Other researchers argued that too few students took challenging coursework, either because they were "tracked" into dead end curricula (Oakes 1985), or because they chose poorly from the vastly varied array of courses in the "shopping mall high schools" (Powell, Farrar, and Cohen 1985). Ted Sizer saw the problem as high school teachers isolated in classrooms, trapped with resistant students within a rampant bureaucracy, and forced to "compromise" their own academic standards (Sizer 1984).

Although the problem of overall performance of high school students, including graduates, still dominates political rhetoric, the polarization of high school outcomes—increased dropouts at one end and increased college attendance for high school graduates at the other end—also has educators and policy makers justifiably worried (Fine 1991). As the Rhoten et al. essay in this volume suggests, it is as much the seemingly dismal performance of schools catering to low-income students as the amount learned by the average student that spawned the most recent rounds of educational reform.

The major educational reform movement of the past twenty years is standards-based accountability. The current wave of assessment-based school accountability reforms combines two traditions in American education: public accountability and student testing. In the past, accountability and assessment were only loosely connected. Assessment was used mainly to divide students into academic tracks or for diagnostic purposes, helping school administrators and teachers see whether students were learning loosely defined state curricula. Accountability has traditionally been based in community participation and parent control, as represented by local school boards. Schools have been accountable to district administrators, who, in turn, answer to elected boards.[1] Parents have also been able to influence schools directly. School test results enter into parental decisions about where to live and fuel parent criticisms of school board actions, especially in higher income neighborhoods.[2] The link between traditional local accountability and traditional student assessment has long been important in neighborhoods with high parent participation. In the majority of schools, however, this link has either been indirect, acting through family residential choice, or practically nonexistent. It has been especially weak in low-income communities and large urban school districts.

In the late 1990s, a group of professors and graduate students at Stanford and Harvard Universities, as part of a Consortium for Policy Research in Education (CPRE) project funded by the Office of Educational Research and Improvement of the U.S. Department of Education, researched this traditional notion of internal (local) accountability in about twenty-five public and private schools—elementary, middle, and high schools—in the Boston area and in California's two major metropolitan areas.

We developed a relatively simple working theory of school *internal accountability* (this is described more fully by Abelmann and Elmore 1999). The theory is based on the premise that schools actually have conceptions of accountability embedded in the patterns of their day-to-day operations, and that a school's conception of accountability significantly influences how it delivers education. We assume that schools must solve the problem of accountability in some way in order to function, and that the way they solve this problem is reflected in the way teachers, administrators, students and parents talk about the fundamental issues of schooling. We also assume that formal, external accountability systems—such as state or district bureaucracies, or market forces—are only one among many factors that influence a school's internal sense of accountability.

Schools form their conceptions of accountability from a variety of sources, including individual teachers' and administrators' beliefs about teaching and learning, their shared understanding of who their students are, the routines they develop for getting their work done, and the external expectations from parents, communities, and administrative agencies under which they work. To capture this construction of accountability, our theory posits a relationship among three tiers—the individual's sense of accountability, or *responsibility*; parents', teachers', administrators', and students' collective sense of accountability, or *expectations*; and the organizational rules, incentives, and implementation mechanisms that constitute the *formal accountability* system in schools. These accountability mechanisms represent the variety of ways, formal and informal, in which people in schools (including parents, in some cases) *give an account* of their actions to someone in a position of formal authority inside or outside the school. Mechanisms are *formal* when they are recorded in a policy handbook or as part of a union contract. *Informal* mechanisms refer to a set of measures that school actors respond to, regardless of what bureaucratic rules and regulations in fact say, that are "organic" to that particular school culture. Mechanisms can also vary in the consequences they carry for success or failure. They can be *low stakes*, resulting only in approval or disapproval by, say, the principal. Or they can be *high stakes*, involving public disclosure or financial sanctions and rewards.

In this working theory, responsibility, expectations, and accountability operate in a mutual relationship with each other. This relationship varies from school to school. A given school's response to the problem of accountability is a product of how it resolves the conflicts and complementarities between individuals' internalized notions of accountability, their shared expectations, and formal and informal mechanisms that push them to account to someone else for what they do. Schools are likely to have more "operative" internal accountability systems if their formal and informal mechanisms are *aligned with* individuals' internalized notions of accountability (responsibility) and collective expectations of the school (Abelmann and Elmore 1999). At the other extreme, a high degree of incoherence among the three levels of accountability translates into a relatively weak or dysfunctional internal accountability system. This would be the case, for example, when a principal forces teachers to adhere to rules that they know result in poor academic outcomes (Chubb and Moe 1980).

We found that schools varied a great deal in their alignment, but that the "default" mode—the most likely system of internal accountability—is one of "atomization" rather than alignment. Most schools we studied operated on internal accountability systems that, beyond the formality of taking attendance, began and ended with individual teachers and parents. In the "default mode," accountability is a classroom and home event and the two are largely unconnected. Far from having "aligned" internal accountability systems, most schools we saw were a collection of "atomistic" accountability systems.

To the degree that individual teachers and parents are excellent educators, with a high level of content knowledge and pedagogical skills, with good information collection systems, such an atomistic accountability system could still produce high levels of student learning. Schools in our sample catering to students with more highly educated parents also tended to have more alignment because of greater parent communication with teachers than schools catering to students with less educated parents. But we found that more learning may actually take place in a highly aligned, low-income, urban school than in many atomistic suburban schools.

Schools not only vary on the degree of alignment between the different levels of accountability, but also on *what* they consider themselves to be accountable for. A school can exhibit a high degree of alignment around student academic achievement or it may organize itself around order and discipline in the classrooms with little or no coherence with regard to academic goals. We also found that private schools were just as likely to be in the "default mode" as public schools.

Because of this tendency for schools to have atomized internal accountability systems and because reformers and politicians believe that greater accountability means better student performance, they have focused on imposing new types of formal accountability from outside the school and the school district—from the state. When we were doing our study of schools' internal accountability systems, external accountability was just coming on line in California and Massachusetts, the two states in which we were conducting our survey. If we had done our work in Kentucky, North Carolina, or Texas, the schools we were studying would have already been heavily influenced by external accountability systems.

Given our new understanding of how schools managed themselves internally and how they may be influenced by district level policies, we wanted to find out how state-imposed accountability would change this management. Does external accountability tend to "align" atomistic schools around clearly defined goals? Does external accountability help less aligned schools more than aligned schools? What does external accountability do to schools that are already aligned but around something different from state standards?

In the second round of our study of accountability, we chose to analyze the impact of state accountability systems on high schools' internal accountability in four states. At least two of these, New York and Texas, had *high stakes* accountability systems for secondary schools. High stakes implies here that there are rewards and sanctions for students and schools associated with the accountability systems. In high schools, this translates into a high school "exit test" that all students are required to pass in order to graduate. Schools whose students fail to pass such a test in sufficient numbers are sanctioned by the state—the principal may be fired or the school may have to accept reorganization.

We chose to focus on high schools for several reasons:

- High schools are now the key institution in the schooling process—as mentioned in our discussion above, they are the "make or break" point for students.
- In evaluating the potential impact of accountability reforms, it is crucial to understand how high schools respond to high stakes testing, the imposition of new course standards (required algebra, for example), and sanctions and rewards for schools that did badly or well on state-mandated tests and standards. We wanted to know whether schools with less "alignment," ostensibly the target of these new external accountability systems, were more or less likely to become more aligned in response to the new demands.
- Given their departmental structure and very size, high schools seem to be especially difficult institutions to "align." We wanted to know whether some parts/subunits of a whole school could be aligned but not others, or whether they could be aligned in different ways.

The expressed purpose of the new state accountability systems is to raise student achievement and, more generally, to improve the quality of schooling. By testing pupils, states hope to provide performance benchmarks for schools that would, in President Bush's words, "leave no child behind." School administrators and teachers, exposed to scrutiny by published test scores, are expected to improve educational delivery to avoid "failing" and to gain the rewards of high academic achievement.

By 2001, forty-nine states had adopted some form of standards-based reform, and thirty-three had established the central components of an accountability system (Goertz and Duffy 2001). While few states have yet to fully meet the ambitious standards set by federal agencies and national advocacy groups, two of the states of the four we chose—Texas and Kentucky—are among the earliest that implemented standards-based reform. New York has the oldest high stakes high school test in the nation, the Regents Exam, which was a voluntary test meant for college bound students, but is now applied to all high school students in the state as a graduation requirement. Vermont is a case where the state brought different kinds of pressures to bear on schools.

The origins of the new accountability systems in Kentucky and Texas were rooted in litigation by lower-income districts to gain greater equality of financial resources and school outcomes. In New York, the reform has its roots at the "top" of the system, where the education commissioner and the legislators issued the mandate that all students would have to pass a redesigned version of the traditional Regents Examination. The underlying theory of accountability in the Vermont model is a hybrid of the state's strong tradition of local control and a recently added, more assertive and visible state role, independent of local boards and schools, in imposing standards of content and performance. Furthermore, New York and Vermont's accountability systems have also been recently impacted by financial equity litigation.

In designing our study of high schools in the four states, we wanted to capture the response of different "kinds" of public schools in each state to accountability reforms. We studied three schools in each of three states (Kentucky, New York, Vermont) and six schools in Texas.

In two states, these schools are all within a single (urban) district: "Tate County" in Kentucky and "River City" in New York. In Texas, the six schools we studied were in "Major City" and "West City" (all district and school names are pseudonyms). In Vermont, the three schools were in different districts. The three schools in each state were "positioned" somewhat differently with respect to accountability policies. We selected one as the "target" of the reform (a school that had not been performing well by traditional measures, but that had not been declared failing or selected for reconstitution). One school was somewhat "better positioned" (not a highly selective exam school, but one that has traditionally performed well on standardized achievement tests). The third school fell into a category we called "orthogonal" (a school, sometimes a small school, with an articulated and distinctive mission, whose standards might not be congruent with state standards or assessments). Examples of orthogonal schools might include career academies, alternative high schools with state waivers, magnet schools, and/or a school with a particularly strong external constituency that drives its mission.

Finally, while we interviewed administrators and teachers across the schools, we focused most intensively on four subjects—two that commonly are tested (math and English), and two that are not (music and technology).

Thus, our design did not assume that "type" corresponded to a static collection of characteristics and qualities determining effectiveness. Rather, typing schools enabled us to identify how schools differed in their "initial" positions with respect to uniform policies. In two of our states, Kentucky and Texas, defining such an initial position was especially tenuous, since by the time we appeared on the scene, these schools had already been subject to the current version of state accountability, for about eight years in Texas and about seven years in Kentucky. Schools in those states had already been "shaped" by accountability policies—they were already used to them. At the other end of the spectrum, we did our interviews in the New York and Vermont schools just as the states were beginning to implement their new accountability systems in the high schools. Nevertheless, in all the states, state accountability systems as they applied to high school students and to high schools, were a work in progress, relatively new in New York and Vermont, much older in Texas and Kentucky, but ever changing. Our study tries to understand how this changing system was incorporated (or not) into these different kinds of schools.

This was not a randomly selected set of schools, but the interviews and additional empirical work we did using secondary statistical data on high schools, particularly in one state, Texas, led us to four basic findings:

- Systems vary greatly from state to state, even though the goals are generally similar. The development of assessment and accountability stems from a common educational purpose—developing new standards that focus on the school as the central unit of accountability and on the academic performance of students as the primary target of assessment. Additionally, all four states have sent strong signals that their policies are designed with particular attention to those schools, students, or scores, at the bottom of their scales. But the underlying politics that drive states to develop current assessment systems differ—they have taken quite different strategic approaches to assessment and accountability

- The high stakes associated with external accountability systems in most states are different in high schools than in elementary or middle schools. At lower levels of schooling, the stakes are highest for schools—"failing" schools are much more likely to get sanctioned than are students. In high school, however, the stakes associated with external accountability are, directly and indirectly, more likely to apply to students than to schools. It is students, not schools, who are rewarded and penalized by higher standards (passing required algebra, for example) or high school exit exams.

- The states' external accountability systems are increasing the attention paid to test scores and increasing the focus on testing in high schools. Testing certain subjects and not others is also having some effect on the curriculum. However, the tests seem to have little influence on how well high school students are doing on national tests or, more important, on persistence rates or graduation rates. Thus, in terms of what really counts for students in high school—graduation rates—external accountability appears to have had little if any impact.

- High schools vary greatly in their capacity to respond to external accountability systems imposed by states. External accountability systems are designed primarily to push low-performing schools to do better. The schools least aligned internally are supposed to get the greatest benefits from the "discipline" of external accountability. Yet, we found that it is precisely these schools that are least likely to be able to respond coherently to external accountability demands. This is especially so when those external demands are not consistently strong, with clear rewards and sanctions for schools. When the system is strong, schools with little internal accountability are much more likely to align themselves eventually with state standards. For example, that appears to be the case for high schools in a state such as Texas, which—when we got there—had had seven or eight years of experience with a high school exit test bearing serious consequences for both students and schools that performed poorly on the test. Even in Texas, however, some target schools responded successfully to external demands only after years of difficulties. This raises serious questions about the value of weak external accountability systems and of external accountability in the absence of improving school capacity.

Organization of the Book

Our study is presented in a series of essays that examine the nature of the new accountability systems in the four states and our findings in the fifteen high schools in our sample.

The first essay, by Diana Rhoten, Martin Carnoy, Melissa Chabrán, and Richard Elmore, describes the varied political origins and implementation processes of accountability reforms in each state. This provides the setting for understanding the measures high school personnel and students are being asked to respond to. The two most important features of the four systems are that they are highly varied yet all end up focusing on the lowest achieving groups in each state, mainly because of law suits challenging unequal financing of schools.

The next quartet of essays analyzes the large amount of interview data collected in the fifteen high schools we visited over a two year period. The first, by Elizabeth Debray, Gail Parson, and Salvador Avila, discusses the responses of schools within each state to the external accountability systems represented in the four states. The authors find that in addition to the variety of incentives and stakes of the different state accountability policies, within each state there was an array of responses that were related to schools' "initial positions," or school type. It appears that when accountability policies are not accompanied by strong repercussions for schools that do not align with the policies, the policies do not improve school performance via alignment with external requirements. In such cases—Vermont is the extreme case—already better organized schools—those with more aligned internal accountability (even those with missions that conflict with the goals of the accountability system)—form more coherent responses to external pressures. In states such as Texas (and perhaps down the road in New York), however, some compression does occur, mainly because strong sanctions bring many target schools into alignment with state policies.

Leslie Santee Siskin's essay focuses on the effect external accountability has on departments that teach tested subjects versus departments, such as music, that are untested, but have a highly structured set of standards and measures of performance. She finds that in addition to contributing to the deemphasis of music, the application of external accountability only to certain core subjects puts pressure on music departments to develop measures of performance that look like the tests given in math and English.

Richard Lemons, Thomas F. Luschei, and Leslie Santee Siskin attempt to draw some lessons from differences in school leadership. They analyze, in an exploratory way, responses to the particular demands generated by external accountability while examining where leadership around these responses emerges. Although the analysis is limited to five schools in two states, Kentucky and Texas, the examples suggest very different responses to the new demands, some with much more coherent forms of leadership than others.

In the final essay of this quartet, Melissa Chabrán analyzes the student response to the new accountability in three states, Kentucky, New York, and Texas. Predictably, students focus on the many more tests they are required to take by the state—in New York and Texas, high stakes exit tests. Surprisingly, she finds that students do not universally condemn the additional testing. Some argue that the tests help students focus their studies and, at least give them a clearer definition of what they need to learn, which is precisely what many educators find most detrimental about the tests.

The essay by Martin Carnoy, Susanna Loeb, and Tiffany L. Smith takes a different methodological approach to analyzing the impact of accountability on high school outcomes in the long-running Texas system. Because the Texas system has been in place so long, and the current exit test, the TAAS, was first used in 1991, Carnoy, Loeb, and Smith are able to trace the effects of the test on survival rates in high school. They also use test results and dropout data over time for approximately one thousand four year high schools in Texas to analyze possible relations between high school dropouts and tenth grade TAAS results. The essay raises questions about the overall impact of high stakes accountability on high school outcomes over time.

The last two essays in the collection attempt to draw lessons about the possibilities and limits of accountability from the papers in this collection and their own observations and analyses. Leslie Santee Siskin asks the rhetorical questions, "What happens when an irresistible force meets an immovable object? When a movement with the force and fervor of standards-based accountability reform hits the massive, highly stable, and reputedly reform-resistant form of the American high school?" Pulling together the analyses of the four papers that form the core of our study, she articulates the six major lessons we learned from the school interviews.

Perhaps the most important of these lessons, developed in depth by Richard Elmore, is that the capacity of the school to deliver high quality education is still the fundamental measure of how a school responds to the increased pressures exerted by the new state accountability systems. Elmore argues that testing schools and rewarding and sanctioning them can only take schools so far in self-improvement. Without the internal coherence (the internal capacity) to make such improvements, schools are less likely to make the organizational changes required for their students to do better as a result of higher standards imposed by states.

Elmore's analysis, combined with Siskin's summary of what happens in high schools in response to the variety of accountability systems in the four states we studied, and Carnoy and Loeb's results showing the weak effects on survival and graduation rates in a "strong" accountability state such as Texas, all provide powerful insights into the likely results of standards-based reforms. All four of the states we studied are ostensibly committed to improving the academic performance of low-performing high schools catering mainly to students from low-income families. Yet, our study suggests that although strong accountability *may* help low-income primary schools and their students make gains at least equal to (but not necessarily greater than) higher income schools and students (Carnoy and Loeb 2003), lower-performing *high schools* are at a distinct disadvantage in changing significantly in response to external accountability demands. This may explain why, when it comes to raising graduation rates, the new accountability systems are showing such minimal success.

The implications of our findings for reform policy are also powerful. Based on what we have observed and measured, we find it difficult to imagine that any reform, including raising standards and school accountability can be successful without building the capacity to execute the reform. All school improvement efforts have had to face this inescapable reality. The new accountability seems to be no exception to this rule.

Notes

1. The definition of community has changed over time, particularly in urban areas, and in many urban communities beginning a century ago, business interests became more influential in school policy than parent groups (Tyack 1974).
2. Evidence suggests that in choosing schools, parents are as conscious of the socioeconomic background of students attending a school as they are of student test scores. See Wells and Crain 1992.

References

Abelmann, C., and R. F. Elmore. 1999. When accountability knocks, will anyone answer? Philadelphia: Consortium for Policy Research in Education.

Boyer, E. 1983. *High school: A report on secondary education in America.* New York: Harper & Row.

Carnoy, M., and S. Loeb. 2003. Does external accountability affect student outcomes? A cross-state analysis. In *Educational Evaluation and Policy Analysis,* forthcoming.

Chubb, J. and T. Moe, 1990. Politics, markets, and America's Schools. Washington, D.C.: The Brookings Institution.

Fine, M. 1991. *Framing dropouts: Notes on the politics of an urban public high school.* Albany: State University of New York Press.

Goertz, M. E., and M. C. Duffy. 2001. Assessment and accountability systems in 50 states: 1999–2000. *CPRE Research Report.*

National Center of Educational Statistics. 2001. *Digest of Educational Statistics, 2001.* Washington, D.C.: National Center of Educational Statistics.

National Commission on Excellence in Education. 1983. *A nation at risk: The imperative for educational reform.* Washington, D.C.: National Commission on Excellence in Education.

Powell, A., E. Farrar, and D. Cohen. 1985. *The shopping mall high school: Winners and losers in the academic marketplace.* Boston: Houghton Mifflin.

Sizer, T. R. 1984. *Horace's compromise: The dilemma of the American high school.* Boston: Houghton Mifflin.

Tyack, D. 1974. *The one best system; a history of American urban education.* Cambridge: Harvard University Press.

Wells, A. S., and R. L. Crain. 1992. Do parents choose school quality or school status? A sociological theory of free market education. In *The Choice Controversy,* ed. P. W. Cookson, 65–81. Newbury Park, CA: Corwin Press.

CHAPTER 1

The Conditions
and Characteristics of Assessment
and Accountability
The Case of Four States

DIANA RHOTEN, MARTIN CARNOY,
MELISSA CHABRÁN, AND RICHARD ELMORE

Introduction

Historically, the American educational system has tried to balance meritocracy and democracy. By pitting the "perfectibility of man" against equality of opportunity, assessment has been important in defining this balance (Hoff 1999). Today's assessment-based reforms are hardly new, but the purpose of assessment has been "transformed" from traditional goals of measuring intelligence, tracking students, standardizing learning, and evaluating applicants into new forms of judging the quality and equality of schooling. Assessment has also been greatly intensified. The convergence of these two trends has led to more state testing and new types of assessment, such as high stakes tests for high school graduation, and the use of assessment in formal accountability systems. Between 1980 and 1998, the number of states that mandated student testing increased from twenty-nine to forty-eight (Office of Technology Assessment 1992; Hoff 1999). By 1998, thirty-nine states were administering some form of performance-based assessment; twenty-four states attached stakes to their tests in the form of student recognition, promotion, or graduation; and forty states used test scores for school accountability purposes (Bond et al. 1995, cited in Stecher and Barron 1999).

Assessment and accountability are not mutually exclusive. Assessment is a test or any planned procedure, method, or series of tasks used to obtain observations, which are then used to guide decisions and actions regarding student learning, curricula, and instruction. Accountability is the use of such tests, procedures, methods, or series of tasks to measure what is taught and learned (Leithwood, Edge, and Jantzi 1999). Accountability is "an arrangement whereby 'an account must be given'[1] to some authority, as an indication of compliance with defined standards, and as demonstrated by improvement on baseline or performance measures" as determined by some form of assessment (Elmore, Abelmann, and Kenyon 1996). A number of states have recently adopted formal school accountability systems that rely heavily on assessment tools. Experts like Robert Linn argue that assessment and accountability systems have become more popular because they offer a "relatively quick, relatively inexpensive, and highly visible way to bring about changes in schools" (Linn 2000).

Yet, research suggests that the mere presence of such a system in a particular state does not drive school change. The nature and the magnitude of the effects that accountability systems produce in schools depend on the characteristics of the particular system, which, in turn, are conditioned by the political-economic origins and the educational context of the state in which the system is implemented.

This essay compares and contrasts the conditions and characteristics of assessment and accountability systems in four states: Kentucky, New York, Texas, and Vermont. The development of assessment and accountability systems in these four states stemmed from a common educational purpose—developing new standards that focus on the school as the central unit of accountability and on the academic performance of students as the primary target of assessment. Additionally, while all four states have sent strong signals that their policies are designed with particular attention to those schools, students, or scores at the bottom of their scales, the underlying politics that drove the four states to develop current assessment systems differ—they have taken quite different strategic approaches to assessment and accountability. These differences help us focus on a number of critical issues.

Assessment and Accountability in Theory

Politicians and policy makers want to make school systems, schools, teachers, and students more accountable. At one end of the spectrum, they advocate more assessment and greater accountability as a "political quick fix"—a means of demonstrating to taxpayers that they are getting reasonable value for their educational dollar (Linn 2000). At the other end, assessment and accountability systems have been promoted as "educational life savers"—the integral cogs and central vehicles of much broader school reform initiatives (Leithwood et al. 1999). In either scenario, the assumption is essentially the same: holding school systems, schools, teachers, and students more accountable by assessing their performance can and will trigger a change in expectations and actions that leads to improvement. It is not an exaggeration to claim that assessment and accountability systems became the "prominent zeitgeist of education" in the second half of the last century and that they are likely to remain so well into this millennium (Leithwood et al. 1999).

Calls for assessment and accountability gathered force in the late 1960s and early 1970s, and then subsided briefly only to reemerge in the early 1980s (Elmore, Abelmann, and Fuhrman 1996). States' initial accountability efforts generally entailed judging schools on the basis of the amount and kinds of inputs they had—library books, lab equipment, condition of buildings, percent certified teachers, and class size, for example. Although schools with greater resources often had higher test scores, the causal link between student outcomes and such inputs was not clear once neighborhood income was accounted for. Partially in response to such weak links, reformers questioned the benefits of focusing policy solely on improving school inputs and moved to restructure accountability systems (Elmore, Abelmann, and Fuhrman 1996). Some states already had considerable centralized control over educational policy; in others, the shift has occurred gradually over the past three decades. Now many states with little tradition of state level accountability have legislated or are in the process of legislating school accountability systems that focus on student outcomes and judge school quality in terms of these outcomes (Elmore, Abelmann, and Fuhrman 1996).

The intensity of the revival was fueled by competing but complementary constructs, such as national standards, local control, and international competition, which have become central features of the most recent wave of the assessment and accountability movement. Arguably, the revival emerged in a new political, social, and economic era—one of rapid economic growth and increasing inequality of income and wealth, a boom in new technology, decreased confidence in government, and severe attacks on public education. This has increased pressure across the entire country to improve the quality of education and to make education a more effective tool for reducing income inequality. Individual states have responded to this pressure differently. In the following sections, we show how the implementation of assessment tools and accountability systems in our four sample states vary, and argue that this variance is largely explainable by the political-economic origins and educational contexts of each.

In the most general terms, education reformers who favor assessment advocate a set of instruments, indicators, and indexes on the assumption that they will:

- Identify student needs, improve student learning, and enhance student life-chances;
- Focus national, state, and/or local attention on the need to improve student skills; and,
- Provide teachers, parents, and students with accurate and reliable information about student performance.

Concurrently, those who endorse accountability systems hope to:

- Increase the use of good educational practices;
- Reduce the use of harmful or wasteful practices; and,
- Identify, diagnose, and change courses of action that do not lead to learning.

They argue that, collectively, assessment tools and accountability systems can improve system, school, teacher, and student performance by evaluating and encouraging valuable kinds of learning for students. Together they show how students are progressing, and can have a major impact on how changes in student, teacher, school, and/or system cognition and action might improve performance. States can only achieve solid assessment and accountability systems if the relationship works to provide good education and corrects problems as they occur. In practice, however, they can use a variety of models, methods, and mechanisms to formulate and implement the relationship (Darling-Hammond 1991).

The current assessment and accountability movement continues to emphasize the fundamental characteristics outlined but also features some significant new trends. These include, but are not limited to, an emphasis on performance-based approaches to assessment, "tests worth teaching to," ambitious content standards, the inclusion of all students, the opportunity to learn, and the use of high-stakes accountability mechanisms for schools, teachers, and sometimes, students (Elmore, Abelmann, and Fuhrman 1996; Linn 2000). The way in which these trends—tests, standards, opportunities, stakes—transform education, however, depends on the micro-context. Generally speaking, there are four fundamentally different approaches to assessment and accountability: state-wide standardization, school- or district-based management, teacher-focused professionalization, and student-driven competition.

The statewide standardization approach focuses on efforts to create more goal-oriented, efficient, and effective schools by introducing systematic management procedures. A basic assumption underlying this approach is that there is nothing fundamentally wrong with the current nature of schooling or with the current structures of state-local-school governance. Rather, the argument is that their effectiveness and efficiency can be improved in order for the system to become more strategic and cogent in its goals and more data-driven about the means used to accomplish those goals. According to Leithwood et al. (1999), " 'cost effectiveness' and 'value added' are phrases that capture the mission of those advocating [state-wide standardization] approaches to accountability, and 'control,' in its various forms, is the mechanism for accomplishing this mission" (50). Strategies associated with this approach to accountability differ from the other approaches in what they aim to control, the magnitude of what they hope to control, and how that control is exercised. Such strategies include: input controls (teacher training, teacher selection), process controls (program specification, performance appraisal systems), and output controls (standardized testing, rating systems).

Reformers also seek to increase accountability via decentralization and school- or district-based management reforms. This approach differs in that it does not tackle school improvement via statewide standardization reforms and does not emphasize the role of the central state in the state-local-school governance triad. In this approach, one of the central aims is not only to increase schools' efficiency and effectiveness, but to do so by increasing the role of local actors in traditional state-local-school governance structures (e.g., Bryk and Hermanson 1993; Weiler 1990). This approach can be categorized in the cluster of reforms referred to as "new managerialism." According to Stephen Ball (1998), new managerialism focuses on the decentralization, deregulation, and delegation of decision-making power and control to administrators and/or the local community at large. There are several variants of this approach to accountability. Ball suggests that they share in common a shift in emphasizing inputs and processes over outputs and in organizational integration over differentiation. Strategies in this approach include local administrative control (financial auditing, district reporting) and local community control (school councils, school profiling).

Within the teacher-focused professionalization approach to accountability, there are two different strategies. This first is the implementation of professional control models of school- or district-based management. The second strategy encompasses the standards movement as it applies to the practices of teachers and administrators (Darling-Hammond 1991; Leithwood et al. 1999; Linn 2000). Both approaches hold in common the belief that improved performance can be achieved via professional practice reforms that enhance the expectations as well as the responsibilities of school-level actors in the state-local-school governance structure. This approach and its two manifestations differ from the others primarily on which practices they choose for their direct focus. In the case of professional control, the focus is on school-level decision making, which holds a school's staff of teachers and administrators, as a group, accountable to parents, students, and the district office for the overall effectiveness and efficiency of the school. Teachers' classroom instructional and curricular practices are the focus of standards, which hold the individual teacher and administrator accountable to his or her clients for delivering services that meet or exceed what is specified by the standards (Leithwood et al. 1999).

In personal correspondence with us, Terry Moe (1996) argues that even with the new wave of assessment and accountability reforms and the modified features of these three approaches, "most of the talk still seems to presume that accountability is a goal we can pursue by coming up with better standards, or by engaging in tougher enforcement, or by promoting more active parental participation or a more vibrant democracy in general." Moreover, he argues that, because "these sorts of reforms are unlikely to work," the system must be radically overhauled.[2] The student-driven competition approach to accountability has emerged from this disillusionment with the bureaucratic public school "monopoly" and its tendency to consider students and parents as clients to be managed rather than as customers to be served. The goal of this approach is to transform schools and school systems by making them more responsible for the services they deliver and more responsive to their customers at the school level. Strategies include the establishment of school choice policies that open the boundaries within or between school districts so as to allow students and parents to select from any school within or across districts. They also include school privatization policies, which are more radical and encourage the development of alternatives to public schools, usually specialized educational facilities such as charter schools, magnet schools, and academies. For at least some version of either of these strategies to occur, it is necessary to alter the basis for school funding so that money follows students (e.g., vouchers, tuition tax credits).

The assessment and accountability systems in our four sample states reflect aspects of one or more of these four approaches. How assessment and accountability systems develop in each state, we argue, depends mainly on the political-economic origins of the reforms and on the traditional educational context of each state. Since three of the states we studied initially developed their accountability systems in response to court challenges on equity issues, we might predict that they would come up with similar systems that, in practice, function similarly. This turns out to be partly but not completely true. In one of the states, the accountability reform had an entirely different origin, yet was rapidly influenced by equity issues. This produced some features of implementation in common with the other states but not all. Thus, despite similar calls for assessment and account-ability in three states and a number of common intents and purposes in all four, each state's approach also has unique characteristics. These, we argue, reflect sets of beliefs and assumptions about the purposes, the services, and the governance of education that are particular to each state.

Assessment and Accountability in Action
Kentucky

The Conditions of Assessment and Accountability In 1983, Kentucky ranked 42nd out of 50 states in education spending per pupil, 38th in teachers' salaries, 41st in pupil-teacher ratio, 42nd in high school gradua-tion, 50th in adults with a high school diploma, and 49th in adults with a college degree (Prichard Committee 1999). Three years later, sixty-six school districts filed a lawsuit against the governor, legislature, superinten-dent of public instruction, and state school board. Unlike Texas, where discrepancies in district funding paralleled racial differences, the discrep-ancies in Kentucky followed geographic divisions between eastern (rural, poorer) and western (urban, wealthier) regions of the state.[3] Thus, it was plaintiffs from primarily rural districts in eastern Kentucky who argued that Kentucky's poor showing on national assessments could be attributed to the relatively low and grossly inequitable levels of educational financing in the state.

At the same time that litigation was unfolding, a debate was developing between the legislative leadership and then-governor Wilkinson over the best strategy to improve elementary and secondary education in Kentucky. As one education advisor remembered it, both parties had "started to wade into the same literature on systemic reform" but were walking out with dif-ferent approaches. Whereas the legislature pushed to continue the state-led reforms that had already been initiated, Wilkinson proposed new "struc-tural changes that involved moving primary responsibility for education reform from the statehouse to the school site, the development of a method by which to hold school personnel accountable for results, and providing a significant financial reward to schools that show progress" (Foster 1999, 9). After a legislative stalemate in 1988 and a financial short-fall in 1989, both sides agreed that they could not reach agreement until after the Supreme Court made its ruling on educational financing.

On June 8, 1989, the Kentucky Supreme Court extended the original 1986 suit beyond issues of fiscal scarcity and disparity and declared Ken-tucky's entire school system to be deficient and unconstitutional in its teaching and learning, as well as funding. The court ordered the Kentucky legislature to create a new and "efficient system of common schools" that would ensure equitable funding schemes and equal educational opportunities for all children by April 15, 1990 (Foster 1999, 9). After months of consultation and deliberation, the General Assembly enacted House Bill 940, or the Kentucky Education Reform Act (KERA), on March 29, 1990. At the time, KERA represented the most comprehensive education legislation in the history of the state and in the memory of the country. And, in its implementation, KERA presented one of the most extensive processes of structural, institutional, and cultural change ever attempted in American education.

KIRIS: The Original Approach and its Characteristics Wilkinson proposed that school improvement be measured on various criteria, including, among other things, student scores on a battery of state tests that would eventually be based on the academic achievement goals set by the state's Council on School Performance Standards. School performance results were to be calculated, using an Educational Performance Index (EPI), as the percentage of students who met or surpassed the specified academic goals. The Council on School Performance Standards, ultimately the cornerstone of Kentucky's reform movement, was chaired by a business person and was comprised of representatives of higher education, business, school administrators, and state education offices. The council was responsible for examining the question: "what is it that students should know and be able to do when they graduate from a school in Kentucky?"

Wilkinson believed that in return for being held accountable for standardized test results and student performance, teachers should be given direct control over all aspects of the instructional process. Moreover, he argued that—and this was the most controversial element of his proposal—personnel in schools demonstrating improvement in the performance of their students should be rewarded with cash bonuses. This aspect of Wilkinson's proposals represented, at least in theory, a significant departure from previous state-led approaches to school accountability in Kentucky and the United States. For various reasons, however, Wilkinson's proposals were not enacted during the 1988 session. Nevertheless, they remained an important part of the education policy debate in the state and a starting point for the debate over education reform and school accountability by the Task Force on Education Reform (Foster 1999).

David Hornbeck, consultant to the curriculum committee of the Task Force on Education Reform, proposed an accountability system that was based on the key policy principles set forth by Wilkinson, but with several important changes. Hornbeck recommended that schools be given clear and significant goals to be met over a two-year period. He argued that improvement toward these goals should be measured by an accountability index similar to the one proposed by Wilkinson, but which also took into account gains for "at-risk" students. Like Wilkinson, Hornbeck also proposed that personnel at improving schools receive cash rewards, but he believed that rewards should be calculated on the basis of individual teacher salaries and not on the basis of the school as a unit. Hornbeck added that the instructional staff at each school should decide how the award money should be spent. Finally, Hornbeck proposed a system of sanctions for failing schools (Foster 1999).

Based on statewide standards and school-based management structures, KERA brought a new system of assessment and accountability to Kentucky. Initially known as the Kentucky Instructional Results Information System (KIRIS), this system was based on a series of objectives. The first of these was to develop the ability of *all* students to meet the six academic achievement goals put forth by the state's Council on School Performance Standards. Because it would take time to develop and implement a reliable and valid assessment tool that would aptly measure students' competencies on these goals, the KIRIS system was initially based on "transitional" paper-and-pencil assessment instruments that were augmented by "performance events"[4] and writing portfolios (Hoff, 1998).

Using transitional assessment tools in the interim and more permanent tools in the long term, KIRIS was expected to influence what was taught by determining the percentage of students who could demonstrate all the learning outcomes required by KERA. Initially, assessment tools were used in grades four, five, seven, eight, eleven, and twelve to assess student performance and to then classify schools based on the percentage of students whose performance was considered novice, apprentice, proficient, or distinguished. In addition to these academic standards, KERA's initial accountability index also included noncognitive measures. These included: reducing truancy, reducing drop outs, reducing the number of failed students, increasing postgraduation transitions, and reducing mental and physical barriers to learning (Foster 1999; White 1998a). Together, these cognitive and noncognitive measures were used to determine the effectiveness of schools and the consequences—either rewards or sanctions—each would receive under the accountability program.

CATS: The Modified Approach and Its Characteristics   After a series of conflicts over and evaluations of KIRIS, the process culminated in 1997 when the state fired the testing company because of scoring errors and investigated more than one hundred schools for cheating (Jacobson, 1999). Shortly thereafter, a new group called the Task Force on Public Education, which had been convened in 1996 to conduct an external review of KERA, presented its final recommendations to then-governor Patton and the legislature. As a result of the KIRIS crisis and the KERA review, Patton signed

House Bill 53 into law on April 14, 1998. Although most agreed that changing the assessment tool of the KIRIS system was essential, educational reformers and clients remained divided into two distinct camps over how to do that: those who wanted a new, improved version of the test, and those who hoped to replace the entire system with a national standardized test (White 1998b).

The new law renamed the KIRIS system, the Commonwealth Accountability Testing System (CATS), to distinguish it from its discredited and defunct predecessor. And, although the law addressed Kentucky's overall assessment and accountability system, its immediate political goal and its primary technical function was to revise the existing testing instruments. At the level of assessment, CATS modified KIRIS by (1) introducing the Kentucky Core Content Test, which tests students on how well they are learning the basics of math, science, reading, writing, and other subjects; (2) requiring a national, norm-referenced portion, which matches the state's core curriculum and provides national comparisons for state students; (3) calling for a pared down written portion of the test; and, (4) expanding the number of grades in which these tests are administered. The state board selected CTB/McGraw Hill to run the norm-referenced component of the CATS testing system. The California company now administers norm-referenced reading, mathematics, and language arts versions of its CTBS to third, sixth, and ninth graders in Kentucky.

In addition to testing students to see how they compare with children across the country, CATS also uses performance-based exams to assess whether fourth, fifth, seventh, and eighth graders meet the state's academic achievement goals and standards in reading, history, the arts, and other subjects.[5] Additionally, the system uses CATS's new "straight line" approach to setting improvement goals, a baseline calculation was established over the course of the 1998–2000 school years, from which each school must improve by a fixed percentage each biennium so that all schools reach the same level of performance—a score of 100 out of 140 possible points—by 2014 (Foster 1999). This new approach eliminates the need for the Department of Education to recalculate a threshold for each school every two years; instead, the bar is automatically raised every two years even if the school did not meet its previous goal. As with the KIRIS system, a school's progress in this new system is determined on the basis of students' academic performance on the different assessments as well as the so-called noncognitive factors mentioned above, such as attendance rates, dropout rates, and so on. The relative weights of these noncognitive factors were calibrated differently for elementary, middle, and high schools.

Finally, the 1998 legislation charged the Department of Education with setting up a rating system in which the cash rewards for successful student performance would be distributed to schools for school-related expenses, rather than, as under KIRIS, to individual teachers for unspecified purposes. At the same time, the law also identified the need to rework sanctions for low-performing schools, although this is, as one policy advocate stated, "the area of the reform that's still sort of murky" in practice. The new sanctions and assistance programs as prescribed by the law include: mandatory audits for struggling schools; eligibility to receive CATS school improvement money; education assistance from highly skilled, certified state staff members rather than, as under KIRIS, so-called distinguished educators, who were experienced, state-paid teachers or administrators; and the option for students at low-performing schools to transfer to successful ones. Additionally, the law required school officials to distribute to parents and local news media school report cards that assess students' academic achievement and provide information on extracurricular activities and parent involvement at the school (White 1998b).

The Outcomes of Assessment and Accountability   As Kentucky redesigned its system, a new education financing formula, known as SEEK (Support Education Excellence in Kentucky), adjusted the state's district allocations from a plan that dispensed comparable funding based on student attendance and teacher experience and certification to one that varied allocations based on the amount of revenues generated by local taxes. Under SEEK, districts are required to meet certain local revenue-raising benchmarks. However, those with small tax bases and/or limited property values are protected and theoretically equalized with additional state funding. As a result, according to *Education Week*, Kentucky has accomplished a level of relative equity in spending per student, with a variation rate of only 13 percent between districts compared to the national average of 23.1 percent. Overall, the state and local financial commitment increased by approximately 73 percent between 1989–90 and 1997–98, with the growth in local shares most substantial in wealthier districts (Prichard Committee 1999). Moreover, from 1989–90 to 1998–99, Kentucky reduced the gap in per pupil expenditures between wealthy and poor districts by 36.9 percent while raising the state's national rank in per pupil spending from 42 to 31 (Heine 2002).

In Kentucky's accountability model, the state testing and rating system is seen as the guardian of progress while school councils make the instructional changes that ultimately drive that progress. The Executive Director of the Kentucky Association of School Councils, Susan Perkins Weston, summarized the logic behind this structure: "the school council was to be dominated by teachers, so the idea was to set the standard of the state and push teachers into a responsible position." In trying to push teachers into responsible positions, KERA specifically avoided mandating instructional practices of any kind. According to Jack Foster, former Secretary of Education and member of the Task Force on Education Reform, KERA purposefully left such decisions to the educators themselves.

In a 2001 letter to Kentucky parents, current Commissioner of Education Gene Wilhoit drew an analogy from business to explain the philosophy of the state's accountability system:

> Nearly all successful enterprises work this way. They set high standards for performance. They provide training, then liberate and empower the people who do the real work to meet the high standards. Then they check to see how well the standards are being met. They reward those who meet the high standards and figure out ways to help those who don't. That's the way it is in virtually every successful American workplace. In Kentucky, that's the way it is in our school system, too (Kentucky Department of Education 2001).

The problem with this aspect of the reform is not in the logic of its formulation, but in the logistics of its implementation. According to the policy makers and practitioners we consulted, Kentucky just "has not gotten the teachers where they need to be." A former consultant to the state's Council on School Performance Standards explained, for example, that the lack of teacher preparedness has "been a big flaw in the system."

According to state officials, the fundamental philosophy behind Kentucky's assessment and accountability system is that "all students can learn at high levels" and "high expectations produce high results." After ten years of reform, the Prichard Committee has found plenty of evidence that Kentucky headed down the right road. Kentucky's schools have moved from their place among the lowest-achieving in the country to the middle ranks of national benchmarks and standards. Yet, despite the reform's success in raising student performance overall, the results have been slow to penetrate all the classrooms equally, leaving too many students within the state behind, especially poor children in urban and Appalachian areas and those at the high school level. "When you put all the improvements in one spot we've made a lot more progress than we thought we had," said Robert F. Sexton, the group's executive director. "There are strong gains in achievement, particularly at the elementary level—but we don't think it's enough" (Keller 1999).

New York

The Conditions of Assessment and Accountability New York's current system of assessment and accountability dates back to 1878, with a state sanctioned course of study and assessments leading to a Regents diploma (Bishop, 1998). Since then, New York has undergone several changes in its accountability system, ranging from competency testing instituted in the mid-1970s to a push for higher standards through assessment in the mid-

1990s. Many of the current reforms in New York state center around testing and high expectations.

The New York Board of Regents, often regarded as the "fourth branch of government," and the State Commissioner of Education have been at the center of changes affecting assessment and accountability in the state (Maeoff 1983, 4–7). The state constitution and statutes provide for commissioners of education under a Board of Regents with vast power, often surpassing that of similar positions in other states. In the same way, the state has relied on strong leadership by the Commissioner of Education and looked to this commissioner for direction.

In 1974, New York, along with a few other states, led the way in adopting minimum competency tests as a requirement for high school graduation. This push to improve teaching and learning intensified when Gordon Ambach became Commissioner. In the 1980s, when states began to increase their high school graduation course requirements in response to national critiques of a mediocre education system, Ambach promised to make New York's standards "the most rigorous in the nation" (Fiske 1983, B-3). Informed by Ambach's vision and design, in 1982 the Board of Regents proposed the Regents Action Plan—a comprehensive reform to improve state education through increased courses required for high school graduation, an expanded school year, and increased teacher training.

Early in Governor George Pataki's term, Richard Mills, former Commissioner of Education in Vermont, was appointed by the Board of Regents to lead New York's educational reform. The Regents had been "grappling with years of halting efforts at reforming and upgrading the state's public schools" (Karlin 1997, C-4). "'They wanted closure,' said Mills, explaining how that translated into the push for higher, more demanding academic standards" (Karlin 1997, C-4). Mills disagreed with Pataki concerning the future of the Regents, although he investigated the Education Department's role and outlined a plan to improve the education system in New York. This included increased expectations, public measurement of results, directed use of technology in the schools, and partnerships between schools and human service agencies (Calarco 1996).

RCT and Regents: The Original Approach and its Characteristics   The 1982 Regent's Action Plan was meant to complement New York's longstanding two-tiered system of awarding diplomas. Mostly students intending to go to college earned the Regents diploma, as it measured college preparation and determined state scholarships. The local diploma was earned by passing the Regents Competency Test (RCT), which measured students' acquisition of basic skills (Sengupta 1997). Graduation requirements under the Regents Action Plan increased from 16 to 18.5 core academic courses for students seeking a local diploma, and from 18 to 18.5 for students seeking a Regents diploma. Requirements were directed at increasing the number of courses students took in English, mathematics, social studies, science, and foreign language, and differed depending on the degree students sought. In 1989, the testing requirement was expanded to allow students to demonstrate competency on the RCT, Regents, American College Testing (ACT) exam, or Scholastic Aptitude Test (SAT) in order to graduate.

Part of the statewide standardization strategy to raise academic levels in the 1980s also involved creating pressure at the school level without actually granting control to schools. In 1985, the State Board of Regents commissioned a study which identified 600 of New York's 6,000 public and private schools as "in need of improvement" based on Regents Competency Test scores in mathematics, reading, and writing and student dropout rates (Rohter 1985, B-3). Seventy-two of these schools were among New York City's 111 high schools. The Board's effort did not include measures to remove schools from the list, but assumed that this public reporting would stimulate advancement toward improving education.

The practice of identifying schools in need of improvement and holding them accountable was redefined in both 1989 and later in 1996 with the introduction of Schools Under Registration Review (SURR). This designation is applied to schools that are furthest away from having 90 percent of students achieve at the state's minimum on the mathematics and reading competency exams. After receiving this designation, schools must develop outcomes for improvement. The Commissioner may remove them from the list if they meet these progress goals (State Education Department 1996). If schools do not make improvement, they may be closed or taken over during a three-year probationary period. Both districts and communities are to play a role in assisting schools to meet the state reference point, and avoid the SURR list. New York does not yet have a mechanism for recognizing above-average performance, although such a policy has recently been proposed (Kadamus 2000). There is little evidence that the SURR policy has had a great effect on educational improvement in New York.

Regents For All: The Modified Approach and Its Characteristics   In 1996, the New York Board of Regents and Commissioner Mills introduced a new system of accountability to the state's schools. They began with new standards in seven core areas meant to phase out low expectations through low-level courses. However, the new standards were criticized as too vague. Indeed, the New York State United Teachers (NYSUT) raised concerns with the Commissioner that far more guidance was needed regarding the standards if teachers were to prepare students to meet the new requirements. Assessments in grades four and eight were also redesigned to reflect higher standards. However, the most visible accountability mechanism came with the decision to phase out the RCT and require that all high school students take and pass Regents examinations in five subject areas: English/language arts, mathematics, global studies, U.S. history, and science. These Regents exams were also redesigned, with the first revised, more difficult, exam administered in June 1999 (DeFabio 1998).

Beginning in the year 1999, students were required to take a six-hour English Regents exam with a minimum score of fifty-five on a scale of one hundred in order to graduate. In 2000, juniors had to pass the Mathematics Regents exam. Tests in the three other subjects will be phased in over a ten-year period with a higher minimum score of sixty-five (Debray 2000). By the year 2005, students will have to pass all Regents exams in order to get a diploma. If they do not pass, the only option will be an equivalency degree (Sengupta 1997). Provisions made for students whose first language is not English included offering the exam in five languages, including Spanish, Russian, Chinese, Haitian/Creole, and Korean, with the exception of the English Regents. Only students with the most severe disabilities are exempted from the new policy. Other students with disabilities must take the Regents exam, and if they do not pass, they can take the RCT.

Despite these significant policy changes, the state still maintains a dual-diploma system. It awards both Regents and Advanced Regents diplomas. Prior to the policy change, all students had to take 18.5 units in the academic core as instituted in the 1980s. This later changed to require those seeking Advanced Regents diplomas to take 20.5 units in the academic core and pass Regents exams in eight subjects. In 1997, however, the course requirements for all students entering grade 9 in or after September 2001 were raised to 22 units in a standard academic core.

This statewide standardization reform requiring all students to take Regents exams was almost instantly considered controversial, as an average of only 38 percent of students in the state formerly earned Regents diplomas (Diegmueller 1996). Concerns also surfaced over how the policy would apply to students with learning disabilities and students whose first language was not English, and whether it would increase dropout rates in the state. A broad-based group of teachers, administrators, parents, and students advocated a multi-tiered system, particularly for students with disabilities. However, Commissioner Mills, a staunch supporter of the new reform, continued to express the need for all students to have a minimum level of education through the respected Regents diploma.

In response to the new policy, many schools applied for and received five-year waivers from the Regents exams. Approximately forty nontraditional schools in New York then requested permission to substitute their own assessments for the English Regents examination, contending that they were more rigorous than the Regents and that they were integral to the mission of nontraditional schools. Commissioner Mills, however, rejected this request for alternative assessments in English, but permitted some of the schools to administer alternatives in mathematics (Keller 2000). Whether alternative assessments in other subjects might be used is the subject of an ongoing evaluation by the State Education Department. Mills agreed to extend the waivers granted earlier for subjects other than English. Previously, a state panel evaluating which alternatives would meet the same standards set by the state found two exams which had been requested for review by their testing companies—the Advanced Placement English exam and the International Baccalaureate English exam—could be used as alternatives and were more rigorous than the Regents exam.

As part of an effort to improve education throughout the state, New York also outlined an ambitious plan to improve teacher quality. Components of this teacher-focused professionalization approach, introduced in 1998, include replacing permanent licensure with a "professional" certificate (Hendrie 2000, 3). To qualify for this, teachers must obtain a master's degree and four years of teaching experience. Teachers also must participate in 175 hours of continuing education every five years in order to maintain their license. Professional development plans are also part of this system and must be developed by districts. Additionally, there is discussion of requiring the accreditation of all teacher-training programs. Lastly, the state is ending the practice of using temporary or emergency certified teachers. It estimates that by 2003, it will ban these types of teachers in the state's low-performing schools (Hendrie 2000).

A final part of the new policy, somewhat overshadowed by the implementation of the Regents exams, is more concentrated accountability at the school level. In 1996, Mills ordered school report cards for grades four, eight, and high school in which the performance of schools could be compared with other schools across the state. The first report cards, issued in spring of 1997, focused attention on individual schools' performance. Partly because of the sustained attention on the Regents exams, it is unclear whether this performance reporting has had any effect on school practice. However, in 1999, there was considerable debate on what teacher information would be placed on the report cards—how many teachers were rated unsatisfactory, what their involvement in reform was, and how many participated in tenure-revocation proceedings (Hendrie 2000). In the end, it was decided that schools must only report how many teachers were temporarily certified. Unlike Kentucky or Vermont, however, these initiatives did not constitute a school-based management approach to accountability, given that they implied a shift in the role of reporting school-level results but did not consider a change in the rights and responsibilities for governing school-level results.

The Outcomes of Assessment and Accountability   In 1999, only 38 percent of eighth graders met the new mathematics standard, while 48 percent met the new English standard. On the new high school English Regents exam in 1999, 78 percent passed with a score of at least 55. Six percent of students failed this exam, and 16 percent still need to take the test. The five largest school districts in New York had an average of 56 percent of students passing this exam with scores above 55. Eleven percent of students in these districts failed the exam (Perez-Pena 1999).

In March 2000, Mills announced that more students were taking and passing the Regents in all required subjects prior to the full implementation of the policy (Holloway, 2000). He credited schools, the increased graduation requirements, and the students themselves with this dual increase. However, critics contend that this is not a statewide trend, and that many students are failing, not taking the Regents, or dropping out of school. In this vein, former Regents board member Norma Gluck asked the state to postpone the full requirements for two years, as she and others feel that a single standard should not be used to hold students accountable for their learning (Holloway 2000).

Our interviews in New York schools suggest that teachers scoring the Regents exams face a number of logistical problems. Although the State Department of Education provides training for lead teachers on scoring and administering the examinations, there is still a great deal of ambiguity on the uniformity of the procedures. Some teachers are also critical of the content of the Regents exams. One English teacher comments on students' performance on the English Regents and the problems with the exam: "While I was disappointed by the poor performance, I was far more distressed by the knowledge that the same students could have written essays that were far more articulate had the test been designed and administered differently" (Mosco 2000, 2).

Although New York is currently in the beginning phase of implementing these new requirements, the State Board of Regents has proposed changes to the policy. These changes, put forth by the State Education Department in a plan entitled "System for Accountability for Student Success" (SASS), affect the identification of SURR schools, cutoff scores, the process for identifying high-performing schools, performance standards for special schools (including progress targets), and the implementation schedule for Regents exams in the state's high schools. The Department crafted these changes after extensive discussion with the public around the state's approach to accountability (Kadamus 2000). This plan proposes four school accountability levels (farthest from state standards; below state standards; meeting state standards; and exceeding state standards). The state has now proposed a reward system for high-performing schools, which requires that they exceed standards for two years and have satisfactory levels of performance for disaggregated student populations in order to be recognized. The plan also calls for districts to address the performance of various disaggregated student populations within their improvement plans when their scores are unacceptable. Special schools such as alternative and vocational schools may be able to submit supplementary performance indicators to inform the state accountability system. In addition, the provisions for exempting students not proficient in English as well as those who have disabilities from the Regents exams are streamlined, although Individualized Education Program Certificates will not be accepted once the policy is fully implemented. Lastly, the state is reviewing the timelines for implementation of this accountability system (Kadamus 2000).

The passage of the federal No Child Left Behind (NCLB) Act of 2001 requires further adjustments to New York's accountability system. Although the United States Department of Education identified New York as one of 20 states in full compliance with the Improving America's Schools Act of 1994, the state must add or change several components of its accountability system to comply with the new requirements of NCLB. Required changes include: (1) implementing tests in English language arts and mathematics for grades 3, 5, 6, and 7; (2) instituting a measure of academic performance in addition to English language arts, mathematics, and science; (3) adding a graduation rate indicator to New York's high school accountability system; (4) incorporating all of the state's limited English proficient students and students with disabilities into the school accountability system; (5) requiring schools to demonstrate annual progress among student groups disaggregated according to racial and ethnic group, socioeconomic status, disabilities, and limited English proficiency (6) establishing a framework to identify "persistently dangerous" schools from which parents will be allowed to transfer their children (New York State Department of Education, 2002).

New York and other states are questioned for measuring students' education with a single set of tests. This criticism, coupled with New York's ambitious timetable, may be an indicator of a bumpy road ahead. At the same time, the state's decision to phase in a 65 cutoff score may help in assisting students to make incremental progress. This, however, assumes that progress is being made toward improving instruction as well as the logistics of phasing in the reform. New York must keep a watchful eye on dropout rates statewide and monitor student scores closely. Although state leaders would like to see evidence of change, they must also be willing to do what is necessary to assist students in their learning.

Texas

The Conditions of Assessment and Accountability Texas's current educational reform has its roots in two distinct conflicts. As in Kentucky, the first was a challenge to the unequal distribution of resources among Texas school districts, a result of supplemental state funding of education with property taxes. These additional taxes created major differences among districts. Unlike Kentucky, where differences were based on geographic location, the differences in Texas were highly correlated with the ethnic composition of districts. Texas's largest minority groups—Latinos and African Americans—went to schools that received considerably fewer resources than predominantly Anglo schools. The second conflict was the rise, in the 1970s, of a new group of businesses based on high technology and services that challenged the hegemony of Texas's traditional agricultural and oil interests.

The first conflict arose from a series of legal suits by Mexican-American parents living in low-income school districts. In 1968, the parents of the Edgewood Independent School District in San Antonio brought a class action suit against the state and Bexar County (San Antonio) on "behalf of schoolchildren throughout the State who are members of minority groups or who are poor and reside in school districts having a low property tax base" (San Antonio v. Rodriguez, 411 U.S. 1, 1973). In 1971, the District Court judged in favor of the parents, holding the Texas school finance system unconstitutional under the Equal Protection Clause of the Fourteenth Amendment. Subsequently, the state appealed to the Supreme Court, and in 1973, by a 5–4 vote, the justices overturned the district court decision. In the majority opinion, Justice Powell argued that the Texas system neither discriminated against any definable class of "poor" people, nor impermissibly interfered with the exercise of a "fundamental" right or liberty. Representing the majority, he argued that the education financed by the supplemental property tax did not represent a fundamental right.

The dissenting opinions of Justices Brennan, White, and Marshall questioned both of these points. By the mid-1980s, other complaints brought by less-funded districts were being heard in District Court. As in the Rodriguez case, the District Court in these later cases ruled against the state and for equalization. Yet, it was not until the early 1990s that the state began to redress the lower educational funding provided to poorer, largely Mexican-American and African-American districts. Thus, for almost twenty-five years, unequal educational funding was a major political issue in Texas, and the powerful Anglo-dominated legislature long resisted directly remedying the complaints of minority groups.

Texas's sweeping 1984 educational reform must be viewed in this context. In the early 1980s, Governor Mark White appointed a commission headed by Ross Perot to review Texas education and make recommendations for its improvement. David Grissmer and Ann Flanagan of the RAND Corporation argue that the commission came about for several reasons, among them a "growing awareness in the business community that a quality K–12 education was crucial to the future economy of the state."

This awareness "appears to have arisen as the state was trying to attract new industry to the state and to diversify the state economy away from dependence on oil and gas" (Grissmer and Flanagan 1998, 26). A longtime leader in the Texas Federation of Teachers agreed with Grissmer and Flanagan's assessment and added the following commentary: "His [Ross Perot's] vision did include a better-educated state, a better-educated work force, because in part his business is such—as he said many times—that he can't work with people unless they're well educated, because he requires a skilled work force." Most of today's analysts focus on these business pressures for reform in Texas.[6] While this was an important element in the reform process, so as the persistent litigation over unequal funding and the poor condition of education for Texas's growing minority populations. It is no accident that the reform was called the Equal Opportunity Act of 1984.

The main recommendations of this act and Perot's Commission in general included: reducing the monetary gap between funding for rich and poor school districts, lowering class size to twenty-two in kindergarten through second grade, moving to a full-day kindergarten, and providing subsidized pre-school education for low-income four-year-olds. It also included a significant increase in Texas's relatively low teachers' salaries. In the first year after the reform, salaries rose 12 percent to $22,648 for the average teacher, and 23 percent to $17,320 for beginning teachers. Expenditures per student rose 15 percent statewide, and 30 percent in the state's 151 poorest districts, where teachers' salaries rose 19 percent. As a result of funding equalization, the poorest districts received a 44 percent increase in state money (United Press International 1985).

All of these initiatives were financed by a major tax increase of $3.3 billion dollars, much of it financed by property tax increases. Despite the intentions of its sponsors, however, the Act did not, in the end, equalize funding. As a result, minority groups continued to litigate against the funding gap. Initially, ten school districts took suit against the state education agency over the funding plan presented in the 1984 Act. Fifty-seven other school districts joined the original ten within a few years. In 1987, a district judge ruled in favor of the plaintiffs. The state appealed to the State Supreme Court and lost. Finally, in September 1991, the state began to comply by increasing spending in the poorer districts.

To Ross Perot's credit, he continued to fight over the course of the 1980s for more spending on education (mostly needed to meet court-mandated equalization requirements) and higher taxes. As falling oil prices reduced state revenues, these tax hikes became more difficult to extract politically. But Perot's business backing and overall credibility with the public, based on the success of earlier educational reforms, gave him a certain degree of influence over the state legislature. In addition to fighting for funding, Perot was intent on cutting bureaucracy in the system, particularly with regard to the State Board of Education. As one teachers' union representative recalled, "The bureaucracy that [Ross Perot] was probably zeroing in on was the State Board of Education, which at that time, was, as Ross Perot said, like the Louisiana Legislature of the 1930s. It was an embarrassment. And we had a commissioner of education who I used to call the commissioner of ignorance. I said he'd gone over to the enemy. He genuinely didn't believe, he did not believe that Hispanic children and African-American children were capable of learning at the same level as Anglos. And Perot figured this out pretty quick."

TEAMS: The Original Approach and its Characteristics Where did assessment and accountability figure into all of this reform? The 1984 Equal Opportunity Act instituted a new bureaucracy, the Texas Education Agency (TEA). The TEA was granted just as much, if not more, power than the State Board, but with an education commissioner who was "with the program." Although Perot's commission secured that victory, the battle for Perot's proposed cuts in bureaucracy was postponed in favor of introducing new roles and responsibilities related to assessment and accountability. One of the TEA's new functions was to evaluate students with a statewide test in third, fifth, seventh, and ninth grades as well as to develop a minimum skills test given to high school juniors that they would need to pass to graduate from high school. The Texas Educational Assessment of Minimum Skills (TEAMS) tests, as they were called, were consistent with a business approach to education, but they were also important politically. The Anglo-dominated legislature was not about to push a lot of new educational spending into low-income Hispanic and African-American districts without some sort of quid pro quo. In the words of one who witnessed the arrival of TEAMS firsthand: ". . . testing was done as a way to guarantee that money given to school boards to educate children would at least be spent, in part, on educating those children and wouldn't be totally wasted, frittered away. And the test was to be a system by which you could tell that something had been done or you wouldn't have students passing a basic skills test . . . it was sort of, 'you want money from us for taxes. We've been giving you money. It's been frittered away. Look at what happens down in the Rio Grande Valley. Look at all the wasted tax money. These kids get diplomas, they can't read. We're not giving you any more money unless we are sure that this money will be spent on educating kids to at least read and write'" (Interview, *President, Texas AFT* 1999). In short, TEAMS established the framework for assessment in Texas, and the attached quid pro quo laid the initial groundwork for accountability.

In addition to Texas's state-wide standardization approach to account-ability that this original quid pro quo implied, a second quid pro quo introduced strategies from the teacher professionalization approach to accountability. All teachers and administrators in the Texas education system were to be given a basic skills test. College students aiming to become teachers were already being tested before the Act was even passed, but this test was only further affirmed by the Act. Of the almost three thousand students—mostly sophomores—who took the competency test in 1984 (before the reform) to qualify as teacher candidates, only 54 percent passed (*United Press International* 1984). In March 1986, District Judge Harley Clark ruled that the competency test for teachers was constitutional. A few days later, the TEA tested 202,000 administrators and teachers (math and science teachers were excluded) with the Texas Examination of Current Administrators and Teachers (TECAT). Of this sample, only 3.3 percent did not pass (those who failed got a second chance three months later). This prompted many administrators to argue that the tests were of little use to management (*United Press International* 1986).

The 1984 reforms were criticized on many fronts, not just for the TECAT. For example, the controversial "no-pass, no-play" rule that kept athletes from playing high school sports if they did not pass required courses drew heavy fire, particularly from rural superintendents and parents. Teachers unions and civil rights groups opposed teacher testing and ultimately stopped the testing of all teachers, but lost on the testing of prospective teachers. Poorer districts continued to litigate over financial inequalities between districts and ultimately won equal funding. Despite these critiques and the fact that initial TEAMS scores were low,[7] the vast majority of the Texas public backed the reform throughout the mid-1980s. So much so that in 1987, when the new Governor Bill Clements threatened to scale back education reform measures because of oversized budget deficits, Ross Perot was able to use the threat of remobilizing massive public support and the business community to back Clements down (LaFranchi 1987).

TAAS: The Modified Approach and Its Characteristics   By 1991, the reform had already gone through two rounds—in 1984 and in 1987—and was now institutionalized into Texas politics and policy. It included a strategic plan that recommended "new learning standards for each grade, measuring learning by linking statewide assessments to those standards, holding schools accountable for results, but not dictating to teachers and principals how to achieve the results" (Grissmer and Flanagan 1998, 28). Under the new governor, Ann Richards, the new local-school management approach to accountability was added to the earlier statewide standardization and teacher professionalization components. It was ultimately completed in 1995–1998 by Richards's successor, George W. Bush.

Unlike Kentucky's version of this approach to accountability, districts rather than schools were given the stronger role. In this role, their primary responsibility was to implement school improvements that would raise student performance as measured by the new assessment tool—the Texas Assessment of Academic Skills (TAAS). The TAAS was still a basic skills test but was somewhat more difficult and more comprehensive than the TEAMS. Under this new model, the TEA also set state curriculum standards (such as requiring three math courses, including Algebra I in the ninth grade, for high school graduation), authorized state tests in grades 3–8 and 10 (the latter required for high school graduation), and identified state accountability rating standards for school and district performance (exemplary, recognized, acceptable, or low performing). With these as the baseline, local school districts could set higher standards and were responsible for implementing improvements that would bring students in their schools to satisfactory performance levels on the TAAS.

While the TEA was empowered to provide technical assistance to school districts and schools having difficulty meeting acceptable TAAS performance standards, the keys to the new accountability system were the local-school management approach to building community and district pressure to improve TAAS scores. Sanctions for continued failure to improve on these scores ranged from peer review and on-site investigations, to notices of deficiency, school reconstitution, and old fashioned public "shame." Many teachers and administrators explain that, as the accountability system has become increasingly institutionalized and the publicity around TAAS scores has intensified, the weight of the "shame factor" has increased significantly. A representative of the Dana Center at the University of Texas elucidated the power and effect of this factor in greater detail:

> The public understands the system. You can talk to bus drivers and taxi drivers, and they know what their school's accountability rating is. And, moreover, they can tell you why their school is rated as it is rated. Having that kind of transparency has been extremely important in empowering the public to come to the table, ask hard questions about what's going on at their school, and help influence change. Also, I believe that another very important part of the system has been the extent to which it isn't just a bipolar system that rates schools good or bad. Meeting the criteria, not meeting the criteria. Instead, in this system, you have four ratings for schools, four ratings for districts: low performing, acceptable, recognized, exemplary. What's been important about that is that school communities have gotten tremendously excited about achieving the higher ratings. In fact, there's a tremendous energy expended in schools trying to get to an exemplary rating. If the system didn't have that categorization, then it's much more difficult to imagine the outpouring of energy that we see currently in hundreds of schools around the state. Schools are saying, wait a minute, there's a school down the road that has kids that look a lot like our kids. They have an exemplary rating. How come we just have an acceptable rat-

ing? And, the system definition of higher levels of school achievement have been important in generating additional change (Interview, November 1999).

This same representative also claimed that, in his opinion, TAAS has most dramatically increased the public awareness of the students and schools in lower-income and minority communities, which were the least likely to get the attention they deserved and the information they needed before the external evaluations began. In 1994, a new set of TAAS tests began with increased hype around policies and practices of assessment and accountability. The TEA raised the level of publicity that schools received for their success, adequacy, or failure on the TAAS. And with the increased national attention given to Texas's success in increasing student performance on both state and national tests, test scores began to take on a life of their own. Because of the momentum and the might that testing had generated and the fact that local school districts and schools were charged with the primary responsibility for responding to testing standards, many administrators and teachers saw that the simplest way to get higher pass rates was to focus on the test itself.

Take the case of Kashmere High School in Houston's low-income near north side. The principal came to Kashmere in 1992, when only 16 percent of the school's tenth graders were able to pass the TAAS minimum competency test for high school graduation. What did the principal do to rectify the situation?

> [He] bought a $4,500 machine to rapidly score practice tests that would diagnose students' weaknesses. He spent $1,800 on a computerized tutoring program designed specifically to help students pass the exams. Daily tutoring sessions replaced homeroom, the band teacher taught fractions, and the shop teacher stressed converting measurements into the metric system because those topics appear on the crucial exit exam. Four times a year, the school sponsored day long Saturday cram sessions. Teachers threatened to dock the grades of students who didn't show up for Friday night tutoring sessions (Colvin 1999).

Similar stories of cram sessions, pep rallies, tutoring programs, mock tests, and class orientations targeting the TAAS were commonplace among the teachers and administrators in the schools visited here. Because the test is constructed to assess student performance on a prescribed curriculum, it can be convincingly argued that programming and teaching to the test is not a "bad" thing. Moreover, because of the way the test results are measured on the Academic Excellence Indicator System (AEIS), minority student scores carry significant weight, thus forcing schools to focus on these populations.

Outcomes of Accountability   The mix of incentives and the nature of standards in Texas have resulted in a bifurcated system of accountability. On the one hand, schools have been pushed to expand their advanced placement enrollments and motivate their teachers to raise the performance of high-performing students on advanced placement tests. In some districts, for every student who gets a 3 or better on an AP test, the AP teacher receives $100 and the student has the test fee waived. Even in those districts without AP incentive schemes, state accountability norms have little influence on high-performing students. On the other hand, schools have been encouraged to improve the scores of their low-performing students and increase their ratings to "exemplary" by increasing attention to the TAAS. Thus, whereas college course requirements, EOC tests, the SAT, the ACT, and AP tests are the accountability measures that drive the high school experience for honors and AP track students, state-controlled and district-controlled basic skills and content drills fuel the experience of the low-performing students. This system begs two key questions. First, what are the implications of this difference in student experiences with state-led basic standards versus private-led college standards in terms of accountability? Second, what is the experience of the middle-performing student?

Although EOC tests could be a much more direct means of making local and school actors more accountable than the state for student performance, this aspect of the statewide standardization approach has not evoked the same kind of reaction as the TAAS test. For one thing, district EOC tests do not overlap with state EOC tests in the same courses,[8] which confuses their relative values and purposes and, consequently, renders them somewhat ineffective as incentives of accountability in the eyes of "over-tested teachers." Moreover, at the school level, both district and state EOC tests count for only part of a student's grade in a course (25 percent), and, at the district level, they are scaled so that more than 50 percent of students pass the tests. For example, in the two urban districts visited here, more than 80 percent of students failed the state's algebra I EOC test, but about 70 percent passed the course required for graduation. A district administrator explained it this way: "You're passing kids that don't know algebra—that's right. But, see, the way we rationalize this is that at least we're calling attention to the fact that these kids can't do algebra. Now, if in fact we went in and we actually flunked them, you'd lose a lot of kids. And we already have a dropout rate that's like 40 percent. I mean, you know, our dropout rate under the state system [the way the state measures dropouts] is under 2 percent, but the real dropout rate's like, you know, over 40 percent" (Interview, November, 1999). Thus, even if a student fails the EOC exams, he or she can pass the course and, potentially, the TAAS, making this a weak tool of accountability from the perspective of either motivating the student or measuring the district. Changes to Texas's accountability system scheduled for 2003 may remedy this situation by phasing out the

End-of-Course exams and replacing the TAAS with a more rigorous and comprehensive exam.

Increasing the number of required courses in math is another direct form of improving student performance under the statewide standardization approach that is used by both local and the state actors of the state-local-school governance structure. Logically, the more math students take, the more math they should learn and the better they should perform on national assessment tests taken at the end of high school, such as the NAEP given to 17 year-olds, the SAT, or the ACT. There is some evidence of increased performance on math tests for those students who make it to their senior year. Assuming that the dropout rate has not increased over the past five years,[9] these might be attributed to increased course requirements. But, as in other cases where states attempted to increase course requirements,[10] the interpretation of what constitutes a math course for low-achieving students is quite broad, and may do little to increase math skills beyond eighth or ninth grade levels. Because increased requirements are subject to such broad interpretations, they do not necessarily produce the desired outcome of higher order skills in the given subject.

An overhaul in Texas's accountability system scheduled for 2003 will introduce a new test, the Texas Assessment of Knowledge and Skills (TAKS). The TAKS is designed to be more closely aligned with the state's curriculum standards, the Texas Essential Knowledge and Skills (TEKS). The new test, which will be administered in grades three to eleven, will be more rigorous and will cover more subjects than the TAAS. The exit-level TAKS exam will be moved from grade ten to grade eleven and will assess the following subjects: English III, algebra I, geometry, biology, integrated chemistry and physics, early American and U.S. history, world geography, and world history. According to proponents of the redesigned system, a more comprehensive and difficult test will steadily increase the standard for high school graduation, making Texas students all that much better prepared for college and work. Critics argue that the current logic necessarily slows down any process that increases the difficulty of the test. Since the state, despite its rhetoric, is doing little to improve the quality of individuals being recruited into teaching or to improve the quality of existing teachers, schools' capacities to improve student learning are highly constrained. Raising test difficulty under such circumstances probably means raising the high school failure rate, not student outcomes. Further, Texas politics could not tolerate either a sharp drop in scores or higher high school dropout rates.

At the heart of the conflict between the two views is whether the present model's underlying assumption of considerable "slack" in the school system is correct. Proponents argue that they have already shown that by simply drawing attention to low-performing schools, the TAAS has been able to force improvement, particularly for minority students. These proponents have a case. But critics may now be on solid ground in arguing that the "slack" has run out. Teaching to a relatively easy test may have led to improvement in basic skills for those at the bottom of the educational ladder, and test teaching probably did not require greater capacity within the system. Beyond that, further progress may be more difficult to achieve. The difficulties currently faced at the high school level, where 80 percent of minority students are failing tests in more demanding courses such as algebra, suggest that more progress requires more fundamental changes.

Vermont

The Conditions of Assessment and Accountability   Vermont anchors one end of our accountability sample. It has a small population, with fewer than 600,000 people (the 49th largest state), and slightly more than 100,000 students in its 350 schools. It is a state of small towns and rural areas. Its largest city, Burlington, has less than 40,000 people. Sprinkled among the state's 285 school districts are some sixty supervisory unions—multi-district administrative units for small or single-school districts—and a number of academies—nominally private schools that provide schooling for students in towns that pay tuition in lieu of running their own schools.

Unlike the other states in our sample, Vermont has a history of strong local school governance, in the New England tradition of face-to-face local democracy. As one former teacher and current policymaker explained, Vermont ". . . has been very typically a local-control state . . . I know a lot of states say it, you know, we always go to places nationally, say, we are the most local-controlled state you can get, and everyone else just laughs because so many states say they're local-controlled. There are central-controlled states like Kentucky" (Interview with state administrator, 1999). Consequently, unlike the other states, Vermont's state government, until only recently, has not been a real presence in local school affairs. Education policy and governance began to shift toward a larger state presence and more high-profile education reform in the late-1980s, with the growth of a strong education reform presence in the governor's office and the state legislature and the appointment of Richard Mills as Vermont's commissioner of education (formerly education aide to Governor Tom Kean of New Jersey, and now commissioner of education for the state of New York).

The hallmarks of the Mills period, from the late 1980s to the mid-1990s, were the development of content standards and a portfolio assessment system. These policies were accompanied by broad participation from the public and professional educators. Participation came in the form of a wide grassroots effort that touched nearly every hamlet and school in the state with initial consultation on the nature and scope of content standards, on the use of standards in the design of curricula, and on the development of a portfolio assessment system to determine whether students were mastering the content in the standards. For a period in the 1990s, Vermont was the leading state in the country in portfolio assessment and was thought to be the laboratory for the development of new broad based measurement techniques for assessing student learning. In the mid-1990s, however, a series of studies found relatively low reliabilities in teacher scoring of portfolios. These studies were followed by a shift toward the use of portfolios primarily as school-level assessment tools and the introduction of the newly developed New Standards Reference Examination (NSRE) as the main required state-level test.

At about the same time that the NSRE was implemented, Vermont entered into an educational financing suit similar to those experienced in Kentucky and Texas. As in the other two states this financial equity case, known as Brigham v. State, began the process of educational reform that culminated in a reform addressing excellence and quality in addition to financial equity. In fact, according to a former Commissioner of Education, "the quality aspect of the bill is the most important part" of the reform. Ultimately, the Equal Education Opportunity Bill, or Act 60 as it came to be called, mandated that schools participate in student assessment as promoted by the State Board of Education as well as develop local assessment plans that at least include but potentially go beyond the state component.

NSRE: The Original Approach and Its Characteristics   The NSRE is a high-level criterion-referenced standards-based test of English/language arts and mathematics given in grades four, eight, and ten. The test was developed by the Learning Research and Development Center at the University of Pittsburgh and the National Center for Education and the Economy, and it is marketed by Harcourt Brace Educational Measurement. Vermont is one of only two states in the country—the other is Rhode Island—using the NSRE as its statewide test; the test is used by some local jurisdictions that are interested in high-level assessments keyed to external standards. Students in Vermont schools have usually done well on standardized tests. However, during the first administrations of the NSRE in the 1996–97 school year, only 30–40 percent of students in the state's highest performing schools scored above the proficiency level—results that made nearly every educator unhappy and concerned.

The NSRE was supplemented with the introduction of the Vermont Science Assessment (administered in grades six and eleven), which was developed around the state's science standards by CTB/McGraw Hill. Due to prohibitive costs, this assessment was terminated, and in 2001 a new science test was implemented in grades five, nine, and eleven. The Developmental Reading Assessment (DRA) is administered in the second grade to identify early reading problems. And the state provides some statewide scoring of portfolios in mathematics and writing in the elementary and middle grades.

The advent of systematic testing and Vermont's statewide standardization approach to accountability in the mid-1990s was viewed by most educators as a dramatic break with the past. One policy advisor recounted the significance of this change in the state of Vermont:

> . . . the 90's, along with beginning with portfolios, they did have a standard math exam and a standard writing test . . . a large group of stakeholders got together and met for about two years talking about, you know, "what did Vermont need in order to understand how well our students were doing and how well our programs were preparing them?" . . . this group of stakeholders came up with a recommendation to have a comprehensive assessment system for Vermont where there was a state component that was mandatory, and this was an enormous departure for Vermont . . . The standards themselves—I understand that Vermont had a thing called the Common Core for a number of years, and then, that transmuted into the framework of Standards of Learning Opportunities. And, the Board, I believe, in January of '96 adopted the standards as being the foundational expectations for students in Vermont schools, but the standards themselves were never mandatory (Interview, 1999).

Former-commissioner Mills gets much of the credit for building legitimacy for reform with grassroots consultation. One major consequence of the relative newness of a state presence in standards and assessments, according to state education department officials, is that many schools are confronting serious testing for the first time. As a result, schools and districts had developed little capacity to analyze and understand data about school performance.

As a result of this "departure," and in the spirit of the early phases of reform, the Vermont State Department of Education, while small by any standard, increased its staff to include experts on standards and assessment. The state department also runs comprehensive consultation and training activities designed to make teachers and administrators more familiar with the reforms. Virtually all the administrators and a substantial portion of the teachers in the high schools we visited in Vermont have participated in a number of state-sponsored workshops on various aspects of the reform or were instrumental in the initial design and construction of the state standards. The state department receives high marks from both outside experts and local educators for its training and professional development activities.[11] Additionally, in an effort to incorporate a teacher-focused professionalization approach into Vermont's accountability model, state institutions of higher education have brought their teacher certification programs into alignment with the state reforms. Student teachers in our sample high schools reported, for example, that they are required to align their lesson plans with the state content standards, that their teacher preparation deals explicitly with state standards, and that their evaluations depend on being knowledgeable about the standards. Supervising teachers in high schools also reported learning from their student teachers about the process of aligning lessons with standards.

The political-economic origins and the educational context of assessment and accountability in Vermont together represent a long-term engagement in a gradual process of grassroots consensus building around standards and assessments; very low capacity and sophistication in many local schools concerning fundamental issues of standards, assessments, and accountability; and reasonably large and targeted professional development and training efforts at the state level designed to improve local capacity.

Action Plans and School Choice: The Modified Approach and Its Characteristics In 1997, the Vermont State Supreme Court issued an opinion in Brigham v. State invalidating the state's school finance system on the grounds of its inconsistency with the provisions of the state constitution and requiring the state legislature to produce a school finance plan that would "insure substantial educational opportunity throughout Vermont." The resulting law, Act 60, passed in June of 1997, creates a steeply progressive redistribution scheme in the school finance system, requiring high-wealth school districts—commonly called "gold towns"—to return substantial amounts of the revenue they raise to the state for redistribution to low-wealth communities. Hence, high-wealth districts that want to continue to spend at current levels must raise substantially more money. The Brigham decision, not surprisingly, has caused uproar among the small number of high-wealth, high-expenditure school districts in the state's winter recreation areas and small urban centers, and political mobilization to modify the law is growing. The high schools in our sample are in both high-wealth and low-wealth communities. The high-wealth district has made two major budget cuts in the last two school years, with significant programmatic impact on its high school offerings, although no appreciable impact on academic core content. Conversely, the low-wealth district has received a significant financial windfall, which it is treating cautiously because district administrators don't believe that Act 60 will survive for long.

Act 60 also made an addition to the programmatic structure of education reform in the state. The law requires all schools to prepare "action plans"—annual plans that set specific goals and targets for improvement and school performance. The action planning requirement is a purely school-level requirement—districts are not required to do likewise—and districts are the monitoring agents, not the state. The plans are reviewed at the district level for consistency with district policy, but they are not reviewed by the state except potentially in audits. One long-time policy maker described this change to Vermont's accountability system as holding "the key to the difference between Vermont and other states."

> . . . in the accountability system in Vermont that's being developed, we're the only state in the nation, from what we've heard from our consultants, that thinks that there should be a local component in the accountability system. Every other state sets the test, says this is the only thing we're going to pay attention to, you know, how you do on this or these, and then we're going to consecrate you based on, you know, kind of how you do. And our approach is to say that, really, if you're implementing a system of standards-based . . . a standards-based system, that, really, accountability is a responsibility, and you've got to have responsibility across the system so when that teacher closes the door—and that's kind of how we imagine this—are they doing the kinds of things that are the things that are going to make a difference for the kids, particularly the kids who traditionally don't learn, because a lot of kids are going to learn anyway, but for the ones who traditionally don't learn? And, what would it take in a system for that? And, part of it's around professional development (Interview 1999).

The introduction of local school "action plans" and the decentralization of monitoring power from the state to the district give Vermont's model a stronger flavor of a school-based management approach to accountability than the models in the other states.

Since 1869, Vermont has had an educational choice system for students who reside in "tuition towns" (towns that do not have their own public high school and do not belong to a union high school district). Of the state's 246 towns, ninety (comprising about 18 percent of the state's high school age population) are tuition towns, thirty of which do not have their own elementary schools. Tuition town students in the seventh through twelfth grades may attend either a public or approved independent school ("academy") located within or outside Vermont. Their town school boards pay their tuition expenses. If the student chooses a public school, the town must pay the full tuition cost. If the student chooses an independent school, local voters can decide whether to pay the full cost or the state average union high school tuition cost. About three hundred Vermont high school students take advantage of this program to attend out-of-state private schools. For towns with no elementary schools, Act 271 of 1990 provides for similar payment of tuition by school boards to both public and independent schools. Parents of these students do not have the legal right to a tuition payment for their children to attend an independent school of their choice, but it would be highly unusual for a school board to refuse a parent's request (Heritage Foundation, 1999).

In addition to questions of fairness and equality, Act 60 sparked a bitter debate over the fairness and importance of local control. To begin with,

Vermont's historical school choice program and—as one local political representative called it—its "taken-for-granted system of accountability" based on student-driven competition, came under scrutiny. As part of Act 60's revision in education financing, for example, there were those who wished to expand the program by allowing parents to use state block grants ($5,000 per pupil) to send their child to *any* approved nonsectarian school, beginning in 2003. The Senate passed such an amendment by a vote of eighteen to twelve, but the provision was dropped at the insistence of House conferees. An identical amendment offered in 1998 was also rejected by a vote of twelve to seventeen. At the same time, a group of state House members sponsored a bill to create "Education Freedom Districts." Under House Bill 393, the voters of a school district would have been able to design their own school system, including options for vouchers, charter schools, an exemption from teacher certification, subject matter examination for teachers, merit pay, termination of union dues, check offs, and privatization. But again, no action was taken. In the meantime, in 1998, Act 71, the "technical corrections bill" designed to "fix" Act 60, mandated that the state board develop and present a "limited choice" public school open enrollment plan for high school students by January 1999 (Mathis, 1999). Unexpectedly, momentum headed in the opposite direction. With no prior warning, rather than producing the plan in 1999, the State Board of Education voted to recommend elimination of the independent school choice options in Vermont. One local decision-maker explained that while "the legal future of school choice may remain uncertain in Vermont, the cultural heritage remains true . . . it is part of our improvement mentality, and this state's always been blessed by that kind of, really, kind of forward drive" toward accountability.

The Outcomes of Assessment and Accountability   Vermont's accountability system is relatively simple in its basic goals and objectives and comparatively clear in its state-local-school governance structure. The state issues content standards in all academic subjects; the extensive process of development of the standards is the main source of their authority. Schools and districts are not monitored for their use of the standards, nor is there any formal requirement that they show evidence of the impact of standards on curricula and teaching. Schools and districts are required to administer the New Standards Reference Examination (NSRE) annually at the fourth, eighth, and tenth grades and to report the scores publicly. There are presently no state-level sanctions that apply to low school performance; there is, however, a state process (called School Quality Standards) for identifying the lowest-performing schools and targeting them for state oversight and assistance. Stakes for schools and districts, then, consist almost entirely of public scrutiny of performance data on the NSRE, plus some possible additional state scrutiny for extremely low-performing schools.

However, in July 2000 the State Board of Education approved the Vermont School Accountability System Based on Student Performance. Under the new system, scheduled to be implemented in the fall of 2002, schools will be reviewed for the development of accountability reports that will document their progress toward state goals set for the 2007–2008 school year. Beginning in the fall of 2004, additional consequences beyond technical assistance will be phased in for low performing schools. However, the Vermont accountability system does not have high stakes for students. Students and their families receive their scores individually on the NSRE, as well as the school-level scores for tested grades, but student promotion and graduation decisions are not based on test performance.

The underlying theory of accountability in the Vermont model is a hybrid of the state's strong tradition of local control and a recently added, more assertive and visible state role. The state has been quite aggressive in asserting its interest, independent of local boards and schools, in higher standards of content and performance as well as equity in school finance. In terms of academic performance, the theory is that clear evidence of student performance measured against high standards will mobilize the public to improve schools through local governance mechanisms. In the finance domain, the theory is that the state is the custodian of equal opportunity education and that it is responsible for creating and administering a system that redistributes wealth. Hence, there is a mix of state assertiveness and deference to local control, indirect incentives for improvement through publicity, and direct redistribution of wealth.

Similarly, the Act 60 action planning requirement is premised on the view that schools should actively engage in the systematic scrutiny of their own performance and the planning of improvement measures, but that it is more important that these activities be carried out at the school level than that they be monitored or enforced by states and localities. The state requires local boards to review and approve school actions, and they provide a specific rubric to use in evaluating plans. However, the consequences of doing a poor plan or of having weak local board scrutiny remain unclear.

Overall, Vermont's approach to accountability has been to set relatively ambitious standards, to use relatively high-end measures of performance, to develop broad consensus through extensive consultation and training, to build up the state department's presence in school-level matters primarily around capacity-building activities, and to lean rather lightly on formal external accountability measures toward schools or students.

Assessment and Accountability in Sum

The movement toward assessment and accountability stemmed from the ideal that all children should receive a fair and equitable education and responded to the call that the best educational policies and practices should be recognized, rewarded, and replicated across states. The application of such policies within and between different states reflects, however, the political-economic origins and educational contexts of accountability within each state. In the four cases reviewed here, we see both variation and correlation.

All four states employ a statewide standardization approach to assessment and accountability. But in each case the reform includes other approaches, albeit to different degrees and in different manners. For example, in response to fiscal discrepancies and educational inequities, Kentucky's reform has centered on a statewide standardization approach to accountability and assessment. Although Kentucky and New York have attempted to introduce components of a school-based approach, each of the state's reforms has been conditioned by the fact that the reform originated in the state government and by the fundamental understanding that it is the state's constitutional responsibility to provide and improve education. However, whereas Kentucky places some emphasis on the role of the teacher in carrying out the state's efforts to improve education, New York focuses on the role of the student in demonstrating progress toward those improvements. By comparison, while both Texas and Vermont believe that it is the state's role to provide educational opportunities for all, they have each introduced district- or school-based approaches with more fervor than either Kentucky or New York. In the case of Texas, this approach was conditioned by the primary role of nongovernmental actors in advocating the reform and by a historic commitment to local control and innovation. Vermont's approach was conditioned by the central role that civic organizations played in pushing this reform and by the intrinsic belief in the power of local actors and their right to choose.[12] Thus, each approach implies a different transformation, stemming from different conditions and with different characteristics. (See tables 1.1 and 1.2 for summary tables.) So, what are the results?

- Between 1993 and 1998, the percentage of Kentucky students scoring "proficient" rose in every subject at every level, except in science among middle school students.
- In the spring of 2002, Texas students completed their eighth consecutive year of increasing scores in just about every grade level in almost every subject tested in the Texas Assessment of Academic Skills.
- More New York high school students took and passed Regents exams in 1998 and 1999 than ever before, with 73 percent of the

Table 1.1 Conditions

	Educational financing per pupil (1998)	Educational structure	Student population pre-K to 12 (1998–99)	Percentage of students who receive free or reduced lunch (1998–99)	Percentage of students who are minority (1998–99)	Percentage of students taking SAT/ACT (1997–98)
Kentucky[1]	$5,622	8 regions, 176 districts	646,190	47.7%	11.9%	53.1%*
New York[2]	$9,321	711 districts	3,293,848 (1997–98)	25.0% (1997–98)	44.0% (1997–98)	77.0%*
Texas[3]	$5,853	1,042 districts	3,945,367	48.5%	55.8%	61.7%
Vermont[4]	$7,155	60 supervisory regions, 251 towns, 285 districts	105,106	26.4%	3.0%	63.0%

[1] Data from the Kentucky Department of Education website at http://www.kde.state.ky.us/comm/mediarel/facts.asp.
[2] Data from the New York State Education website at www.emsc.nysed.gov/irts/ch655_99/home.html.
[3] Data from the Texas Education Agency website at http://www.tea.state.tx.us/perfreport/aeis/99/state.html.
[4] Data from the Vermont Department of Education website at http://crs.uvm.edu/cfusion/schlrpt99/vermont.cfm.
*This calculation represents the number of students going on to post-secondary education. The estimate for students taking SAT/ACT was not available.

Table 1.2 Characteristics

	Source	Advocates	Approach(es)	Overarching objectives	Instruments	Stakes/incentives	Outcomes
Kentucky	Regional fiscal disparities and educational inequities	Governor Lesislature "Grass-tops" business groups	Statewide standardization School-based management	Equalize educational financing and educational opportunities Enhance overall state image and economic prospects	High level competency as measured by norm-referenced CTBS tests, performance events, and writing portfolios (grades 4–12) School rating in accountability index (CATS) based on tests and performance events as well as non-cognitive measures	Student financial incentives to take KIRIS/CATS test Teacher-school financial rewards for high CATS index rating/ school sanctions for low CATS index rating	All regions improving, but the gap between regions still exists No student performance gaps based on SES or race, but gap based on gender Student text scores improved most in elementary school, less in middle school, and least in high school
New York	Educational discrepancies between academic and non-academic students	Governor Board of Regents Commissioner of Education	Statewide standardization Teacher-focused professional-ization	Prepare all students for post-secondary education	High level competency as measured by Regents exams (grade 11)	High school graduation requirement Post-secondary matriculation requirement School sanctions for low student scores	More students taking Regents exams, but percentage of students passing is constant Student performance gap prevails on the basis of race and special needs

Texas	District fiscal disparities and educational inequities	Governor Texas Business and Education Coalition	Statewide standardization District-based management Teacher-focused Professionalization	Equalize educational financing Graduate all students on grade level Increase local control and innovation	Minimum competency as measured by criterion-referenced TAAS test (grades 3 to 8 and 10) School and district rating in accountability index (AEIS) based on TAAS test, SAT/ACT and AP/IB tests, and noncognitive measures	High school graduation requirement School financial rewards for high AEIS index rating/school sanctions for low AEIS index rating Student, teacher, and school financial incentives based on SAT/ACT and AP scores	Overall student performance has improved on TAAS, particularly among minority students, yet the percentage of students passing TAAS still varies significantly by ethnicity
Vermont	Local fiscal disparities and educational inequities	Governor Legislature Department of Education "Civil society" organizations	School-based management Teacher-focused Professionalization State-wide standardization Student-driven competition	Equalize educational financing and educational opportunities Sustain local control and improve local capacity	High-level competency as measured by student portfolios, criterion-referenced NSRE tests, and locally developed assessments (grades 2, 4, 5, 6 and 8–11) School rating in accountability index based on state tests and portfolios, local assessments and non-cognitive measures	There are intentionally no stakes Sanctions are in development	Percentage of students who met or exceeded the state's standards has increased in math and language arts at elementary level, increased in math but decreased in language arts at middle school level, and decreased or stayed the same in both at high school level

state's twelfth graders passing the English Regents exam in 1998 and 78 percent passing in 1999.
- In the three years of the state's testing program, the percentage of Vermont's fourth graders who have met or exceeded the state's standards in reading and math has risen every year, as has the percentage of sixth graders with respect to math.

Is this evidence that assessment and accountability systems really can ensure higher academic performance for students?

Perhaps. But these trends do not tell all. In Kentucky, a significantly higher percentage of suburban students are scoring "proficient" or higher than are rural and urban students, and the overall rate of improvement in student scores has been much lower among high school students than elementary or middle school students. In Texas, TAAS and NAEP test results show that the performance gaps between minority students and white students remain large, particularly at the high school level, and the NAEP results suggest that the gap is not narrowing. More and more high school students are taking and passing Regents exams in New York but a high percentage still do not pass, with most of those left behind being minorities and students with disabilities. Although scores are increasing in Vermont among elementary and middle school students, the results for high school students are mixed at best.

In addition, increasing test scores in states such as Kentucky and Texas, where the accountability systems have been in place for many years, are just beginning to have an impact on high school graduation rates. In terms of students' economic futures, graduation rates are much more important than performance on a state test in the primary and middle grades. Thus, test scores have improved but not for everybody and, in our four sample states, accountability has a much smaller effect on outcomes than in any other level of the system. This raises serious questions about why, when all is said an done, educational accountability, no matter what its political origins or ultimate shape, seems to have so little impact on high school outcomes, at least until now. Is this simply because accountability needs many years to work its way up the educational ladder? Or is there something about high schools that makes them relatively unresponsive to accountability efforts? We explore these questions in the essays that follow.

Notes

1. This definition of accountability was originally coined by Robert Wagner, *Accountability in Education*, New York: Routledge, 1989.
2. See also Paul Hill, Lawrence Pierce, and James Guthrie, *Reinventing Public Education* (Chicago: University of Chicago Press, 1997) and Moe (1996).

3. Kentucky is a very racially homogenous state, with 92 percent white, 7.2 percent black, .7 percent Hispanic, .6 percent Asian-Pacific Islander, and .2 percent Indian. Government Information Sharing Project: http://govinfo.library.orst.edu/cgi-bin/usaco-list98?01-state.kys.
4. "Performance events" are structured activities that students are required to perform in order to demonstrate their ability to use certain concepts or processes to solve one or more problems (Foster 1999).
5. It should be noted that, according to one of the consultants and advocates of the process, the performance events for the arts are a "fraud." She reported that even though arts performance events are mentioned in the new law as something that will be accomplished under CATS, as of now, Kentucky is "not doing anything through performance events that would move up the quality of what schools are doing in the arts."
6. In addition to Grissmer and Flanagan (1998), see, for example, Peter Schrag, "Too Good to be True," *The American Prospect* 11, no. 2 (2000).
7. In 1988 there was "marked improvement" in the third, fifth, and seventh grades, but not in the ninth grade (*United Press International* 1988).
8. Except in algebra I, where a district test may be given in the first semester and the state test at the end of the course.
9. Peter Schrag argues that they may have (Schrag 2000).
10. See, for example, PACE, 1985, for an assessment of California's efforts in the 1980s.
11. See, for example, Susan Lusi, *The Role of State Departments of Education in Complex School Reform*, New York: Teachers College Press, 1997.
12. For more on the role of civil society in Vermont's historical and contemporary educational context, see Bill Mathis, "Civil Society and School Reform: Vermont's Act 60," prepared for the annual meeting of the American Educational Research Association, April 24–28, 2000, New Orleans, LA.

References

Ball, S. 1998. Big policies/small world: An introduction to international perspectives in education policy. *Comparative Education* 34: 119–30.

Bishop, J. 1998. *Do curriculum-based external exit exam systems enhance student achievement?* CPRE.

Bryk, A. S., and K. Hermanson. 1993. Educational indicator systems: Observations on their structure, interpretation, and use. *Review of Research in Education* 19: 451–484. Washington: American Educational Research Association.

Calarco, T. 1996. New commissioner tackles hard tasks ahead. *Capital District Business Review* 22: 1–3.

Captioning Unlimited. 1999. New York learns: Parent night "Getting ready for the Regents English exam." Transcript, February 11.

Colvin, R. L. 1999. Texas Schools Gain Notice and Skepticism. *Los Angeles Times*, Part A Section, July 6, Home Edition.

Darling-Hammond, L., and C. Ascher. 1991. *Accountability in big city school systems*. Digest Number 71. New York: ERIC Clearinghouse on Urban Education.

DeBray, E. 2000. *A comprehensive high school and a shift in New York state policy: A study of early implementation*. Unpublished Qualifying Paper, Harvard Graduate School of Education: Cambridge, MA.

DeFabio, R. Y. 1998. (Director of Curriculum and Assessment, New York State Education Department). Interview by author for CPRE. Albany, NY, 3 August.

Diegmueller, K. 1996. New York backs tougher exams for all students. *Education Week*, May 1: 13.

Elmore, R., C. Abelmann, and C. Kenyon. 1996. Working paper on accountability. CPRE, June.

Fiske, E. B. 1983. Action plan by Regents. *The New York Times*, 1 August.

Foster, J. 1999. *Redesigning public education: The Kentucky experience*. Independently published.

Grissmer, and Flanagan. 1998. *Exploring rapid achievement gains in North Carolina and Texas*. National Education Goals Panel: Washington, D.C.

Hartocollis, A. 1999. New York's chief pushes agenda of change. *The New York Times*, 1 April.

Heine, C. 2002. Kentucky school updates: A parent/citizen guide for 2002–04. Lexington, KY: Prichard Committee for Academic Excellence and the Kentucky Department of Education.

Hoff, D. 1998. Kentucky to include norm-referenced test in accountability plan. *Education Week on the Web*, 21 October.

Hoff D. 1999. Made to measure. *Education Week on the Web,* 16 June.

Holland, H. 1999. Putting parents in their place. *Education Week on the Web,* 22 September.

Holloway L. 2000. Students getting jump on Regents exam requirements. *The New York Times,* 8 March.

Jacobson, L. 1999. Kentucky district questions fairness of accountability proposals. *Education Week on the Web,* 17 February.

Kadamus, J. 2000. Memo to the Board of Regents: Design of a system for accountability for student success, 26 January. Albany, NY: New York State Education Department.

Karlin, R. 1997. Education chief aims for higher standards, *The New York Times,* 6 July.

Keller, B. 1999. After 10 years, landmark Kentucky law yielding dividends. *Education Week on the Web,* 17 November.

Keller, B. 2000. New York chief deals blow to alternative-assessment plans. *Education Week,* February 2: 13.

Kentucky Department of Education. 2001. Testing in Kentucky. Keys to understanding accountability: A parent's guide to the commonwealth accountability testing system. Part two: Accountability. Lexington, KY: Kentucky Department of Education.

Leithwood, K., K. Edge, and D. Jantzi. 1999. Educational accountability: The state of the art. Gütersloh, Germany: International Network for Innovative School Systems. Bertelsmann Foundation Publishers.

Lewis, A. 1998. *Assessing student achievement: Search for validity and balance.* CSE Technical Report 481. Los Angeles: CRESST: University of California at Los Angeles.

Linn, R. 2000. Assessments and accountability. *Education Researcher* 25: 4–16.

Maeoff, G. L. 1983. New York's Regents climb down from their ivory tower. *The New York Times,* 20 November.

Maeroff, G. I. 1984. Regents adopt stricter standards for high school diplomas in state. *The New York Times,* 24 March.

Mathis, B. forthcoming. Vermont. In *Public School Finance and Programs of the United States and Canada.*

Moe, T. 1996. Some brief thoughts on accountability. Correspondence.

Mills, R. 1996. Report to the state Board of Regents. Albany, NY: New York State Education Department.

Mosco, M. 2000. How Albany failed English. *The New York Times,* 5 February.

New York State Education Department. 1996. Board of Regents meeting minutes, July.

New York State Education Department. 2002. *No Child Left Behind: Implementing a System of Accountability for Student Success to Meet the Requirements of NCLB.* Albany, NY.

Olson, L. 2000. Quality counts 2000: Who should teach? The states decide. *Education Week. Special Report* 13 January [http://www.edweek.org/sreports]

Patton, P. 2000. State of the Commonwealth Address. Frankfort, KY, 4 January.

Paul, L. 1997. Great expectations: In his demand for higher standards, State Education Commissioner Richard Mills has shaken the foundations of New York public education. *The Buffalo News,* 22 June.

Perez-Pena, R. 1999. 78 percent have passed Regents, but experts raise concerns. *The New York Times,* 13 October.

Policy Analysis of California Education (PACE). 1985. Curricular Change in California's Comprehensive High Schools. Berkeley, CA: PACE.

Prichard Committee. 1999. Gaining ground: Hard work and high expectations for Kentucky schools. Lexington, KY: The Prichard Committee for Academic Excellence.

Rohter, L. 1985. City lists high schools rated deficient by state. *The New York Times,* 28 November.

Schrag, P. 2000. Too Good to Be True. *The American Prospect,* 11(4): 46–49.

Sengupta, S. 1997. Tougher tests? Bring 'em on!; State's stiffer standards for graduation are embraced by many in class of 2000. *The New York Times,* 18 June.

Stecher, B., and S. Barron. 1999. Test-based accountability: The perverse consequences of milepost testing. CRESST and RAND Education. Paper presented at the annual meeting of the American Educational Research Association, Montreal, Canada, April 21.

Vermont State Board of Education. 2001. The equal educational opportunity act: Measuring equity. Montpelier, Vermont: Vermont Department of Education.

Weiler H. 1990. Comparative perspectives on educational decentralization: An exercise in contradiction. *Educational Evaluation and Policy Analysis* 12: 433–48.

Winter, M. 1985. New York Regents exams: Emulated and criticized for toughness. *The Christian Science Monitor*, 23 August.

White, K. 1998a. Kentucky senate gives ok to measure that would replace KIRIS test. *Education Week on the Web*, 1 April.

White, K. 1998b. Kentucky bids KIRIS farewell, ushers in new test. *Education Week on the Web*, 22 April.

CHAPTER 2

Internal Alignment and External Pressure

High School Responses in Four State Contexts

ELIZABETH DEBRAY, GAIL PARSON, AND SALVADOR AVILA

Introduction

A main goal of the new accountability systems in the four states we surveyed is increasing quality of education for lower-income rural or inner city students. If this goal is to be realized, high schools that start out "behind" would have to improve their students' academic performance more than high schools where students are already doing better. States such as Texas claim that they are succeeding in helping low-performing schools catch up, at least in the primary and middle grades. The claim is at least partially supported by National Assessment of Educational Progress (NAEP) score gains in the 1990s. Blacks and Latinos represent a large proportion of low-scoring students in Texas, and in both fourth and eighth grade NAEP math, these students made larger gains than whites. The high percentage of black and Hispanic students in New York also made relative gains on the math NAEP test in the same period, especially in the past four years. But the gains in these two states may have been partly an artifact of excluding more minority students from the test in later years (Carnoy and Loeb 2003). Writing scores on the Kentucky state test increased more in the eastern, lower income counties, largely because writing had not been taught systematically in those schools before the state test was implemented. Yet in Kentucky and Vermont there is no evidence that disadvantaged groups have made relative gains over time in NAEP math or reading scores.

Moreover, where lower performing groups made NAEP test score gains in the primary and middle grades, these gains did not appear to carry over into high schools. As Carnoy, Loeb, and Smith show in their essay in this book, toward the end of the 1990s, blacks in Texas did improve compared to whites in high school survival rates—the proportion of eighth graders who reach twelfth grade four years later. But we have no evidence that this improvement is related to the Texas accountability system. Indeed, for most of the decade, high school survival rates for these disadvantaged groups did not change in Texas or in the other three states we studied.

Why the difficulty for standards-based reforms in equalizing student performance? This essay attempts to analyze how state accountability systems geared toward pulling up lower scoring schools by delineating clear goals and incentives actually affect schools. Using observations and interviews in schools, we try to understand the barriers states face in improving learning, particularly at the high school level.

Our method for unraveling this puzzle was to select high schools that were differently positioned with respect to the reform. We designated these schools as "target" (T), "better positioned" (BP), and "orthogonal" (O) schools. We defined a "target" school as one with a low socioeconomic class and a large disadvantaged minority student population that performed at relatively low levels of academic achievement. A "better positioned" school was defined as one whose student performance, prior to the onset of the policy, was deemed adequate with regard to existing assessments. "Orthogonal" (differently angled) schools were those viewed as potentially having a mission or purpose that differed from the official goals of state policy. This "angling away" from the direction of state policy is the one common criterion these three schools shared. They "angled" differently according to their missions and purposes, and were therefore as different from each other as they were from the common characteristics of the BP and T schools. Examples of orthogonal schools might include career academies, alternative high schools with state waivers, magnet schools, and/or a school with a particularly strong external constituency that drives its mission. The rationale for including orthogonal schools was to leave open the possibility that school-level accountability can be constructed in response to a variety of constituencies or missions. The study hypothesized that the orthogonal schools might or might not align with state policies.

Thus, our design did not assume that "type" corresponded to a static collection of characteristics and qualities determining effectiveness. Rather, typing schools enabled us to identify how schools differed in their "starting positions" with respect to uniform policies.

A major methodological issue in typing the schools in our sample was defining school starting position in states with long-running reforms, such as Kentucky and Texas. There we were selecting schools that had already been subject to standards for a number of years before we arrived on the scene. In the case of orthogonal schools, we picked schools in those two states that had been orthogonal for the entire period of the reform. We designated the targeted schools in Texas, for example, by their high proportion of disadvantaged minority, low socioeconomic class (school lunch) students, and relatively low scores on the TAAS in the early and mid-1990s. We had four targeted schools in our sample, but two of them had a magnet program that had been added in the mid-1990s. The magnet programs were added specifically to make the schools more attractive to high SES students, and they did make rapid gains on the TAAS; yet, we still considered these schools as target schools because they had started at a much lower performance level.

Common Embedded Expectations of State Policies: Relatively Uniform Response over Time

As Rhoten et al. describe in their chapter, performance-based accountability systems all share the common assumption that their combination of mandates, incentives, and sanctions will bring schools into line with state policy and the goal of increased student performance. Performance-based educational policies, by and large, also share the goal of creating a greater degree of outcome equity for a state's students.

Though the mechanisms and policy "logics" differ, they assume that over time the demands of the policy will be stronger than the existence of local factors, such as culture, tradition, and expectations, which may determine a school's beginning position. So, as envisioned by policymakers, schools' performances, relative to each other, become more compressed over time toward alignment with the policy. This represents the political drive to generate outcome equity.

Each state's time frame for achieving the goal of compressing the range of performance levels is different. In Kentucky, policy makers envisioned a time frame of twenty years. In Texas, the system has been in place for almost twenty years, and is still pushing for reducing the minority-white test score gap. In Vermont, no time frame is given. In New York, the timeline for all students to pass the exams necessary for a diploma was equivalent to the five year phase-in time for the tests.

Figure 2.1 represents the linear assumption of many state policies—a progression over time toward a goal of more uniform outcomes, even though schools begin at different places in terms of their performance. One possible finding in the fifteen high schools we studied is that all the

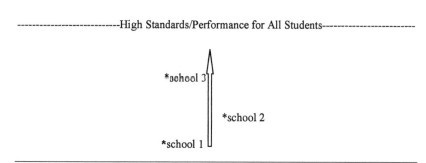

Figure 2.1 Linear Assumptions of Most State Policies

schools in all the four states are more or less equally aligned with state external accountability systems. This alignment would be independent of school type and independent of the "strength"—the degree of rewards and sanctions—that characterizes the state's accountability system.

An alternative possibility is that the state accountability systems are accomplishing their goal of "aligning" most forcefully the least internally aligned schools—the targeted schools in our sample—with state standards. In this scenario, the schools in our sample might produce a pattern of response like that in Table 2.1—a pattern in which external accountability coming from the state consciously focuses on differences in school type to push greater alignment in target schools, and the design of the state accountability system drives response to policy differentially across types of schools. In this scenario, we might also find differences among states with stronger and weaker accountability systems, but in all states target schools would align more with external standards than other types of schools.

In this essay, we suggest that neither of these two patterns of response seems to be playing out at the high school level in the four states we studied. Contrary to expectations among state policy makers, target schools tend to be less aligned with state policies even in Kentucky and Texas, two states with many years of strong external accountability (although there are targeted schools in our sample that were able to align themselves with state standards). Better positioned schools seem best able to incorporate external accountability into their internal accountability systems, and orthogonal schools tend to focus on their mission and avoid defining themselves in terms of external accountability, or, in some cases, resist alignment if they feel it compromises their mission.

We also suggest that "stronger" state accountability systems are more likely to produce alignment with state standards, and that this effect is felt most in the target schools. Thus, we suggest that the weaker the direct

Table 2.1 Expected Response Based on School Type in Four States, 1998–1999

State	Schools with relatively high alignment with policy	Schools with relatively low alignment with policy	Schools where accountability is defined primarily in terms of mission/identity
New York			
High stakes for students	Robinson (T)	Rivera (BP)	Ring (O)
Kentucky			
High stakes for adults and schools	Binghamton (T)	Byrd (BP)	Baleford (O)
Texas	Calin,		
High stakes for students and schools	Miramar, Eames, Ricki Lee (T)	Texoma (BP)	Cityscape (O)
Vermont			
Low stakes beyond test score publicity	Garrison (T)	Glen Lake (BP)	Graham (O)

sanctions and incentives from the state, the less likely target schools are to align themselves with state standards.

Not only do incentives and stakes within the four different state accountability policies vary considerably, but schools within each state also tended to respond differently to these policies. The difference in response was least pronounced among the best-positioned schools. These schools tend to be better able to incorporate and utilize external standards in school improvement. Our study also suggests that, rather than state accountability goals driving alignment with policy, as in our second scenario, it is the internal accountability system, or the capacity, of the school that tends to drive alignment with policy. Since target schools have less capacity to align themselves with standards, this tends to interfere with state goals to compress outcomes.

We also find variance *within* this pattern. Since we sampled a larger number of Texas schools in the target category, we were able to observe differences within that "type." Whereas generally, there were important differences in response to state policies between target and better-positioned schools, some targeted schools that started out with relatively poorly aligned internal accountability were able to align themselves with state policies better than other target schools.

Adding the orthogonal schools to our analysis further deepens our understanding of schools' internal accountability as capacity for response. Because of their commitment to missions other than those defined by the policy, they also illuminate the power and influence of existing school culture and identity. For every school in the sample, the response to policy emerged not only from capacity and collective expectations, but also from the connections the school may forge with outside networks and similar schools based on its self-conception. While the stories of each of the orthogonal schools were quite different – some resisted the external policies while others aligned with them—they show the range of how organizations mediate uniform demands.

State Policy Environments, School Type, and High School Response

In analyzing how a high school's internal accountability interacts with state attempts to align schools to standards, the two main variables are the incentives and sanctions of the state accountability system and the conditions within each school.

All four accountability policies we studied are standards-based systems with mandated testing; they differed substantially in three key ways: location of stakes, strength of incentives and assessments, and state policy context. The accountability policies of these three states from a continuum, from low stakes (Vermont), to organizational stakes and stakes for adults (Kentucky), to high stakes for students (New York), to organizational high stakes for adults and high stakes for students (Texas).

For each state, we describe how certain features of the accountability policies shaped schools' responses, and how these responses varied among types of schools within each state. Specifically, the differences in placement of stakes in the system were an important factor in schools' responses, and partly account for the variation of responses within different types of schools. At the same time, the alignment of the internal accountability system in each school affected how it was able to respond to the sanctions and rewards in each state. As we show, the interaction between the two accountability systems is crucial to understanding how schools incorporate state standards, and hence, how the reform plays out in terms of school improvement and student outcomes.

Vermont

Vermont's accountability system does not have stakes for either students or adults. The underlying theory of the system is a sort of "market communitarianism." In the context of fierce local control and community action, policy makers assumed that publishing schools' assessment results would stimulate local pressure on schools to implement reform. The response to this pressure would be building-level instructional improvement. Educational policy makers in Vermont also seem to have a business theory of total quality management and continuous improvement through effective data analysis to monitor and stimulate organizational improvement. Each community is expected to do things its own way and, as in the other states we studied, schools themselves are supposed to figure out how to meet state standards.

In contrast to New York, Kentucky, and Texas, the accountability policy for high schools in Vermont attached no stakes to its two primary mandates, the New Standards Reference Exam (NSRE) and school level "action planning," other than publication of test scores and/or school rankings. There were no graduation stakes for students, no clearly defined stakes for adults, no specified roles for districts, and no organizational incentives or consequences for schools. The policy assumed that schools had the local motivation and capacity to create and implement effective action plans, using test scores as performance incentives.

The three schools in our Vermont sample contradicted this assumption of uniform capacity and intrinsic local incentives to effect change and improvement. Figure 2.2 shows where our three sampled schools were located after two years of standards reforms in terms of both their alignment with the external accountability system and the strength of their internal accountability system.

The *target school*, Garrison, is an example of a small school with an extremely weak internal accountability system and a low level of alignment with the state policy. State policy makers' assumption that the local community would pressure for change and improvement in response to Garrison's extremely low test scores was undercut by the reality of Garrison's demographics. The highly transient working class and immigrant community was not actively engaged with the school, and several staff members seemed to read this parental and community silence as acceptance and reinforcement of their own low expectations of students in general. In the late 1990s, less than 30 percent of Garrison graduates went on to college.

We were not able to find a coherent internal accountability structure in Garrison. Longstanding problems with communication, discipline, and attendance had created a leadership focused on crisis management and operations, resulting in a habituated laissez faire approach to instruction. The curriculum coordinator described the early years of the reform policy in Vermont, when the Department of Education sent packages of standards out to each teacher in the state. He expressed frustration about the lack of attention and interest in these packs of standards materials. "My goal at one point," he said, "was just to get folks here to take the shrink wrap off the standards that were sitting on teachers' shelves."

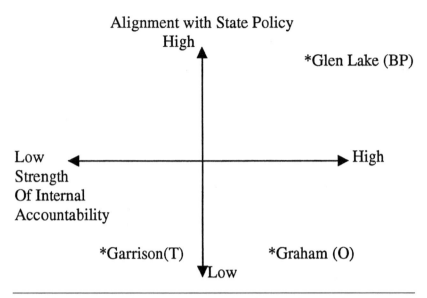

Figure 2.2 Vermont Sample Schools: Alignment with State Policy and Strength of Internal Accountability

We found that the highly idiosyncratic and isolated teaching staff, including many who had not been formally evaluated in years, acted individually in some cases to align their teaching with state standards and tried to improve practice. However, they worked in isolation or networked with colleagues around the state, the school functioning only as a coincidental venue, not a source of, professional growth. Most teachers, including those in tested content areas like English, expressed that changing or improving practice was solely a matter of individual discretion. One English teacher described the lack of pressure to teach to the standards in the school: "There is still a sense in my mind that this is the fad for the next two or three years. We've had so many other fads. What I've done is taken the standards and forced them into the courses I'm already teaching . . . And so what? It hasn't changed all that much the way I deliver education to the students . . . Is [my teaching] standards-based? In a sense it is. I can make it look standards-based. But I don't sit down every day and say, what standard am I teaching today? Which maybe I should be. But I don't."

The combination of collective low expectations and minimal demands that had long dominated the school, resulted in a culture where instructional dysfunction and incompetence remained unidentified or ignored and unchallenged. Action planning was pro forma, a process that met minimal compliance requirements, and resulted in a document submitted to the state. But there was little meaningful staff participation in its development (it was essentially written by an outside consultant) and it did not include performance goals addressing the low scores in math and reading.

Among the staff we interviewed, no one seemed to have a full sense of what the action plan included, its impact on them, or of the specific goals the school was addressing. Garrison illustrates the wide gap between policy compliance and effective policy alignment in a school lacking the capacity, leadership, and internal accountability structures to use policy strategically in the service of improving student achievement.

The orthogonal school in Vermont, Graham, represents a case of a school with the ability to adopt the state policy selectively. Graham is a private academy with a tradition of accepting tuition vouchers from the surrounding local towns. Its internal accountability structures focus on maintaining a rigid tracking system and a strong local identity as a college prep institution in competition with similar prep schools around the state. International students and students attending from other states are exempted from taking the state test. Policy alignment appears in the efforts of the math and English departments to focus on improving scores among those students who actually take the test. To this end, the school uses the two-year "grace period" before the state begins releasing test scores to the public to ensure that Graham's scores will exceed the standard, or at least exceed the scores of similar rival schools. The story of Graham's test scores inadvertently being sent to a neighboring rival school repeatedly struck a note of anguish. One administrator told us that the faculty had not been unanimously receptive to the Vermont frameworks being introduced at Graham: "The only tensions I see with the advent of the Vermont framework is some people saying, 'Whoa, is she trying to make us a public school, because she thinks that the Vermont framework is a fairly good document, a healthy document.' I think that's less so than it was three years ago. When I introduced the Vermont framework to this school, that was the first reaction—we're private, that's public. Then as teachers started working with it more, they saw that it was healthy and they came to respect it, and also my focus has been, 'We're not trying to get you to rewrite your curriculum based on the framework. Take what you do as a department and align it, see where the holes are.'"

Graham does not use the tests strategically as kind of school-wide assessment to challenge current instructional practices or tracking structures. Department heads and the academic dean were fluent in the tests and scores, but staff in general seemed much less involved and informed. Collective expectations and staff development activities over the course of our visits addressed curriculum alignment with standards (with little real progress according to the outside consultant who came twice a year to facilitate the work) and preparation for switching to a block schedule.

The better-positioned school, Glen Lake, started out with internal accountability structures and processes already in place that not only supported, but jump started the new state mandates. Their pace of implementation was rapid because their identity as a high-performing school was important to them. The staff shared a disposition to accept the new standards as a barometer of their academic success. Departments were already aligned organizationally with both attainment and departments/subjects/standards. School and department leadership worked together to make the required action planning an active tool to get all students to meet high standards. In response to local control, public reporting stakes, and action planning, Glen Lake had a rapid ramp-up, an enthusiastic disposition to comply with the standards, a positive identity alignment with the demands of the policy, and leadership with the skills to facilitate alignment and improvement.

The culture at Glen Lake is geared toward exceeding any external initiatives and mandates, maintaining an identity of "being out in front." So initial alignment with state policy was relatively high, and this alignment increased with each of the two years of our study. Interestingly, this drive to work successfully and collectively was internally driven and seemed independent of community interest or attention to particular test scores. In fact, Glen Lake is an example of a school that used state policy strategically to bolster ongoing efforts to improve achievement, a momentum of prior habit and history. Prior to the state required school action planning, for example, the school had already had its own version of a committee in which representatives from all departments focused on setting goals for school improvement. Aligning to meet state policy was a way to improve and intensify this process. The math department chair, who had been at Glen Lake for thirty years, told us that this approach to meeting external goals is typical of the school: "We're involved in everything in this school. We just buy into everything that comes down the pike. We try to meet every state standard. We try to meet the needs of all the parents. Do you know what I'm saying? We're just that kind of a school. We're not a school that very often says no. That kind of explains us."

Individual departments at Glen Lake developed target goals and action plans, gathering data from the state tests and other sources to drive departmental plans and decision making. The teachers in the English department reacted immediately to surprisingly low scores in reading comprehension by taking the test themselves and by radically altering the ninth grade curriculum. (A pre-state policy action plan had resulted in the hiring of a new reading teacher to address the needs of struggling students.) The math department created a two-year algebra I class to give students more time to acquire tested math skills and emphasized technology and hands-on instruction.

The action plan that Glen Lake eventually submitted to the state was deemed "too ambitious" by some state officials, but the school was not deterred. For departments less skilled in data gathering and analysis, there was in-house training and support for all departments to make effective plans that could be executed. The school's internal expectations provided the incentive to align with the external requirements, rather than any pressure from the state or district. Action planning was a school-level activity, subject to virtually no external stakes. The school board did not choose to review or approve the state-mandated Action Plan at all in the last cycle, and the state's only feedback was to ensure Glen Lake conformed precisely to a state rubric. And that, according to the chair of the School Development Team (responsible for action planning), suited Glen Lake just fine: "We're doing this because we think it's valuable for us. And we're going to keep doing it, even if the state backs off . . . We're conforming to the state series of boxes, but we have something we want to get out of it . . . I know there are other schools that are just filling the boxes just to get past this . . ."

Glen Lake's teachers and administrators were eager to respond to the external changes when they easily might have coasted on their preexisting successes without extreme pressure from the community to change. Its existing organizational structure, with strong academic departments, was able to smoothly align its strong internal accountability with state policy. The testing brought to the surface the relatively invisible strata of students who were struggling, and enabled a collective response and an effort to bring high standards to all.

Kentucky

Kentucky's accountability system focuses on rewarding and sanctioning schools (not students) for compliance or noncompliance with state standards and goals. Specifically, principals of nonimproving schools can and have been replaced by distinguished educators who are given administrative authority over the schools. If a school continues to fail to improve, it may be taken over by the state. As in Vermont, there is a strong theory of action about continuous improvement—a school is measured and compared not only in terms of absolute performance but is also compared to its own previous performance for determining rewards and sanctions. The two-year improvement measurement cycles are supposed to get every school to the same level of high standards within twenty years (Elmore, Abelmann, and Fuhrman 1996).

Given schools' familiarity with the state accountability policy after ten years and the policy's system of sanctions that affect the school organization and incentives for building-level improvement, we had expected to observe considerable "compression" of the cluster of schools in our sample

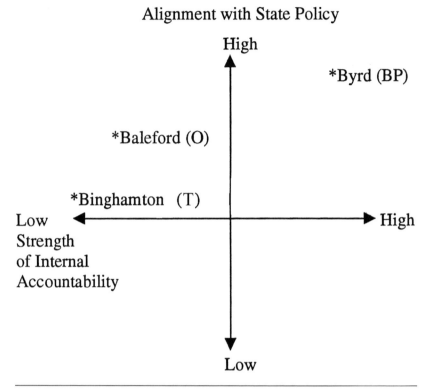

Figure 2.3 Kentucky Sample Schools: Alignment with State Policy and Strength of Internal Accountability

(i.e., all schools' internal accountability systems becoming more highly aligned with external standards) compared to Vermont. To some extent, this was the case. However, in terms of alignment, the schools in Kentucky still remained dispersed.

The target school, Binghamton, represents a case of a school aligning with policy at the level of compliance, but failing to improve student achievement on the CATS tests. Over the course of KERA, this school has consistently failed to improve its performance, and thus has never received a reward from the state. The school has a conception of itself as the "school of last resort" in the district, the "holding tank" for chronic low performers in the district and students who are not accepted into the selective magnet schools. Binghamton's self identity as the helpless victim of an inequitable district assignment system appeared to block the staff's belief in its capacity to change instruction and improve student performance.

Binghamton struggled, having the district's highest dropout rate, high student mobility, attendance problems, and numerous discipline referrals.

According to the vice principal, many of the school's problems are a result of Binghamton being the "dumping ground" of the district, the last resort for parents: "I think the district knows exactly what it's done to this school . . . and I think it's naïve for anyone to assume otherwise . . . I think it's a sad state of affairs that there is not awareness that there is going to be a Binghamton High School every time you have [screened and selected] schools set up."

In recent years the school has added a vocational magnet, which neither increased its internal alignment with KERA goals nor attracted academically oriented students from the district. This, and a patchwork of smaller programs and initiatives to remediate and encourage lower-performing students was not part of a larger, more coherent plan for the school and has had a fragmenting effect on the school. This added to an already atomized culture in which teachers and departments were isolated from each other.

There have been state, district, and school-level responses to Binghamton's needs. In the most recent KERA cycle, the school was assigned a "Highly Skilled Educator" by the state. This sanction, however, was a weak one because the HSE was not given the full authority that the policy had delineated, namely, to take over the school administratively. The HSE was present on an observer/consultant basis, offering advice and rendering observations to district authorities. The district awarded the school a large grant for targeted staff development in the areas of reading and writing throughout the curriculum. At the school level, the freshman curriculum was revised to give all ninth graders a double-block each of math and English. A testing committee, led by a department chair, designed test taking processes and procedures that involved the entire school staff and supported specific content areas.

These various interventions during our two years of fieldwork increased the school's alignment with state policy. However, this alignment, combined with a fragmented and weak internal accountability system, and a lack of consistent attention to the instructional core, has resulted in minimal improvement in student performance. The staff at Binghamton represents a bifurcation of experience, energy, and expertise. Whereas a cadre of younger reformers and "activists" seek to challenge the school's identity and culture, there is an equally strong cultural tenor of resignation, victimization, and despair. The HSE told us, "[The teachers] are really very defensive. They can't stand the big magnet schools. That's what I've heard over and over, 'if we just had our kids back from the other schools. They took all our advanced program kids. If they'd just close x high school and let our kids come back home.'"

Baleford, the orthogonal school in our Kentucky sample, kept a strong sense of mission to the community while also aligning with the performance-based accountability system. As administrators describe it, this is a trend that did not happen immediately after the Distinguished Educator arrived in 1994, but has been evolving gradually since. Baleford is a public magnet with career academies and with strong historic ties to the local community. It is not characterized by strong internal accountability, nor does it have a particularly coherent system of evaluating teaching. However, we found evidence that Baleford was *not* resisting KERA's demands for improvement, as we had hypothesized for all the orthogonal schools in our sample. Rather, probably because of its strong commitment to its career academies, the school was making efforts to align its activities with the policy's demands.

For instance, performance on the CATS tests are being used as the basis of identifying action items in the school's consolidated plan. A good example is the shift to an instructional focus on science and math, including enhancing opportunities for teachers to attend professional development workshops, based on disappointing performance scores. Several teachers told us that scores were being discussed at the school level, with the entire faculty present. Second, there is evidence that Baleford focused on the kinds of teaching and learning that were demanded by KERA following its identification as "failing to make improvement." The school examined its curriculum at that time. Third, administrators describe a cultural shift that has taken place since the changes of the reforms. An assistant principal described how KERA affected the way teachers saw themselves and their work, noting teachers' initial resistances to change several years ago: "At first you had a very negative opinion because there was a big change, change in the way you deliver education to the students because they went from old traditional to a performance-based education and teachers didn't, most teachers except maybe English teachers, didn't use a lot of the open-ended type questions. When you start changing people's procedures, then you've got a lot of complaints . . . you know after they realized that this was in place and this is going to reflect on how well they did their job and that we weren't dictating it, they were no longer angry with us as administrators locally. Now they may, you know, not really like KERA, but they say, 'We're here, we're educators, we got to live with it—we'll do our job.' Actually when you think about, and you look at what was being requested, it wasn't a bad idea."

Typical of the administration's view that student test performance reflects on Baleford's reputation, the Friday before testing week in April, the school principal exhorted the students to "Do your best. Junior classes have done well and brought greater respect in the academic community. Do your best so that we'll continue that reputation. Let's all work together to make Baleford a beacon for this community. We know you're bright, smart, intelligent, and wise, we want the community to know likewise."

The school has also made special efforts for its lowest-performing students. The freshman team and ESS are all part of this infrastructure, and the school's staff credits the programs (as well as the schoolwide focus on reading) with the movement of students out of the lowest CATS performance category.

Baleford is not teaching to the test to the same degree as the better-positioned Kentucky school. Part of the explanation for this is that the career magnet programs have their own curricula and course work, as well as internships. However, teachers consider KERA learning goals to be compatible with the school's mission: preparing a diverse student body for higher education and the world of work. Baleford has adapted to the external demands of KERA while retaining its special sense of mission and accountability to the community.

At Byrd High School, the better-positioned school, we found a strong, coherent internal accountability system. The school had been "in rewards" throughout the course of KERA. The administration's latitude in selecting students who were seeking the academic orientation and traditional curriculum strengthened its position with regard to meeting external goals. Indeed, the administration had some power to dismiss students if they were not deemed a good fit academically or behaviorally. The majority of students at Byrd came from feeder middle and elementary schools that were part of a traditional "path" within the district's magnet system. An assistant principal confirmed that as a student and an administrator, you must "buy in" to the culture of the school.

The principal played the role of "standardsbearer" in the school; that is, she oversaw the interface of the state content and performance standards with the school's own curriculum. She favored "selective abandonment" of some of the state standards in the English curriculum, encouraging staff to set a few standards and have students master them. Staff, too, was monitored for teaching ability. A "problem" teacher was removed from teaching her English class to eleventh graders who would be tested, providing an example of internal alignment with the external system. Similarly, through a partnership with a national standards organization, the math department chose to focus on three or four math standards in a given year. The school was a department-driven organization, which facilitated sharing of test scores and identifying topics for improvement. As was the pattern at our other better-positioned schools, the administration put many academic supports in place to help the students at the greatest risk for academic failure. An English teacher described these efforts: "One thing we do is the pull-out sessions. We take the whole junior class, we put them over in the [professional development academy] auditorium and [the principal], she's up there in front of them and works with the entire class . . . Sometimes she'll look at a previous example of an average response and then in front of the whole class, in front of [all of the] juniors, they'll talk about how to raise that average response up to a distinguished response. And she points out how easy it is with just a few subtle changes to move that average response up to distinguished. And so we're really encouraging them to do that."

New York

The accountability policy for high schools in New York is one that puts a single set of tests in place, places stakes squarely on students to pass those tests in order to graduate, and regulates little more than that assessment and those stakes. The policy offers virtually nothing extra in terms of capacity building or extra resources. It is a standards-based accountability policy, in the sense that the state publishes content frameworks aligned with the Regents examination. These content-specific Regents examinations are in many ways the "standard," as they drive what is to be taught and tested. Alternative high schools such as Ring, the orthogonal school, could only be exempted from the requirement of having students take the Regents exams because they demonstrated that their students were meeting the states performance standards via their own assessment system.

Whereas the state uses this uniformity of testing as its theory of change, the three schools in our sample varied widely in the degree of their alignment with the external policy. The target school, Robinson, provides an example of an institution with an atomized and weak internal accountability system—typical of many large, comprehensive urban high schools. We found pockets of efforts to align with the new policy, for example, in the mathematics department. But we found no overall school response. Many individual teachers inside the school espoused beliefs that the higher academic expectations of the new Regents policy were positive for the students; yet, the policy itself was refracted by the school's complex structure of career academies and academic departments, each of which had to individually determine how to respond to the demands of the tests. In figure 2.4, we placed Robinson near the middle of the axis of alignment with the external policy.

Robinson was not aligned with the Regents policy when we began our study. Three percent of all students earned Regents diplomas before the policy came online in 1996–97, so the external accountability measure that had been most important to the school in the past was the Regents Competency graduation requirements. Therefore, Robinson's ramp toward alignment was a steep one to begin with. While some segments of the school are trying hard to align curricula with the Regents, and a new principal who

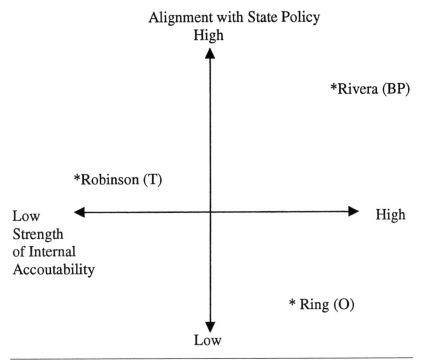

Figure 2.4 New York Sample Schools: Alignment with State Policy and Strength of Internal Accountability

arrived in the 1999–2000 school year aspires to place greater emphasis on standards-based teaching, the imposition of the new testing requirements have not caused Robinson to align to any significant degree.

This is not to say that individuals in the organization do not take seriously the state's placement of stakes on students. The interviews we conducted reveal great concern about students failing to pass the English Regents exam not graduating, and concern that the requirements of the new policy, while basically laudable, are completely unrealistic given the weak academic preparation of the student body. But in an organization where there are no mechanisms for tracking and disseminating information about who has passed and who has failed, it was virtually impossible to marshal a response that could be characterized as "alignment."

In our first year of data collection, we did not hear about any use of data in preparing for the exams. The former math department chair stated that she did not have the capacity or resources to make use of the data from the Regents results: "Last year, [the state] did give us results, where they showed how many kids you had in your class and how many passed the Regents . . . But it could have been done better; it should have been done with support, training, supplemental material, extra resources, consultants, everything. If they thought this was really important, it should have been done with the teachers, not told to the teachers." One ESL teacher told us, "I'm not going to be accountable. Nobody is. If they look at my class list and see that ninety-nine percent of my students fail, is anything going to happen to me? No."

The orthogonal school, Ring, represents a case of a school with a strong, coherent internal accountability system but low alignment with the Regents policy. Ring had a state waiver exempting the school from having to give the Regents before our fieldwork began in 1998–99. The school's mission was to educate students who scored below the twenty-first percentile on the Language Assessment Battery. The administrators maintained that the school could best meet high standards with its own system of performance-based assessments and student defense of individual projects for graduation. The principal and many faculty members saw the Regents system as a threat to the school's particular instructional goals and system of standards. One English teacher told us, "I think [the state policymakers] have lost sight of why alternative schools have existed in the beginning, because these students did not thrive in a regular school system; that's why we started alternative schools. They have special needs one way or another . . . So that's why portfolios were developed in the beginning, and I think people who really don't understand what a successful portfolio is, or what a successful alternative means of learning is, they just don't have a clue. The school system's failing, so they're trying to get a quick fix . . ."

Ring's principal was active in a network of leaders of alternative high schools joining together in a political effort to challenge the state's plan to lift the waiver after 2001. A large part of this challenge included extensive documentation of Ring's performance standards, which the school claimed were even more rigorous than those the new Regents tests demanded. However, Ring and the rest of the consortium of alternative high schools were unsuccessful in this effort. In the middle of the second year of our study, the state's commissioner of education decided that the consortium would have to start giving the English Regents exam in 2000–01, along with all other high schools. When this decision became real to the school, the faculty began to prepare to give the tests. Thus, while figure 2.4 shows Ring's as a relatively low alignment with state policy, this situation is changing. By the end of the second year of our study, its position was moving toward higher alignment with the state testing system (although not yet in all subjects—so far the Commissioner had only required English). Ring's strong identity and coherent internal accountability system led to a fairly strong response to state accountability policies—in this case resistance.

At the better-positioned school, Rivera, we found an established system of internal accountability and shared expectations that prepared students for Regents exams. Thus, the school started out relatively highly aligned with the state's new policy, and increased this alignment over the course of the two years we were in the school. The state testing mandate was readily embraced as the driving force behind the school's efforts, and was accepted as the measure against which Rivera educators judged their success and the success of individual teachers (DeBray, Parson, & Woodworth, 2000). An English teacher explained that ". . . there's a school report card that comes out, and it's broken down by subject area and then by individual class . . . This is a really public place. Everybody knows what's going on behind closed doors. Everybody knows if a teacher is having problems, just everybody knows. It's not a big school."

In turn, teachers shared the common goal of preparing students for college, and accepted the Regents system as a means to do that. As one English teacher said, "I'm not here to prepare them for their career. I'm here to prepare them for college . . . I want to teach them how to write analytically. And I think the Regents is a good assessment of it." The principal stated clearly that preparing students to pass the Regents had long been a school-wide "reality": "There's very . . . little flexibility in what we need to teach, if you care about your kids passing that test . . . [it's] the reality of this school, and now it's really a reality for everybody. I mean, it's been a reality for us for . . . many years, because we were always very . . . concerned about our data, and about the kids doing well here." Rivera's response was to use its existing capacity to align its internal accountability with the state policy even further. As one teacher remarked: "The first week that I taught in the school, the principal had already made an appointment, scheduled an appointment to sit in on one of my classes, just to be sure that I am following the standards of [Rivera], which is tremendous. I felt that that showed that even the principal was actively involved in every single one of his staff's performance, and how they're carrying through their objectives." For those students identified as the most at risk of failing the examinations, a set of interventions was put into place, from after-school tutoring to practice examinations. Like the better-positioned schools in both Kentucky and Vermont, Rivera, partnered with a national reform network, focused on performance standards that aided the school in refining even further its standards-based curriculum.

Texas

Since the mid-1980s, Texas has been a prime example of standards-based accountability reform. The main instruments of the reform have been state testing in grades 3–8 and 10, high stakes for high school students, and sanctions and rewards for schools at all levels. The Texas Education Agency reports passing percentages for students by race/ethnic group, and rates schools as low-performing to exemplary, depending on average scores and scores for each group. High school students are required to pass the TAAS exit test, first taken in tenth grade, to graduate. In addition, high school students must pass ninth grade algebra to graduate. If a school is rated low-performing two years in a row, the principal of the school is replaced.

Schools take the state testing seriously, and parents pay attention to test scores in evaluating school quality. In general, passing rates on the TAAS have been increasing steadily since the early 1990s. In 1997, the year before we first interviewed in Texas, the passing rate of economically disadvantaged students (highly correlated with the average passing rate of African-American and Hispanic students) on the tenth grade test was 71 percent in reading, 55 percent in math, 75 percent in writing, and 47 percent in all tests taken. For white students, the passing rate in all tests taken was 78 percent. By 2001, the passing rate for economically disadvantaged students had risen to 82 percent in reading, 82 percent in math, 82 percent in writing, and 68 percent on all tests taken. For whites, the rate in all tests taken was 89 percent. In 1997, 35 percent of all schools (elementary, middle, and high schools) were rated exemplary or recognized, and by 2002 this figure had risen to more than 60 percent. Low-performing schools had also increased, from 1 percent to 2 percent of the total.

In Texas the stakes are high for both schools and teachers. The incentive structure is designed to recognize the performance and degree of school improvement, which is measured by the scores obtained by the students in standardized testing, end-of-course exams, percentage of students taking the SAT, and attendance and dropout rates. The sanctions for failing to improve as a school range from removing the principal, to an on-site investigation, or a total reconstitution. Public shame is also always a threat (see table 2.2).

Our Texas sample of high schools was larger (six) than in the three other states, and we sampled in two cities (West City and Major City). We also arrived on the scene many years after the assessment system had been put into place. Our sample of schools had a better-positioned school, an orthogonal school, and four target schools. Unlike in the other states, the better-positioned school in our Texas sample did not look very different from at least one of our "target" schools—in part because in large Texas cities, most public high schools have a substantial fraction of low-income minority students.

In the two years we interviewed in the schools, two of the target schools fell into the low-performing category, one in the 1998–99 school year and the other in the 1999–2000 school year, based on the previous year's TAAS

Table 2.2 Main Features of Texas's Accountability Policy

Standards and assessment	Unit of accountability	Primary target of assessment	Accountable to	Stakes in accountability system	Policy history of state
Statewide standardization. State-mandated policy. Passing the 10th grade TASS required for graduation.	Mainly focused on schools and high school students.	Student academic performance; focus on low-performing students.	Students, parents, district, state.	Public reporting about school performance, school sanctions, and student graduation.	State mandated, district managed and supervised, implemented by school. The Texas Essential Knowledge and Skills (TEKS), the end-of-course and the Texas Assessment of Academic Skills (TASS) exams. Some other special tests by district, such as the Academic Course Performance (ACP) in Major City.

scores. In both cases, the schools avoided sanctions by recovering to "acceptable" status the following year. The orthogonal school, to the contrary, was a "recognized" school when we interviewed, and has more recently attained exemplary status with well over 90 percent of the students passing the exit test.

In contrast to the results in other states, we found great variation among target schools in their alignment to state accountability policy. The two schools with the highest proportion of disadvantaged students in our sample probably had become most aligned to state policy by the time we interviewed, even though our interviews suggested that several years before our arrival, one of them was on the verge of reconstitution, and the other also had a low level of internal accountability. This suggests that Texas may have been more successful than the other sampled states in aligning low internal accountability schools to state policy. It also suggests that leadership in the school is an important variable in determining how schools respond to state policy and what the ultimate result of that policy is. But our results in Texas may be the result of more experience in the state of getting low-performing schools to align with state policy, or simply that we chose a nonrepresentative sample of target school(s) either in Texas or in the other states. As we also suggest here and in another chapter (Carnoy, Loeb, and Smith), it is unclear what meaning this alignment has in Texas for the quality of education students in these schools received.

Figure 2.5 illustrates this finding. The schools with initially low levels of internal accountability varied greatly in where they ended up in their alignment with state policies. The orthogonal school, as in some of the other states, was moderately aligned with state policy, although even there, we could argue that in what counted for high rating by the state, the school was highly aligned. The better-positioned school was not as aligned with state policy as in the other three states, but more highly aligned than the less well-aligned target schools.

The four target schools in our sample, two in West City and two in Major City, were all able to compress outcomes relative to the better positioned and orthogonal schools. But this was mainly in terms of the exit test, not on other variables, such as performance on the SAT or eighth to twelfth grade survival rates. The schools vary in strength of internal accountability, but are generally characterized by internal accountability systems that depend heavily on leadership from the top.

The two schools in West City, Calin and Miramar, have student bodies that are almost 95 percent Mexican-American, mostly economically disadvantaged. Calin's students are almost 60 percent disadvantaged, and Mirarmar's, 80 percent, the highest of the seven high schools in West City and the highest of our sample's four target schools. Both schools have been

Alignment with State Policy

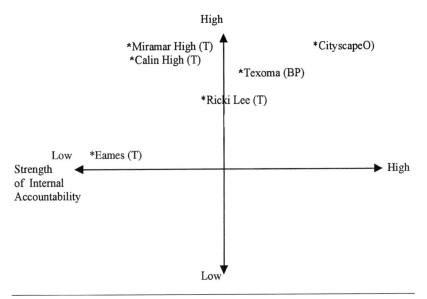

Figure 2.5 Texas Sample Schools: Alignment with State Policy and Strength of Internal Accountability

mainstays in the community for many years, but both faced crises in the early 1990s because of their poor performance on the state exit tests. In a sense, the TAAS test revealed that these traditional community high schools were low performing, at least in terms of state standards. Ironically, even in the crisis period of the mid-1990s, more than 50 percent of Calin's graduates attended two- or four-year colleges, and school attendance was always high. Nevertheless, both high schools were threatened with sanctions by the school district, Miramar's with reconstitution—further, if the district had not acted, Miramar probably would have been reconstituted by the state. As Miramar's principal told us,

> [The school] was the lowest performing school in the district at the time, and perhaps one of the lowest performing schools, I'd say, in the city. And we did an evaluation of the school when I got here in the summer . . . We evaluated the teachers and what was going on and by January of '96, the superintendent called all of the faculty and staff together, from the cafeteria all the way through the assistant principals, called everyone together and made the announcement at that time: everyone would have to reapply for their jobs. I was the only person hired that afternoon. So, then, we went through a process. Everyone went through an interview process over the course of that spring . . . approximately

50 percent of the faculty and staff was rehired at the time, so we made a major, major turnover. And the idea was that we were all held accountable for our students, regardless of where they live in this community.

Also under a district initiative, both high schools began magnet programs in the mid-1990s—Calin got a dance and music magnet and Miramar a health magnet and a fine arts magnet. This diversified the student bodies somewhat by drawing about 10–15 percent of students from outside the neighborhood. It also helped raise test scores. But the most important change that took place at both schools was their alignment with the state testing system and the focus on testing more generally. Standardized testing (the TAAS tests in particular) is a central organizing principle in Miramar and Calin's curricular agenda. School administrators describe how state-mandated assessments have catalyzed programmatic reforms at Calin in order to align school requirements with the state examinations.

Recognizing that the state was going to require [the TAAS] as a graduation requirement, several years back, maybe five years ago . . . the principal said "I need to you to come up with an idea of how we can increase our TAAS scores. What areas are we lacking in? And how can we address those academically and curriculum-wise?" We put together a package that would entail a course that students, all students, would take.

In the summer, before we start school, I give every faculty member . . . this campus summary sheet. This is a summary report from the state that delineates exactly how we did objective by objective. From this, I prioritize, campus-wide, what we need to focus on . . . So I say, okay, campus-wide, here are our weak objectives, and I develop activities, reading and writing activities, that can go cross-curricular and I give these to all content area teachers. All teachers at this campus are responsible for all of the reading objectives, because every course has their content to teach; and if students cannot read and comprehend, they cannot learn. We're all responsible for all the writing objectives, because, likewise, they need to be able to articulate what they have read in that content area. And then, we're all responsible for problem solving, because problem solving is cross-curricular. So, we all are responsible for these objectives. I show them how to teach these objectives in their own content area. So, that's what the campus is given.

Miramar and Calin aligned themselves almost totally around state testing. In addition, they both moved on to opening the pre-AP and AP courses to all students and teaching to those tests as well. This approach yielded remarkable test score gains at both schools. Calin's principal put it this way: "Because of our focus on the test, because of our focus on instruction, and because of the change in attitude that we had to undergo among the teachers, we increased in one year. Just by focusing, just by making the accountability system important to teachers and students and to the parents. And, in one year we went in reading from 62 to 78; in mathematics, from 38 to 62; in writing, from 75 to 86. In one year. We just focused."

But the advancement in TAAS scores has not necessarily translated into academic improvement in other mandated tests, such as end-of-course exams. During the same academic year, only 37 percent of students at Calin passed the English II end-of-course exam, and 0 percent the Algebra I exam. The results were similar at Miramar. Although these pass rates went up in subsequent years, they continue to remain quite low. SAT scores are also low. Without the pressures of high-stakes accountability, "official" requirements other than the TAAS are largely procedural.

The two target schools where we interviewed in Major City did not show the rapid student gains on the TAAS test as in Calin and Miramar, although both Eames and Ricki Lee high schools reached acceptably high pass rates on the TAAS tenth grade test by the 2000–2001 school year. Eames had undergone a series of crises during the 1990s, beginning with the shooting of a student in 1992. When we first arrived at Eames, the school was in disarray because its popular principal, Dr. Channing, had been promoted to a job in the district office, and a new principal had been brought in from another city. The community organization that had been working with Dr. Channing to mobilize parents in support of higher student attendance and increased student motivation and commitment, was now leading protests. The test scores on the tenth grade test dropped precipitously in 1998–99, and the school received a "low-performing" designation. That first year we interviewed, Eames not only had a low level of internal accountability, its teachers were struggling to maintain a positive sense of purpose. A typical complaint was that no one was helping solve the serious academic problems at Eames: "The one thing I can tell you that I know for a fact the district is not supportive of is we have classes of fifty, still. Some of my classes are thirty-nine. But, that does not create very conducive circumstances to learning, and the district says we have no teachers. And they have refused, systematically, to give us teachers. They have refused, systematically, to put math teachers on this campus. We still have subs. Here we are low performance, [and] we still have subs teaching the math courses. They say they have no math teachers. Now, I bet they have them at other schools."

Student motivation was another complaint at Eames, and this was usually connected to the kinds of problems the students faced in their daily lives. As the new principal told us, ". . . most of them appear to not have that much direction, and trying to get them to understand that they must have direction is the biggest challenge. There are some who do, so it's not everybody. Then, it makes it very difficult and challenging for the teachers, as well, who really don't know about their backgrounds and are not familiar with what most children are really up against at home. That makes it a challenge for everybody, a tremendous challenge."

A third complaint was that the best students from the feeder middle schools applied to and were accepted at a number of magnet high schools, such as the orthogonal school in our sample, Cityscape, and that Eames was viewed by both parents and students as a "second choice."

In this context, teacher attitudes toward state attempts to align on test performance were much more mixed than at Calin and Miramar, with some at Eames saying that "They won't be as prepared for college, because we are teaching the basics so much on how to pass the TAAS test, and we need to teach them beyond that, because education [goes] beyond the TAAS test" (teacher interview, 1998), and others that "One way or another everyone at Eames feels the pressure of getting students through this hoop and fears the effects of not making it . . . a low-performing rating hurts school pride" (Teacher interview, 1998). Some of the teachers we talked to kept themselves going by teaching one of the relatively few AP courses, where students were much more motivated.

Despite all these difficulties, the new principal at Eames managed to reestablish a good relationship with the community organization during her first year there, and test scores went up sharply in 1999–2000. When we returned in the first quarter of that school year, students and parents were back "on board." None of the underlying problems of the school had gone away, but at the least, the school was able to align itself sufficiently around the state test to achieve an acceptable rating.

The situation at Ricki Lee was different but just as complex. Ricki Lee is a big school (2,300 students), but the staff views it as quite tightly knit. Eighteen of its teachers and one vice principal in 1998 were former students, which brings a special flavor to the school. However, this environment was experiencing a dramatic transformation when we got there in 1998. The area's white middle-class population was selling its homes and moving into the suburbs. As Mr. Isaacs, the principal, told us, this was "bringing in a different sort of demographics" into the school, lowering the proportion of white students from 48 percent in 1994 to 36 percent in 1998. "Our poverty rate is going up now so that we have about 68 to 70 percent of our students qualifying for reduced lunch," Isaacs told us.

Unlike Eames or West City's high schools, in the early 1990s Ricki Lee had a reasonable level of internal coherence and was crisis free. But like many high schools with a majority middle-class white student body, Ricki Lee built its internal accountability system around student stratification. Even when the student population changed rapidly, the school held on to its pedagogical approach, superimposing new state requirements, but also resisting many of the changes needed to achieve high TAAS pass rates among black and Hispanic students.

"It [the TAAS] warps the environment," one instructor suggested. Some complained that it limited their capacity to use innovative approaches in their classes. Others stressed that teaching to the test detracted from other important dimensions of learning and ways of thinking. An English teacher argued: When you become so test-oriented in your teaching, you forget to relate the subject matter to their lives. You lose the life lessons of literature because you're more concerned about the elements of genre and figurative language that are in there so they can answer the test.

> *Math teacher*—So you spend a lot of time preparing [students for tests] . . . Because, well, you know, gee, "We're going to judge you on the result of your kids." Well, of course, then you're going to do a little time drill in there. I find myself [doing so], yes.
> *Interviewer*—How do they judge you?
> *Math teacher*—Well, they look at the scores that your kids get.

This ambivalence may have been one reason that the school did not meet state standards in the 1998–1999 school year. African-American students fell below the "acceptable" level on math, and Ricki Lee was designated "low performing." Dr. Isaacs was put in jeopardy of losing his job—if a school performs below state standards two years running, the principal is transferred.

When we returned to interview in fall 1999, the school was mobilized around raising TAAS math scores. The mobilization was a success, Ricki Lee received an acceptable rating based on its spring 1999 results, and Dr. Isaacs kept his job. Although teachers did not change their views of the TAAS, they were willing to conform to external notions of accountability in order to protect their popular principal. By stepping up TAAS preparation among the most vulnerable students and creating extra courses for students who had failed in the previous year, they were able to raise the math scores of African Americans substantially.

In other states in our study, the better-positioned schools surveyed differed sharply from the target schools. This was not the case in Major City, in part because so-called better-positioned schools there have a significant percentage of disadvantaged students, and magnet schools draw off many of the gifted disadvantaged. The school we picked for our better-positioned case, Texoma High School, was demographically similar to Ricki Lee. It differed primarily in two ways: Texoma had a more coherent vision of its stratified approach to teaching and learning, and thus teachers were more accepting of a major emphasis on TAAS preparation in the "regular track." In addition, Texoma, much more than Ricki Lee, focused on security and student control. The emphasis on order and security was apparently a change that came with the arrival of the new principal in 1995, and this created a sense of self-confidence in the school's faculty

In brief, Texoma not only increasingly aligned its internal accountability systems with the state's external policies, it was able to make these policies "fit" its prior mission (see DeBray, Parson, and Woodworth 2001, for this characterization of BP schools). As in Ricki Lee, this prior mission was to preserve and extend an AP program with a "private school atmosphere" within the school, while successfully meeting state TAAS requirements for students in the "regular" track. However, Texoma's internal accountability was just that much more coherent to be able to reorganize its regular track around preparing students for the TAAS. According to Texoma's dean of instruction, ". . . we can get together and see where we can support each other, see were we have some overlap. There is no TAAS test for social studies. There's no TAAS test for science. Sometimes, those people have trouble seeing what the math and English people are so hyper about. The math and English people do have a real sense of responsibility to help those kids pass that test, because if they don't pass it, they don't graduate. That is the bottom line in the state of Texas, passing the test is a requirement for high school graduation. So they . . . they bear that burden and very seriously. But, then, we come back . . . their discussion, then, in that CILT team, the social studies chair can say, oh, well, here's where we can support that. And the science chair is, well, we do this all the time in science. Well, great, now when you do that in science, help us make connections because that's what it's all about. It's not this learning in isolation, it's everybody working together."

The Texoma case suggests that a better-positioned school does not have to differ all that greatly from a target school in its demographics and academic organization. Nor does the mission of a BP school have to be one where all students learn according to a homogenous model of learning objectives. Rather, the school's success was largely based on accentuating its commitment to different learning goals for different groups of students. Even so, in both regular and AP classes, these objectives were defined by external tests.

On the other hand, Cityscape, the orthogonal school in Major City, had a highly coherent internal accountability system, a well-defined magnet mission for its selected mostly minority student body, and was able to achieve very high TAAS results even for its lowest-performing students. It did so by acting like a better-positioned school in terms of using its high level of internal accountability to make sure that every student passed the TAAS exit test, but was able to maintain its overall mission of producing college-bound graduates by putting a high percentage of its heavily (more than 90 percent) minority student body in more demanding math and English courses. Even so, the TAAS emphasis, particularly in math, did cause dissension among some teachers. As the head of the math department of one of the seven magnet modules told us, "The administration here is more worried about TAAS than they are about AP. So they want the better teachers teaching TAAS wherever there's a tenth-grade kid. They want me to teach the regular geometry kids because they're going to be taking the TAAS. The honors geometry kids are ninth-graders, so where are my problem teachers teaching? They're teaching the honors kids. Because the priority of the administration is TAAS."

The feature that distinguished Cityscape from its urban neighbors was its focus on training students in particular occupational fields and securing them college admission. As a magnet school for disadvantaged minority students, Cityscape's mission was less high test scores and more college access. Nevertheless, its reputation as a school still depended on its students scoring very high on the TAAS. The school administration could not afford to ignore alignment to state testing.

In sum, all the Texas schools we surveyed did reorganize their courses and teaching to conform to the state's external accountability standards. All made sure that teachers with vulnerable students in their classes taught the TAAS tests. Two of our target schools had difficulties doing that successfully during the period we interviewed in them. Nevertheless, they did recover enough so that all the schools were performing at an acceptable or better level in 2000–2001. Our orthogonal school catered to a high disadvantaged minority student body and was able to both achieve excellent results in the state test and to fulfill its vocational and college attainment missions for its students. The other schools in our sample, however, varied in their high school graduation rates, and even in their ability to reach reasonable pass rates on the ninth grade algebra requirement. Our Texas target schools, in varying degree, also were able to close the "gap" in internal alignment compared to better-positioned and orthogonal schools by aligning with external accountability. By the 2000–2001 school year, all the schools we surveyed had committed themselves to preparing low-income students for the state test—a clearly defined objective that focused teaching/learning activities in math and English departments. Similarly, for higher achieving students, these schools focused on preparing students for AP tests.

Conclusions

At the start of this essay, we hypothesized that since state accountability systems were mainly geared toward improving the academic performance of lower-income, at-risk students, we would expect to observe a "compression" of internal accountability among schools with large differences in their initial alignment. We found that compression did occur in Texas and somewhat in New York, but not in Vermont and Kentucky.

One conclusion is that the nature of external accountability is important in how schools react to external pressures. In Texas, the stakes were clear and the system had already been in place for many years before we began our school observations. In New York, the system and the stakes were still being formed—considerable conflict still characterized the high school exit test, and the state was still convincing schools to accept new state requirements. Kentucky had no high school exit test and no sanctions for either schools of students associated with high school state test scores. Vermont's external accountability was essentially voluntary.

A second conclusion is that whether stakes are low or high, the better-positioned schools are generally likely to incorporate state requirements quicker and more easily into their academic activities. These schools were able to make the policies "fit" their prior missions. For example, the head of a school planning team at Glen Lake said: "We're doing this because we think it's valuable for us. And we're going to keep doing it, even if the state backs off." Byrd High School in Kentucky also increased its internal accountability system with the external policy demands. The strong departmental structure provided a way for the testing policies to take hold. When the CATS scores in English were deemed too low, the principal put pressure on them to improve through a schoolwide professional development session where their practice was analyzed by all.

A third conclusion is that when stakes are low, target schools are *unlikely* to align themselves to external requirements, and when stakes are high and consistently enforced, many of these same target schools, usually with weak internal accountability structures, are likely, over time, to accept and successfully incorporate new state demands into their teaching/learning structures. In Vermont, Kentucky, and New York, the targeted schools we observed had a much more difficult time aligning to external demands. We identified a pattern of "compliance without capacity;" that is, the tendency to meet basic requirements pro forma, often with minimal meaningful or productive engagement on the part of the staff. In our view, this occurred because the new external demands of state policy were often eclipsed by "survival" issues (things such as large-scale student course scheduling problems, attendance, and discipline), and because incoherent internal accountability mechanisms provided a weak or nonexistent structure with which the external policy could align (such things as inconsistent professional development, few collaborative structures or collective expectations, and little or no data sharing and analysis). Yet, in states such as Texas, we observed target schools that were as well as or more highly aligned with state external accountability than better-positioned schools. Despite initially weak internal accountability structures, some schools were able to reorganize themselves around the external policy—that policy served as the new internal structure.

The fourth conclusion is that there is great variance in target schools' reactions to state pressures. Our larger Texas sample suggests that picking one target school in each of the other states may have biased the results. It is also critical to remember that in complex organizations like high schools, pockets of an organization can align with or resist a policy. Even in those target schools that did not wholly align with external pressures, we saw some pockets of alignment: for instance, the instructional interventions at Binghamton and the hiring of a new math chair at Robinson.

The fifth conclusion is that the way orthogonal schools react to external accountability policies again depends on the state context. Some orthogonal schools actively resisted aligning themselves with external policies, whereas others incorporated them but not at the expense of their well-defined missions, which usually had little to do with new state requirements.

Thus, response to external accountability varies across states and across types of schools. In some states, state policies do not appear to be achieving greater compression through the implementation of external accountability systems, and some seem to be having more success. Our studies suggest, however, that the only chance of the desired alignment of schools with weak internal accountability structures is a state accountability system with clear goals and strong sanctions and rewards. Even then, however, many target schools may not have the capacity to respond adequately to external demands.

References

Carnoy, M. and S. Loeb. 2003. Does external accountability affect student outcomes: A cross-state analysis. *Educational Evaluation and Policy Analysis*, 24(4): 305–332.

Debray, E., G. Parson, and K. Woodworth. 2001. Patterns of response in four high schools under state accountability policies in Vermont and New York. In *From the Capitol to the Classroom: Standards-based Reform in the States*, ed. S. Fuhrman, 170–192. Chicago: National Society for the Study of Education, University of Chicago Press.

Elmore, R., C. Abelmann, and S. Fuhrman. 1996. The new accountability in State Education Reform: From Process to Performance." In Helen Ladd (ed.) *Holding Schools Accountable*. Washington, D.C.: The Brookings Institution.

CHAPTER 3

Outside the Core
Accountability in Tested and Untested Subjects

LESLIE SANTEE SISKIN

Standards-based accountability policies entered the public schooling system at the end of the twentieth century as a major reform effort, one that has the potential to dramatically change the face and function of the comprehensive high school. For the past hundred years, the pattern of high school change has mainly been one of enrollment growth. In the middle of that period, the Conant Report (1959) posed the primary challenge to high school organization: could high schools accommodate the "horde of heterogeneous students that has descended on our secondary schools" (p. 602)? To do so, high schools would grow not only in size but in structure, offering a widely differentiated array of courses aimed at the "heterogeneous" tastes and talents of diverse students, and organizing teachers and content into discrete departments.

Conant argued that high schools would also have to develop differentiated expectations. Some courses would "maintain high standards" for those of high ability, while others, by necessity, would have "another standard." Just what those standards would be, however, were not specified by reformers nor standardized by policy makers. Instead, they were quietly and locally negotiated—classroom-by-classroom, track-by-track, subject-by-subject. The American high school grew, as Powell, Farrar, and Cohen (1985) vividly described it, into a version of a "shopping mall" with something for everyone, where "some [students] shop at Sears, others at Woolworth's or Bloomingdale's" (p. 8)—but where not every neighborhood was likely to attract a Bloomingdale's.

It is against that pattern of practice that current reformers press, arguing for high standards that will be the same for all schools, and for all students within a school. But when policies directed at the whole school hit the high school, they collide with that differentiated structure, refracting at different angles through different departments, bending and even reconstituting different subjects. Through establishing standards, choosing which subjects (and what content) will be tested, and then attaching stakes to achievement scores on those tests, the states materialize what kinds of knowledge count, and how much. In some cases, policy makers explicitly quantify how much.

Kentucky, which includes music (or at least humanities) among the tested subjects, counts performance in that area as worth 7.13 percent of the school's total score. Performance in English, on the other hand, counts for 14.25 percent directly. But, recognized as a basic skill needed for performance in other subject areas, English is understood to count much more. An English teacher in Kentucky talked of how the state standards have made teaching her subject more central to the work of the whole school: "Now, it's not just up to the English teachers. It's up to everybody in the school." Those subjects outside the core, less central to achieving a good score, are likely to see their value go down. As the pressure for schools to perform on accountability tests rises, and resources are reallocated to provide extra time to students in the tested areas, teachers in untested subjects wonder what will become of their subjects, and whether their jobs are at stake under high-stakes accountability policies.

To understand how high schools are responding to new state accountability policies (or why they are not), we need to take account of the internal differentiation which characterizes the comprehensive high school. We need to examine the ways in which different subjects and departments receive and respond to the call for common standards and standardized tests. To understand the kinds of changes that are taking place under this policy shift, we also need to look to evidence at the level of the subject and the department. Even large changes taking place at this level may be lost if data are aggregated or averaged to the level of the school.

Drawing on interview data gathered over two years of fieldwork though the CPRE project on accountability and the high school, this essay examines the case of one subject "outside the core"—music. To do so, I adapt, to the level of subject departments, a framework that has emerged out of our analyses of school-level responses to accountability. That framework suggests that to understand school response we need to consider three distinct but interrelated factors: the initial position of the school, relative to the policy; the internal conditions already present—the organizational structures, internal accountability systems, and collective expectations; and then, within that context, the strategic choices and actions of those within it.

In applying this framework to subject departments, we distinguish between the *subject* as a knowledge category that extends across schools and the *department* as an organizational sub-unit within a school. Thus, we need to analyze:

- The initial position of the *subject* relative to the policy;
- The internal conditions of the *department*— the structure, internal accountability system, and collective expectations; and then
- The strategic choices and actions of those within them.

Initial Position

Even before the accountability reform kicks in, some subjects start out positioned favorably within the schooling system. They have high status and high levels of agreement on what the subject is, what should be taught, and even, in some subjects, how the subject should be taught (Goodson 1993; Siskin 1994). Math, for example, commands a relatively high status position, and is considered to have a relatively tight paradigm (agreement and coherence about what counts as knowledge). As one math teacher explained, "every math teacher" across the country knows what should be known in algebra II: "Algebra II, you have to do certain things, and every math teacher knows that when you're done with Algebra II you know these things."

Moreover, math content is considered highly stable, and the sequencing of what topics are to be covered is firmly established—so much so that past reforms have found it almost impossible to dislodge (Leinhart and Smith 1985; Siskin 1994; Stodolsky 1993). When high stakes accountability has encountered a subject that begins from this position, the problem has not been figuring out what should be on the test, but rather how to get students into the sequence so they get to algebra II and "know these things" before they take the test.

English may also be part of the academic core but it does not command the same status or demonstrate the same tightness in its paradigm, stability in its curriculum, or solidified sequence. Coming to consensus on what things a student should know at the end of tenth grade English, and therefore what the state can reasonably expect its testing to assess, is a different problem.

Music, as a subject, occupies a position that, as one Massachusetts teacher explained to me, "has pretty high status; it's somewhat elite, but also . . . marginalized." Music is not typically considered a core subject, or a top contender for the lists of "what every high school student should know and be able to do" that are central to accountability policy. One science teacher in New York, for example, argued that there should be high standards and testing for (almost) all students—but only in some subjects:

"For the majority? Yes, there should be, certainly, the English standards, and the social studies standards, and the math standards. I actually disagree on the science standards for some, and I'm a science teacher." He did note, however, that there should be some standards in science for everyone, since "everybody should know how their body works, so they can make informed medical decisions." But the possibility of standards for everyone in the arts does not even enter the conversation.

Among music teachers, however, the contention is widely made that they do have standards, and that they have had them since long before the terminology of standards-based accountability came into vogue: "We tend, I think—and I'm speaking generally—I think as musicians, we've always tended to be sort of standards-based without knowing it." In almost all the interviews, teachers talked of how they have "always" had standards, "for a long time," or "for centuries." A Vermont teacher described the lineage of a discipline with a well-established history of shared standards: "I think we've always had a standard. My joke in front of the staff and the audiences here in [Garrison] has been that standards for us were established over five hundred years ago. Bach in the 1600s developed the equal temperament, and that's how we've been tuning our pianos ever since. Pythagoras came up with the original scale that we use. So we can go a long ways back for the standards."

For these teachers, it's not simply that there are standardized instruments and scales, but that there are widely shared standards about what should be taught in music, and even about what the order is for learning the essentials. A Kentucky teacher explained that "you can't skip levels. I guess it's sort of like math." A Vermont colleague concurred that "for a long, long, time music has always been taught sequentially." Teachers can be quite precise about just what it is that students need to know to meet these standards: "They need to know note value . . . Quarter note, eighth note, sixteenth note. They need to know note value. They need to know the letter names of notes, lines, and spaces. They need to know rhythm, be able to identify rhythm. . . Name it; perform it. They need to be able to sing, that's a category. You need to be able to sing alone and in a group. . . . You should be able to know music terminology, basic music terminology . . . Dynamics . . . Degrees of loud and soft . . . Vivace, which means lively, fast . . . Allegro, which is also a form of fast. It's not as fast as vivace . . . Be able to recognize grande, or dolce."

Mixed in with the lists of standards for what students need to be able to "recognize" or to "know" are the verbs for what they need to be able to *do*—to sing, to "perform." For, as teachers across the schools and states consistently point out, music as a subject has "for centuries" been not only standards-based, but performance-based. Ultimately, it is the performance of their students that counts: "I realize I've got to teach these students how to play their instruments. Bottom line."

Especially in group-performance oriented subjects, such as band or orchestra, the essential importance of having shared standards becomes immediately and concretely apparent. After all, explained one teacher, "to tie it all together consistently, we're all using the same evaluation pieces. So I know when the flutes come in to join the band rehearsal, they've had the same material as the clarinets and the trumpets." One of the remarkable aspects of music in this area is that the need to "tie it all together" so that students can "join" in for a group performance operates not only within the school, but also across schools. Several teachers describe preparing students to go out to regional and state-level performances where they may perform all together in a larger orchestra, or compete against other groups performing the same piece. The need to have everyone on the same page—to know and to be able to perform the same material in concert—transmits and reinforces the establishment of common standards throughout the musical community.

That focus on performance to a commonly shared standard, on the skills students need to be able to "tie it all together" to perform a musical piece, has put music teachers ahead of their colleagues in shifting to standards-based accountability. As three music teachers told us:

> One thing that we always found interesting was that music and fine arts are performance-based. We have products. We have outcomes. And they tried to take what we do and move us out of the performance area so they could put us back in. And instead of looking at what we have done through the centuries . . . a lot of the other areas have not bought in to this idea that we are where they want to be.

> We didn't have to change the way we taught. We didn't have to change the curriculum. We didn't have to change anything. It's like, now everyone is catching up with what music has been doing all along, which is really interesting. We've been performance-based all along. How we grade is how you perform.

> I think the folks who have been in the arts have been on the front edge of this for many, many years . . . And when I've gone to different classes and so forth, on how to use rubrics and things, we've had instructors that have said, "you folks in the arts always seem to be so far ahead. You already know what it is you want to assess, you know what you want for results." And so for me, the biggest thing is learning this new language of "how do we want to assess kids?" And once we came up with a rubric, it was pretty easy to just go ahead.

State rubrics and standards seem "pretty easy" in part because they don't introduce accountability into the field. Instead, music teachers have long seen themselves as accountable to their communities for the performance of their students—not on tests, but in the public arena. As two teachers told us:

> If I teach the [state] standards, well, maybe they'll be able to think about music better, which is good. But when we're at a basketball game, and when they're playing a song and it sounds awful, everybody's going to say, well, that's a bad band director.

> [That's what my] role as a teacher is, and that's to have these students play when I'm no longer around. And they can't do that unless they learn certain skills. And that's what I'm accountable to. The community has had a great deal of pride, even though it's a very small school . . . concerts are always well attended here, basketball games, football games.

And unlike the state accountability system, in this kind of arena, the stakes can be very high, and attach directly to individual teachers:

> So, yeah, the theory behind having the test, those questions—the theory behind the [state] standards, [the district] standards, is great. But the real practical aspect is, I've got to get those kids to learn how to play these instruments. If I don't do that, the band will sound awful; therefore my job can be on the line.

The subject of music thus provides a certain anchoring in a culturally valued and long established discipline, one where standards are widely shared, where the work is highly performance-based, and where that performance is embedded in a system of public accountability which predates, and may even compete with, new state accountability policies. But to understand why this teacher's job would be "on the line" and why that would be so consequential, we also need to look to the conditions of music as a department within the current organization of the high school.

Internal Conditions of the Department

In the complex organization of the comprehensive high school, teachers are likely to identify themselves, not only as subject specialists, but as members of a particular department that provides them with the primary social, political, and intellectual context for their work (Siskin 1994). These departments, especially in large high schools, can be like different worlds, where English teachers may never have met their science colleagues, and have little or no structured opportunity to see themselves as part of the same collective professional community, to develop shared expectations about student work, or about what teaching should be (Siskin 1991). The distances between departments and the "two worlds phenomenon" tend to be even more pronounced between teachers in the "core" academic departments and those in the "special" subjects like vocational education or the arts (Little 1993; see also Goodson 1993; Siskin 1994).

In this study music teachers also described feeling like they were in a different world from their academic colleagues: "Nothing against the school, but it seems that we're kind of in a world of our own. The choral department, the band, and the orchestra." Even when there was an effort to have the whole faculty focus on state tests, teachers had a hard time "relating" to the work of their distant colleagues: "There has [been discussion of how the school is doing]. And the way I work, it's hard for me to relate to things, or students, or student bodies that I don't know about. Or if they're talking math, or English, you know, there's no point of reference for me personally."

Another teacher we asked about school discussions of state tests (in Vermont, where music is not tested) believed that such discussions probably were taking place, but ". . . not that I'm aware of. I'm sure it takes place within the academic communities who are mandated to reaching [those scores]. And since we're not, we kind of fall by the wayside and in the cracks, and don't really . . . aren't really part of that circle."

The distance between the "two worlds" is not simply one of physical or social geography, but often takes the form of material difference. Some departments have more status and more resources; some, like music, may derive cultural status from their discipline, but little material resource or political support for their organizational status. Resources, even the basic resource of *having* a job, can be hard to come by. A music teacher in Vermont noted that "we have three music teachers in our district." Not in the school, but in the entire district. Another, in New York, explained that: "Music positions are not very easy to come by. Most of the teachers who have music or art positions, they hold on to them for life because the chances of them finding another job are pretty much zero. It's not easy to find a music opening."

Moreover, the positions that music teachers do find are in many cases quite different from the jobs of their colleagues in other subjects. Across the schools we studied, these three teachers described positions that cross school boundaries:

> I'm here every day, last block, but I also go to four elementary schools, and a middle school.

> Well, this year, they started this vertical teaming, and I'm actually assigned to elementary now. So, since we have set up here on a block schedule and you have A days and B days, on my B days, I go twice a day to the elementary and I teach there.

> This is my home school, and then I have eight elementary schools.

The assignment to nine different schools mentioned by this teacher may be an extreme case, but part time assignments across multiple buildings are not unusual. As the nine-school teacher also told us, that can make organizational accountability a complex and difficult issue: "To figure out with all the principals, whose schedule you are on, who you're responsible to, and that kind of thing . . . Every principal thinks you work for them, and each school has a different music program, so you've got to go in and figure out what they want, what's expected of you, what you can expect from them. Trying to figure out who, indeed, you do answer to, and who, indeed, you don't answer to." Each school may have a different music program (although in our sample, one school, Ring, does not have a music program or music teacher), but each school does not have a different music department.

Instead, when it comes to departmental status, music is often in the position of the transient stepchild, put into the arts family in one school, for example, or into the English department in another. But while that might make bureaucratic sense, given the small numbers of music teachers, it creates a "problem" when departments are expected to be the site for substantive conversation about working toward standards: "The principal has told us to take a couple of hours in our department meetings to talk about the standards and how to use them. The problem is, they're always putting me with foreign language and arts teachers. And I guess they kind of group us all together in the arts." As that teacher continued, the "best thing" the school could do would be to have "all the band directors from across the county get together, and we could talk about the standards, and we could wrestle with them." Wrestling with English teachers, or foreign language teachers, however, doesn't seem to help. Nor can many of these music teachers turn to their department heads for substantive support. When we asked one teacher, in Kentucky, about department support, he replied that the person he would go to is another music teacher—but not his chair: "But again, being with the arts and humanities, we answer to, actually, a French teacher. Well, not answer to, but that is our department chair."

What it means to "answer to" a chair in such a multidisciplinary department illustrates one weakness of internal school accountability systems with regard to subjects like music. For when asked if he has been evaluated in this workplace, this same teacher replied, "I have not. Well, not to my knowledge." And when he described what he thought that evaluation would look like, it seemed unlikely that it would actually inform his practice: "I mean, you probably know; in any workplace that they seem to pick out the least important things, and make the most of them. For the most part."

At the one school in our study that does have a strong, single-subject music department, there are other reasons why teachers still feel outside the core—in this case literally, since they are housed in a separate building. Even at this physical distance, however, they view themselves as part of the school community and as an essential part of school pride—at least as long as they keep doing well in regional, state, and even national competitions. They turn to that other public accountability system—external to the school but integral to the field of music—for meaningful evaluation, for professional support, and even for fiscal resources.

As a department, as a subunit of the school, music does have a claim to a share of the school budget. As one teacher there explained, the school does honor that claim, but the amount is minimal: "the school gives up $2,800 a year . . . I don't do anything but buy a computer or a piece of equipment with that." Music is an expensive subject, especially when students need, not only equipment, but funding to travel to the essential competitions or stage performances at home that will bring public support: instruments, costumes, sets and scenery—costs that this teacher estimates at over $400 for a student in chorus, over $700 for one in band: "Then we find a way to earn it. Then we do a show, and we have 2,000 seats in the auditorium. We do $10 a seat. We pack the house several times. Do the math. We clear $40,000 a show. Our budget is just under half a million dollars every year. And it all comes from fundraising and performances." Although music teachers often describe feeling "outside the circle" of the school's departmental system, it is not clear that they really want to move into it, or that they feel themselves accountable to it. The principal doesn't have time to evaluate them, the department chair is not in their field, but they do have strong ties to, shared expectations with, and accountability mechanisms developed among the other music teachers in their district, region, and professional community. Like other teachers in the arts studied by Sikes, Measor, and Wood (1985), these teachers see (or hear) themselves as active participants in their field, not just as subject teachers but as practitioners and performers of music: music teachers are musicians in a way that physics teachers are not physicists.

To Test or Not to Test

Music teachers are concerned about being pushed further outside the technical core of schooling by standards-based accountability actions of the state and by the predictable responses of their schools. From the vantage point of the Kentucky music department, teachers relate how, as a department and as a subject group, they received and responded to the shift in policy. They responded early, with direct action, and with unanticipated results.

Once it seemed clear that the state of Kentucky was moving to a new testing system, and that testing would be the new measure of school success, music teachers recognized the shift as a direct threat to their survival. Jobs might be lost altogether, or music turned into more of a "dumping ground" to relieve the "real" teachers of the discipline problems that interfered with their academic work: "For so long, music teachers were thought of [as if] the only reason we existed was to give the real teacher an off period. And we're still dealing with that issue, and it's tacky . . . but it's a real issue all across this country. Music teachers are not real teachers. But we are." Under this new wave of accountability policy, to be real is to be tested. So these music teachers, and others across the state, joined together to orchestrate a movement to have their subject count.

While music might be weak in terms of departmental status, as a subject it has significant strengths. Teachers were able to unite their forces through powerful cross-institutional professional connections (music teachers across our states are remarkable in the number and intensity of references to subject associations), to invoke national standards (widely shared), to mobilize parents who saw in the subject knowledge to be valued in and of itself, for its connections to adult life after school, or for its ability to connect students, who might otherwise be disengaged from high school (and any high school or district official can testify to the latent power of band parents). They were able to successfully lobby to have music on the agendas of state accountability policy makers.

They were not, however, able to convince policy makers that all high school students should know and be able to demonstrate the kinds of standards embodied in the national standards for music—and it is almost impossible to imagine a policy system that could agree that every student in the state should really be able to read, compose, and perform to any meaningful standard. So what Kentucky adopted was a required standard for the humanities, including music, but including it along with other arts.

There are two profound and problematic consequences of this compromise. First, music as a tested subject had to become something new, something that all students could be expected to do (although many students had never been music students) and that could be "done" on a paper and pencil test. That entails a major shift within the subject, one that many music teachers see as a both a transformation and a lowering of the centuries-old standards of the discipline: "It makes it real difficult when we're in performance mode with all the competitions and performances coming up . . . when we're doing so much performance, it's a little difficult to have them talking about the rhythms and the Brandenberg concertos, as opposed to getting out there playing."

Second, the act created a new subject—humanities—that no teacher had ever taught and no student had ever taken: "Some of it is music, some of it is art. Some of it deals with historical-type things as far as art, how it's related, and dance. There's some dance. And what I found phenomenal about the dance part, is there are only select schools that teach dance. And the PE teachers are supposed to teach dance . . . I haven't seen any of those teachers teach that in the ten years I've been teaching."

Across Kentucky, teachers scrambled to construct new curricula, to identify places in the existing curriculum where the required knowledge might fit, and to compose a new subject—one that crosses both disciplinary and departmental boundaries:

> My first year, we had no one teaching humanities . . . and basically we rotated the kids [the juniors] two weeks before they were to take the test. So we had all the juniors lumped together, and we divided them, thirty each, divided them amongst five different majors [PE, dance, history, art, and music]. So we divided those kids between all five of us, because some of those kids had never had music. In all the years they had been in school, they'd never had music. Meaning if there was a music question on the test, they would never understand what a treble clef was . . . so that's how we did it the first year I was here. We split them into groups of thirty and rotated them every thirty minutes. Then we filled them with as much knowledge as we could fill them with.

That kind of new subject, in which established disciplines are truncated into two-week bursts, decontextualized and disconnected from the performance standards that have long characterized the field, changes not only the knowledge of the subject but the nature of teaching. One music teacher noted the irony in that now "we're embracing the fact that we're going to become reading and writing teachers who also teach music."

The example of music dramatically illuminates one of the major problems confronting high-stakes accountability at the high school level. Once we move beyond (or arrive at) required standards for reading and writing, is there actually agreement on what all high school students should know and be able to do to earn a high school diploma? Are high standards possible across all subjects? Will we expect all students to achieve high standards in chemistry or to "know how their body works, so they can make informed medical decisions"? To perform the *Gloria Vivaldi* or to correctly label the kind of dance illustrated by a picture of dancers in poodle skirts and flat tops? In transforming subjects into something all students need to be able to demonstrate on a test, do we inadvertently lower performance standards, weaken existing professional accountability systems, or lose knowledge outside the core altogether?

The knowledge that standards are supposed to measure—to ensure that the next generation receives it intact—is being altered by the act of measuring itself. In an irony that Heisenberg would have appreciated, accountability policies may well be held accountable for changing the very disciplines they were devised to perpetuate.

References

De Brabander, C. J. 1993. Subject conceptions of teachers and school culture. In *School culture, school improvement, and teacher development*, ed. F. K. Kievet and R. Vandenberghe, 77–107. Leiden: DSWO Press.

Goodson, I. F. 1993. *School subjects and curriculum change*. 3rd ed. London: Falmer Press.

Kliebard, H. 1986. *The struggle for the American curriculum, 1893–1958.* London: Routledge and Kegan Paul.

Leinhart, G., and D. A. Smith. 1985. Expertise in mathematics: Subject matter knowledge. *Journal of Educational Psychology* 77: 247–271.

Little, J. W. 1993. Professional community in comprehensive high schools: The two worlds of academic and vocational teachers. In *Teachers' work: Individuals, colleagues, and contexts*, ed. J. W. Little and M. W. McLaughlin, 137–163. New York: Teachers College Press.

McNeil, L. M. 2000. *Contradictions of school reform.* New York: Routledge.

Powell, A. G., E. Farrar, and D. K. Cohen. 1985. *The shopping mall high school: Winners and losers in the educational marketplace.* Boston: Houghton Mifflin.

Sikes, P., L. Measor, and P. Woods, eds. 1985. *Teacher careers: Crises and continuities.* London: Falmer Press.

Siskin, L. S. 1991. Departments as different worlds: Subject subcultures in secondary schools. *Educational Administration Quarterly* 27: 134–160.

Siskin, L. S. 1994. *Realms of knowledge: Academic departments in secondary schools.* London and New York: Falmer Press.

Stodolsky, S. S. 1993. A framework for subject matter comparisons in high schools. *Teaching and Teacher Education* 9: 333–346.

Young, M. F. D., ed. 1971. *Knowledge and control.* London: Collier-Macmillan.

CHAPTER 4

Leadership and the Demands of Standards-Based Accountability

RICHARD LEMONS, THOMAS F. LUSCHEI,
AND LESLIE SANTEE SISKIN

Public schools and their leaders face a new political landscape, one where standards-based accountability is the "distinctive hallmark" of state educational policy (Abelmann and Elmore 1999). While details of the particular policies vary, almost every state has now established a centralized curriculum and/or performance standards, assessments to measure student learning, and stakes for schools, staffs, and/or students. They have, simultaneously, decentralized the decisions about how to reach those standards, thus providing a theoretical horse swap of increased accountability for greater autonomy. By directly confronting the technology of teaching and learning, and by forcing schools to assume responsibility for educational outcomes (often in terms of test scores), these policies present new and dramatic challenges for schools (Elmore 2000). However, while standards-based reform is purportedly designed to improve student achievement for *all* children, it is less clear how (or whether) schools will achieve this critical goal. Policy, be it accountability or otherwise, is not good at mandating the actions of individual schools and their leaders; policy can only establish incentives to encourage or motivate desired actions or behaviors. Thus, the ultimate success of delivering on the goal of increased student achievement for all children will require leadership to mobilize organizational resources to change the way schools operate.

This essay is an exploratory analysis of the leadership in high schools in terms of how they respond to standards-based accountability policy. For the purpose of this essay, we define leadership as the *interactive relationship among multiple leaders and followers as they enact, implement, and respond to standards-based accountability.* This definition is useful for a number of reasons. First, though leadership exists around much more than just responding to standards-based accountability, such a highly focused examination is appropriate for this project on accountability and high schools. Second, this definition is broad enough to encompass the work of both formal leaders—those in positions of formal authority—and informal leaders—those who do not hold formal positions of authority but who influence the thinking and behavior of their colleagues. In using this definition, we are using the school, not particular "leaders," as the unit of analysis.

In order to conceptualize leadership, we adopt a distributed theory of leadership, one that examines multiple sources of school-level leadership and how this leadership is distributed across the organization. In this effort, we are highly influenced by the work of Spillane, Halverson, and Diamond (2001), who have developed a conceptual model for understanding the social distribution of leadership. In order to develop a comprehensive understanding of leadership, one that accounts for the work of formal and informal leadership as it flows through a school, Spillane et al. argue that researchers must take into account the tasks of leadership (the enacted work of leaders), how leadership around these tasks gets distributed, and how school context constrains and enables the distribution. For the purpose of this exploratory analysis, we look at how leadership, broadly defined, emerges and is distributed in high schools responding to standards-based accountability. Informed by Spillane et al., we examine the responses of high school leadership to four discrete *presenting problems*—discrete demands or challenges posed by standards-based accountability as it lands in schools. In addition, we examine where leadership around these responses emerges in the high schools and whether it is "stretched over" multiple leaders. In those cases where leadership appears to be concentrated in one or two key individuals, we explore the possible effects of accountability policies on the distribution of leadership.

Our research in the six high schools we examined in two states suggests that successful responses to external accountability requirements in schools with relatively low "capacity" (the target schools in our sample) usually come from the top—from the school principal, who has the most at stake in a strong, sanction-based accountability system. Moreover, the concentration of leadership tasks in the hands of the principal increases with the stakes placed on him or her by the accountability system. Alternatively, the greater the capacity of the school in terms of its coherent internal accountability (the well-positioned and orthogonal schools in our sample), the more likely the leadership around these responses takes place at multiple points in the school—the principal's office, department heads, and individual teachers. The success of such schools on standardized tests can also reduce the threat of sanctions and allow for more "stretching" of leadership tasks. We also conclude that principals in orthogonal schools are constrained by special educational missions from taking more "total" responses to state directives. Leadership in those schools must fit state incentives and sanctions into their broader set of educational goals.

Presenting Problems

Standards-based accountability represents a new phenomenon in the environment of public schools, one that introduces new measures of performance, shifts the evaluation of success from inputs to outcomes, and exposes that evaluation to public scrutiny. In this regard, standards-based accountability presents schools with particular organizational problems, what we choose to call "presenting problems." Because these presenting problems do not arrive with self-evident solutions, there is potential for a range of organizational responses.

Standards-based accountability has generated a variety of these presenting problems. Our identification of these many presenting problems has been inductive. In other words, we have not begun with an exhaustive list of demands for which we were observing responses. Instead, we observed these presenting problems in practice, as they lived in the perceptions, anxieties, and work of high schools in four states. Consequently, we have chosen to narrow our focus and examine four presenting problems that consistently surfaced in multiple schools across our multi-state sample. These presenting problems are: (1) Interpreting the policy and relating it to the preexisting story of the school, (2) Interpreting/making sense of the data generated from the policy, (3) Determining what to do about teachers and determining who is going to teach the content demanded by new standards and assessments, and (4) Determining what to do with students at risk of not meeting the standard.

Relating the Policy to the Preexisting Story of the School

As policies land on schools, they do not necessarily come with self-evident accounts of their purposes, meanings, and implications. They also arrive within schools with varying degrees of supportive information—information that provides explanations, interpretations, and specifications. Whatever amount of information they arrive with, how they are received and understood can vary greatly. In addition, accountability policies land in schools with prior histories and organizational identities. It is therefore reasonable to assume that schools, and the leaders within schools, make sense of and construct meaning around standards-based accountability policy, attempting to place the accountability in context.

Interpreting/Making Sense of the Data Generated From the Policy While schools and school districts have long had data concerning student achievement, standards-based accountability policy has generated new (and frequently more) data, often in concert with specific incentives for using these assessment results to inform school practice. That said, how to employ this data is not self-evident, leaving schools with latitude to find their own approach.

Determining What to Do about Teachers and Determining Who Is Going to Teach "This Stuff" Under standards-based accountability, states are faced with new curricular demands, demands that value certain standards and place an emphasis on certain tested subjects. These new standards and assessments may not align well with what and how teachers previously taught. Schools and their leaders are faced with determining what to do about the teaching staff, those who have to provide students with the instruction necessary to reach content and performance standards. In some schools, this may require determining who teaches the tested subjects. In other schools, attention may be given to improving the skills of those teaching certain or all courses.

Determining What to Do with Students at Risk of Not Meeting the Standard Standards-based accountability policy seeks to make schools take account of the achievement of all students. While this is sought through different policy formulations, one of the common demands upon schools and their leaders is to help all students reach the standard. In some states, this appears an absolute goal for each child, as graduation is tied to passing the state tests. For others, where raising school-wide averages is the goal, the focus is on increasing the number of students reaching the standard. Ultimately, schools are left with the question of what to do with those students at risk of not meeting the standard. This demand seems particularly salient and acute for high school leaders because high schools represent a finality in terms of K–12 public education.

Kentucky Schools: Byrd, Baleford, and Binghamton High Schools

First legislated in 1990, the Kentucky Education Reform Act (KERA) was an ambitious attempt to improve the quality of schooling and, ultimately, student achievement, for all public school students. KERA mandated an assessment system that monitors the academic achievement of students and holds schools accountable for their relative progress. In 1998, the Kentucky Board of Education created a new assessment system to replace the existing one, which had been plagued with controversy. Under the Commonwealth Accountability System (CATS), Kentucky schools are held accountable for making continuous progress on a battery of academic assessments and against certain nonacademic measures. The academic and nonacademic measures are combined into a single index score for each school. During the biennium of 1998–2000, each school's index score set a baseline for measuring the targeted annual growth toward 2014, when each school is to reach a common level of performance.

Movement in the index score over subsequent biennia determines the rewards or sanctions schools face. Schools whose index scores fall above their respective goals receive monetary rewards to be used for school-related expenses. Schools whose growth in index score falls below a certain minimum threshold are eligible for state intervention, which can take multiple forms, such as an external audit of the school. In addition, these schools are eligible for technical and financial assistance from the state.

Binghamton High School

Binghamton High School, the target school in our Kentucky sample, consistently scores toward the very bottom of the CATS. Though situated in a school district with a complex assignment program centered on choice, Binghamton's population tends to not actively select any schools. As a result, they tend to come from a particular residential area, one characterized by high poverty. Despite state intervention and an infusion of district resources, Binghamton has failed to make noticeable gains on state assessments. Binghamton educators commonly describe the dramatic obstacles the school's urban student population faces in finding academic success. Binghamton's self-identity as a victim of the district assignment plan is a defining component of its professional culture and the school's identity.

Relating the Policy to the Preexisting Story of the School   In our interviews, teachers and administrators consistently described the particular and extreme characteristics of the Binghamton student body as the defining characteristics of the school. According to teachers and administrators at Binghamton High School, the reason so many of their students face such dramatic problems is because of the school district's assignment system, which permits the most talented students to select into other schools and pools the least academically motivated and most needy in schools like Binghamton. As a result, Binghamton faculty and administrators expressed little hope for being able to improve the achievement of their student population.

Interpreting/Making Sense of the Data Generated from the Policy Bing-hamton administrators and teachers used state assessment data, in con-junction with other data, to target general areas for school improvement. The principal and the School Based Decision Making team (SBDM) exam-ined state assessment results, in conjunction with other sources of achieve-ment information, to establish broad school improvement priorities as part of an improvement plan.

Binghamton administration expected the departments to "look at the scores." For example, the math department chair explained how he first ex-amined the math results alone, looking for obvious areas of weakness. Af-terward, the entire math department collectively examined the results, attempting to "make some generalizations off of it" and to determine what "we need to do as a department." Out of this effort to draw generalizations from math results, the math chair and the math department pushed to alter the school's block schedule by providing ninth graders more time in algebra I. Specifically, the department encouraged the school to allow alge-bra I to meet every day of the week, while other courses only meet every other day.

Though the math department, led primarily by the math chair, took the initiative to analyze math data, determine weaknesses, and influence school organization, data analysis across the school was more sporadic. Though administrators told us that the departments were supposed to an-alyze data, few were sure of whether it had been done. Departments did not have consistent approaches or expectations about how data was to be used, and therefore only certain department leaders who were personally motivated—like the math chair—led this response.

Determining What to Do about Teachers and Determining Who Is Going to Teach "This Stuff" At Binghamton High School, references to issues of "who is going to teach this stuff" emerged in relationship to two issues. First, Binghamton found that there were gaps between the school's cur-riculum and the annual state assessments. This generated action to fill the gap by teaching the missing knowledge and skills. For example, Bingham-ton created an arts and humanities mini-course that would help prepare students for the arts and humanities portion of the state assessments.

Binghamton teachers and administrators explained that the other main concern with determining who was going to teach this stuff was directly connected to an absence of certified teachers. Binghamton's faculty con-sists of a sizable portion of emergency-certified teachers, most of whom are English as a Second Language (ESL) teachers. Filling open vacancies in this school, which possesses a relatively negative public image in the dis-trict, proves rather difficult according to teachers and administrators. De-spite the widespread agreement about the teacher recruitment problem,

Binghamton had not developed a schoolwide response to overcoming this challenge. The math chair, who complained about the problem of recruiting qualified math teachers, took this upon his own shoulders, working to strategically fill empty math positions. When trying to find more math teachers for supplemental math classes designed to accelerate learning, he negotiated with a business teacher and a Title I teacher, both of whom are qualified to teach math, to pick up a certain number of algebra I sections. On another occasion, the math chair simply refused to post a math position, fearing that a particularly bad math teacher in another school would have transfer rights, an outcome worse than being short a teacher.

Determining What to Do with Students at Risk of Not Meeting the Standard
At Binghamton, where a large percentage of the students are at risk of not meeting the state standard, there were multiple efforts to improve the achievement of these students. These efforts fall into one of two categories of initiatives. The first includes schoolwide programs, which make up the majority of Binghamton's efforts to target those students most at risk. For example, over successive years, the teachers and administrators at Binghamton have declared schoolwide foci on reading and math. The result of these foci were regularly scheduled time blocks where each teacher stopped his or her normal classroom lessons to either teach a common math problem or allow students to read silently.

Another example of this schoolwide approach was the creation of a double class period of math for all algebra students. The origin of this double math class emerged from the math chair and the math department, who, after analyzing the achievement of entering students, discovered that far too many of their freshmen possessed huge deficits in math skills. According to the math chair, "Our students are coming in way below grade level next year—seventy, eighty percent in the one, two, three stanines, I think, or something, real low." Again, leadership emerged in a smaller subunit of the organization—the math department—and was not connected to other school responses to accountability.

Binghamton Leadership
At Binghamton, leadership, in regards to the presenting problems, appeared to emerge from different leaders and groups of people within the organization. Paralyzed by a collective sense of hopelessness, responses to standards-based accountability arise from various pockets of leadership in the school, pockets that may be working in virtual isolation from other leaders. For one presenting problem, the leadership comes from the formal site-based decision making committee and for another, leadership emerges from an isolated department chair who appears on a singular mission to

improve student math achievement. As a result, responses to standards-based accountability are sporadic, fragmented, and minimally distributed. For example, while the math department examined math scores and used its analysis to drive a structural change in students' schedules, it is less clear how or whether other departments examined state assessment data.

Byrd High School

Byrd High School, the better-positioned school in our Kentucky sample, has achieved great success in responding to state assessments, scoring consistently toward the top of state rankings. Byrd is a district-wide magnet school possessing the ability to carefully select among a large pool of applicants from across the entire district. As a specialized magnet, Byrd has a focused academic mission that attracts students (and parents) who are drawn to a philosophy of order, structure, and patriotism and who actively chose to enter the district's application process. Following the selection process, the resultant student population is skewed in comparison to the rest of the district, especially along lines of class, as only 10 percent of the students qualify for free or reduced lunch (the district's free and reduced lunch percentage approaches 50 percent). Teachers who work at Byrd agree with the school's mission when they are hired, openly committing to uphold the school's purpose. Bolstered by the student selection system and the relatively large demand to teach there, Byrd has created a strong internal accountability system that highly influences teachers' professional behavior and senses of their own responsibility (see Abelmann and Elmore 1999).

Relating the Policy to the Preexisting Story of the School   Byrd High School is a performance-oriented school, one where teachers, administrators and students strongly emphasize school success, especially in academics. Internally prepared documents, from promotional brochures to Internet postings, highlight the school's instructional focus and tout its high academic standards, its challenging curriculum, and its repeated awards for academic achievement. As such, KERA, with its accountability metrics and academic focus, aligns well to the academic orientation of Byrd, especially as annual assessment results tend to reinforce the school's sense of pride and accomplishment. In fact, Byrd High School actively advertises that its student body repeatedly outperforms those from the vast majority of other Kentucky high schools, as measured by CATS.

Despite the fact that KERA aligns and reinforces the academic and performance orientation of Byrd High School, faculty and staff did not always greet the demands and expectations of accountability policy warmly. When new state expectations trickled down to the school, Byrd's principal took deliberate steps to help guide the faculty's collective interpretation of the policy. The first way he did this was by openly distancing himself from "the state," presenting the Kentucky legislature and the bureaucrats at the Kentucky Department of Education as outside enemies, ones against whom he must rally his troops. Assistant principals and teachers described a consistent pattern of how this principal introduced his faculty to the new demands and expectations of the Kentucky accountability policy, whether it be guidelines on how to assess student writing portfolios or new benchmarks for school performance. The principal, as one assistant principal explained, "always blames it on the state, which is really cool." The effect, one English teacher described, was that the principal "doesn't get challenged" by the faculty. Instead, the faculty receives an explanation of what the state and district expected, and whether the principal thought that it was "good for kids." Moreover, in establishing the state as the enemy imposing stringent requirements, the principal reinforced the legacy of Byrd's academic success, charging the faculty to respond to these new demands because, "If we have to do it, let's do it as well as we can."

Beyond motivating teachers and administrators to not rebel or resist the policy, Byrd's principal also took deliberate and strategic steps to customize and internalize external demands so that they were more meaningful and useful to Byrd teachers. One prominent example of this effort to "take it, filter it, and customize it" was the development of school-specific standards, called "classic standards" or "vital content." Overwhelmed by the quantity and multiplicity of district, state, and subject association standards, the principal, administrators, and department chairs designed a process through which Byrd subject departments generated, course by course, a list of three to five most critical understandings. These critical understandings became the school's homegrown standards and the working curricula. As the math chair explained, the district, state, and the National Council for Teachers of Mathematics had each produced lists of standards that were "just different packages of the same thing." She also explained that creating the classic standards allowed Byrd to "customize it and internalize it," which "helped bring [standards] down instead of being just this nebulous thing that's out there floating around." In effect, school personnel personalized and customized state and district performance standards, generating a more manageable curriculum, one perhaps more directly owned and followed by Byrd teachers.

Interpreting/Making Sense of the Data Generated from the Policy Byrd High School administrators and faculty employed accountability data in a number of ways, from schoolwide diagnostics to subject area item analyses for the purpose of curriculum alignment. Each fall, when Byrd received the complete set of test scores and performance indicators from the Kentucky Department of Education, the principal assumed primary responsibility for examining the data and presenting the larger trends to the faculty, so as to send powerful messages about broad areas for improvement. This presentation occurred in a faculty meeting, where the principal shared and analyzed the school's scores, lauding the efforts of departments whose scores improved and indirectly drawing attention to departments whose scores were areas of weakness. At the onset of one recent academic year, the principal stood before the faculty and robustly congratulated the subject departments whose scores improved, which left only English. As a result, the English teachers received a dramatic signal, one that led them to think, "Oh, we must really be bad."

Beyond these public efforts to formally acknowledge both success and areas of relative weaknesses, Byrd teachers and administrators used state-generated test results to target improvement efforts within the school. For example, following a year of stagnant writing portfolio scores and the before-mentioned faculty meeting where all but the English department were celebrated, the administration and certain teacher leaders targeted the English department to receive special administrative attention to raise the quality of student writing. This special attention first materialized in a professional development day where the principal designed and led an intensive in-service for the English department while all other Byrd teachers worked independently in their rooms. During this in-service, the department examined the state assessment results, came to an agreement about the urgency of improving the writing program, and agreed upon an ongoing process for collaboration.

In addition to targeting attention to departments with weaker test scores, the principal required each department to examine state test results for trends about and implications relevant to each subject area. The math department, for example, subsequently conducted an item analysis of state math results and recognized a specific weakness in student performance.

Determining What to Do about Teachers and Determining Who Is Going to Teach "This Stuff" At Byrd High School, responses to demands on human capital—how to utilize the employed adults in the building—in relationship to the new demands of standards and accountability manifested in two general ways: (1) the development of teachers that state performance measures revealed were in need of improvement, and (2) filling the curricular gaps created by newly tested curricula. The principal's intervention into the English department provides a case in point for the development of teachers. In general, Byrd's principal and the English department chair placed concerted effort into assisting the department, writ large, in strengthening its writing instruction. The cornerstone of this larger effort, however, was a targeted approach to improving two senior English teachers, teachers who, according to colleagues, "envision themselves as literature teachers and not writing teachers." The principal, an assistant principal, the English department chair, and a district-level resource teacher planned and required specific professional development activities for these teachers. As a result, the resource teacher spent numerous hours over the course of the year working directly with these two teachers.

To make sure that all students possessed the knowledge and skills to perform adequately on the state test, Byrd High School responded with two strategies. First, Byrd created a new course for students who currently took no music courses. Second, Byrd High School embedded the new knowledge and skills within preexisting music courses. These two means of dealing with newly tested material—embedding within preexisting courses and creating new courses—reoccurred in other subject areas across the school.

Determining What to Do with Students at Risk of Not Meeting the Standard
In addition to using state assessment data to inform instruction and monitor student achievement, Byrd High School developed a system of internal data gathering where all teachers administered regular and formal assessments to measure student performance against CATS-tested skills and knowledge. Closely connected to this program was an effort to collaboratively examine the work that students produced on these assessments. Byrd's administration required that each teacher attend and participate in meetings of small groups of teachers, which assembled on designated dates of the year to examine student work. However, instead of examining the work of all or even random students, teachers were asked to bring the work produced by two students designated at the beginning of the academic year not reaching the "proficient level" on Kentucky state assessments. Following the periodic administrations of internal assessments, individual teachers submitted the work of the same "apprentice"[1] students throughout the academic year, which allowed the teachers to collectively chart the progress of these identified pupils. Strategically, the principal did not want teachers bringing samples of work from the most successful students. In addition, he didn't want teachers to bring examples of the worst student performers, what he called the "zeros and F's"; instead, he focused on students "who almost made it."

In addition to monitoring select students over the course of the year, another response emerged that may or may not be directly related to state assessments. Byrd High School, by the nature of its particular magnet status within the district, has the ability to carefully select students. In addition, administrators and teachers at Byrd possess the ability to review the behavior and academic progress of students who attend, and to determine which, if any, should be "returned" to whichever district school serves his or her residential neighborhood. As an administrator explained, students who "look like they are going to continue to struggle all the time they are here or even fail while they are here, it would be better for them to return to a situation which is a little less rigorous than what we demand."

Byrd Leadership Byrd's principal played a central role in leading school responses to accountability. Teachers continually describe this principal as "strong," "respected," and one of the most "effective instructional leaders" many had worked for. That said, leadership at Byrd is not simply unidirectional and top-down, where the administrators are mandating and controlling all activities. Instead, the principal, along with other administrators, has worked to create an infrastructure through which the responses occur and through which multiple leaders can emerge and share in the work. For example, the principal and a supportive leadership team helped develop and refine the plan for developing internalized standards for each content area. Once the expectations were clearly developed, it was up to the departments to determine how to develop these standards. The math department, facilitated by the math chair, took the lead and piloted the process for the entire school. Working collectively, the chair and the rest of the math teachers negotiated their own process and the ultimate standards. As such, leadership around work of developing internalized standards was distributed, or "stretched across," multiple formal and informal leaders, from the principal to subject chairs to teachers.

Baleford High School

Baleford High School, the orthogonal school in our Kentucky sample, is a magnet school with a business and vocational focus. During their freshman year, students at Baleford cycle through the multiple and varied magnet business programs before selecting one to join for the remainder of their high school education. Demand for Baleford High School is high, especially among the African-American population, and students from across the district apply through an intense admissions system that takes into account an essay, letters of recommendation, and previous grades and attendance. Baleford educators possess a strong sense of the school's purpose, which concerns serving the community by providing a critical, life-changing educational experience for the adolescents in their care. While it is unclear whether demand to teach in Baleford High School is high throughout the district, teachers at Baleford seem to be in no hurry to leave. Turnover over the last few years was minimal and resulted primarily from promotions or retirement, not transfers. Despite its strong sense of the school's purpose, Baleford possesses a relatively weak internal accountability system (see the essay by Debray, Parson, and Avila in this volume).

Relating the Policy to the Preexisting Story of the School   Baleford High School educators possess a strong sense of the school's purpose, which they generally describe as serving the inner-city and predominantly African-American community. Educators at Baleford describe KERA, with its standards-based curricula and its accountability system, as aligned with the general purposes of the high school. In other words, helping students to achieve success on the CATS assessments actually helps Baleford students find more success later in life. This framing of standards-based accountability in relationship to the preexisting story of the school comes directly from the administration and the key teacher leaders in the building. Ultimately, teachers at Baleford, like at Byrd, tend to see KERA and preparing students for the CATS assessments as part and parcel to serving the community and preparing the students in their charge for the realities of life.

Interpreting/Making Sense of the Data Generated from the Policy   At Baleford, leadership has used standards-based accountability data for two general purposes: motivating school and department performance and signaling areas for targeted improvement efforts. As in other schools in our sample, in faculty meetings, the principal at Baleford used the test scores to demonstrate which academic areas were performing relatively well and which academic areas needed to improve. In addition to this public use of data as a source of motivation, Baleford educators also used data to inform and focus schoolwide and department improvement efforts. During the school improvement planning process, which creates a strategic plan for two years, the school uses professional development days so that the entire faculty can participate in a needs assessment. As part of the needs assessment, administrators and faculty members collectively examine multiple and varied sources of data, from test scores to enrollment figures, identifying areas for improvement, setting performance goals, and determining schoolwide strategies.

Determining What to Do about Teachers and Determining Who Is Going to Teach "This Stuff"   KERA and CATS have challenged traditional paradigms of what being a high school English teacher means. This has led Baleford, much like Byrd, to intervene in the English department to assure that English teachers are direct teachers of the writing process, not simply teachers of literature and grammar. According to English teachers and administrators, Baleford's recent success in its portfolio scores is the result of a two-fold strategy. The first component of the strategy was to move two specific English teachers out of teaching senior English, where much of the final portfolio work was conducted. A few years earlier, the state assigned Baleford a "distinguished educator" because of insufficient gains under

CATS. This distinguished educator, who possessed wide-ranging power over the school, worked with the department chair to move the two senior English teachers into earlier grades. Moving these two teachers, who reportedly "had no clue what process writing was," minimized their impact on the quality of student portfolios. The second component of the strategy was to partner with a local professional development organization around process writing. As a result of this partnership, a critical mass of the department's teachers have worked together to develop an elaborate English teacher resource guide. The result of these efforts was greater consistency across the department in what it meant to teach English—which at Baleford was now directly connected to teaching writing—and greater collaboration on how best to improve the quality of writing that results in students' portfolios.

In addition, Baleford has also implemented a test prep program to make sure students have practice with certain forms of assessment, particularly open response questions. In previous years, when Baleford was under scrutiny for insufficient gains on the CATS, the school implemented "open-ended question" days, where the entire school would focus on how to best answer these forms of questions, which are staples of the CATS. In more recent years, Baleford has done away with the open-ended question days, but the teachers are expected, under the school's improvement plan, to provide content-specific open-ended writing practice within the scope of each course.

Determining What to Do with Students at Risk of Not Meeting the Standard
At Baleford, where teachers and administrators equate the school's mission, in part, with helping students who face greater obstacles find success in school and in life, there are multiple programs designed to help target students at risk of not meeting the standards. These programs, which service a large percentage of the student population, vary in the degree to which they directly relate to KERA. Certain Baleford programs are nonacademic, such as a program designed to build self-respect and leadership skills among girls. Other programs, such as the Title I reading program and the pilot ninth grade team, are more directly tied to improving student performance on the CATS.

In addition to the schoolwide reading program, the school has also implemented a pilot program in which certain ninth graders are organized into a single ninth grade team, where a common group of academic teachers work together to integrate the curriculum and provide a more personalized learning environment. According to a math teacher in this team, various teachers recognized that many entering ninth graders possessed weak study and organizational skills. These teachers also felt that the students were ill prepared for the independence of high school academic work. A group of these teachers worked together to develop a proposal for an integrated, team approach for the freshmen that would provide a structured, yet nurturing educational environment. Ultimately, Baleford implemented the proposal that served 150 students. The ultimate success of this program, according to an administrator, will depend on how well the participating students perform on the state assessments they will take in forthcoming years.

Baleford Leadership

Leadership at Baleford, though an orthogonal school, has mobilized the school to respond to standards-based accountability in multiple observable ways. Leadership for this work emerged in multiple places through the high school, from the principal who is described by teachers as a culture-setting "visionary," to an English department chair and a distinguished educator who take on entrenched English teachers, and to teachers who develop an alternative way to organize the teaching of freshmen. These leadership efforts are only loosely woven together, connected in the explanations of teachers and administrators only by the school's mission of serving the community by providing students opportunities to succeed in school and in life. In addition, Baleford's strategic planning process has provided multiple means through which broad-based leadership can emerge in response to the demands of accountability, though on paper the ultimate improvement plan seems only to minimally unite the disparate school responses.

The case of Baleford suggests that internal accountability systems are not necessarily consistent across departments. In recent years, the English department has strengthened its internal accountability system relative to the school's more general system. This may have begun with an intervention led by the distinguished educator, but has continued through the leadership of a critical mass of English teachers. These teachers have gradually developed a clearer and more collective sense of professional expectations, particularly around what it means to be a teacher of writing. This stronger internal accountability system has enabled the English department to respond coherently (as a department) in an effort to improve student portfolio scores, achieving recognition for its success while the rest of the school struggles to ratchet up its CATS performance.

Three Texas Schools: Ricki Lee, Miramar, and Cityscape

Texas's system of accountability places high stakes on both schools and students. Students must pass the tenth grade TAAS exit exam to graduate from high schools, while schools face stakes ranging from peer review to school reconstitution.[2] In the two Texas districts we visited, the threat of being designated as a low-performing school based on low TAAS scores weighs heavily on teachers and administrators. As an official from the district of our first school observed, "that is the real fear, that is the death sentence, for sure."

In the district of the second school we visited, principals only receive multi-year contracts if eighty percent of their students pass every part of the TAAS. During the seven-year tenure of the district's controversial superintendent—who was fired by the school board shortly before our first visit—thirty-two of fifty-one principals were replaced and two thirds of teachers were either fired or chose to leave the district.

For our analysis of leadership and school response to standards-based accountability, we chose to examine three of the six schools in our Texas sample. Two of these schools, Ricki Lee High and Miramar High, are target schools, and the third, Cityscape Magnet High School, is an orthogonal school. We first visited Ricki Lee High during the 1998–99 school year. We returned in 1999–2000 to find that Ricki Lee had been designated as a low-performing school, based on the low TAAS scores of a student subgroup. We visited Miramar High first in January 1999 and again in September 1999. The school had been reconstituted several years earlier due to low academic performance; as a result, the principal and most of the teachers we spoke with were relatively new to the school. We visited our orthogonal school, Cityscape Magnet High School, in October of 1998 and November of 1999. In both years, students were performing well on the TAAS, but administrators and teachers continued to feel pressure to improve test scores.

Ricki Lee High School

Ricki Lee High School is a large urban school with nearly 2,300 students. For years, Ricki Lee High enjoyed a strong reputation for scoring well on standardized and Advanced Placement tests, but in 1999 the school was designated as low-performing by the state of Texas due to low math scores on the TAAS among African-American students.

Interpreting the Policy and Relating It to the Preexisting Story of the School
During the period that we observed Ricki Lee, school personnel's interpretation of Texas's accountability policies went through two distinct phases. In the first phase, the principal and many teachers viewed the state's concentration on the TAAS as an annoying distraction that victimized a small population of struggling students. The year before we arrived, low scores had prevented fourteen students (out of over three hundred seniors) from graduating. According to Mr. Isaacs, the principal, one of the hardest parts of his job was "calling them up and saying, 'I'm sorry, you're not going to graduate.' It's very, very traumatic for them, their families, and the teachers who have worked with them."

When Ricki Lee High received its low-performing designation in 1999, the school entered its second phase of interpreting accountability policies. One other high school in the district was designated as low-performing at the same time, and according to Mr. Isaacs, the principal of that school had already been reassigned. Asked about the importance of Ricki Lee's TAAS scores, Isaacs responded, "It's the number one factor. And I will not be here if it's . . . low-performing next year. I know that."

Ricki Lee received its designation as a low-performing school because only 42.7 percent of the school's African-American tenth graders passed the TAAS, 2.3 percentage points short of the 45 percent passage rate required to achieve an "acceptable" rating. The principal and teachers of Ricki Lee reacted incredulously to their bad luck. As Mr. Isaacs explained, "We only needed three more black kids to pass the test or we wouldn't have been low-performing." Teachers characterized the designation as a matter of a "fraction of a point," a "clerical error," or the result of "x amount of students who shouldn't have taken the test." An administrator argued, "although our scores aren't as high as I would have liked for them to have been, I don't think that our low performance ranking is indicative of what happens on this campus."

Despite their belief that Ricki Lee continued to be a top-quality school, the threat to the school's reputation—and the principal's job—forced school personnel to direct attention to a population of students that had under-performed their classmates for years. Ricki Lee's test score data reveals that passage rates for African-American students had fallen below campus-wide rates by an average of twenty percentage points over the previous five years. In 1996, only 31.3 percent of African-American students passed the math component of the TAAS, compared to 60.1 percent of all students who took it.

Led by the principal, who faced the highest stakes, personnel at Ricki Lee elevated school activities to a new and frenetic level of TAAS preparation, centered both on improving math scores and targeting the African-American student community. The administration moved experienced AP calculus and geometry teachers to freshmen algebra classes, and all teachers, regardless of subject, were required to teach daily "math boosters" in their classes.

Motivated to save the job of their popular principal, several teachers undertook individual efforts to improve math scores and to intervene positively in the African-American student community. An experienced math teacher started a school task force on freshmen algebra that resulted in the reorganization of freshmen math instruction into "double-blocking," or teaching long daily blocks of algebra to all freshman students. Another teacher organized a mentoring club for African-American students. Administrators and teachers also organized a field trip to a local university for African-American students.

Being designated as a low-performing school served as a wake-up call for Ricki Lee, and forced the school to redefine its self-conception and mission. While maintaining pride in the school's academic tradition, the principal and teachers we spoke with had come to realize that a significant segment of the student population was struggling with math. In effect, the staff at Ricki Lee related external policies to the school's preexisting story by simultaneously reaffirming and modifying their story.

Interpreting/Making Sense of the Data Generated from the Policy   As a result of the numerous tests that high school students in Texas are required to take, Ricki Lee and its district were awash with student test score data. A district official insisted that the district provided its schools with a "mass of data." In our interviews, Mr. Isaacs reeled off pass rates of student subgroups on the TAAS, AP, SAT, and ACT. He also described the importance of sharing test data with other administrators and teachers in order to assess students and improve instruction.

While everyone we spoke with at Ricki Lee agreed that it was important to measure students' knowledge and progress in school, personnel were more skeptical about the use of data to evaluate teachers and schools. Mr. Isaacs lamented increasing pressure from the district to use test score data to evaluate his teachers. Ricki Lee's staff expressed similar wariness regarding the use of data in the school's designation as a low-performing school. In fact, several administrators and teachers characterized the school as a victim of mis-specified or misleading data.

Ironically, Ricki Lee's concentration on sorting out data about who was tested may have obscured a larger truth. Our interviews revealed that Ricki Lee's staff attributed their low-performing designation to the TAAS participation of African-American special education students who should have received exemptions. In fact, the year of the school's low-performing designation, 13.1 percent of Ricki Lee's African-American tenth graders received special education exemptions, compared to a campuswide exemption rate of 9.5 percent, and a districtwide rate of 7.5 percent. Despite the fact that exemptions were already disproportionately large in the African-American student population, Ricki Lee's dean of instruction assured us that counselors would take great care in the coming year to check the list of exempt students much more carefully. Indeed, the percentage of African-American students receiving exemptions increased to 15.3 the next year.

Determining What to Do about Teachers and Determining Who Is Going to Teach "This Stuff"   In our first interview with Ricki Lee's principal, Mr. Isaacs described his job as a "facilitator" for his teachers. He lamented the fact that his job did not allow him to take much time to visit classrooms and observe teachers. Instead, he delegated the role of evaluating and advising teachers to an assistant principal. When we returned after Ricki Lee was designated as a low-performing school, Mr. Isaacs reported that he had changed his approach toward assessing teachers. "This year," he insisted, "I'm in every ninth grade math and every tenth grade math class, because if I'm going to lose my job, I'm going to go down knowing that I was in those classes." Mr. Isaacs also called on the teachers themselves to offer solutions.

When recruiting new teachers, Mr. Isaacs focused on ninth grade algebra and tenth grade geometry, interviewing "only people that either were comfortable in algebra or geometry, which are the two beginning levels for the test, or had affinity for ninth graders, because it's amazing how many people don't like them." Frantic to recruit good math teachers, Mr. Isaacs explained his frustration at the lack of support he received from the district and the state, complaining, "I was on the phone, I was on the internet—I acquired teachers through the internet—so it's like you're out here by yourself, I guess. And I don't think it should be like that."

Determining What to Do with Students at Risk of Not Meeting the Standard
Even before Ricki Lee's designation as a low-performing school, the school administration had established tutoring programs and "repeater classes" for struggling students. With the new designation, these efforts accelerated. A math teacher formed a task force on ninth grade algebra that instituted "double-blocking," or teaching double periods of algebra to freshmen daily, rather than every other day. In addition to repeater classes, the math department also instituted "accelerated double blocks" of algebra for tenth and eleventh graders who had already failed the TAAS.

The administration and some teachers also began to target the academic performance of African-American students, whose scores on the TAAS had triggered Ricki Lee's low-performing designation. Mr. Isaacs characterized the school's relationship with African-American parents as a "me-they syndrome" in which lack of communication caused misunderstandings on both sides. Additionally, the principal observed that many African-American students "are not part of anything" and had no personal connection to the school. As a result, one of the teachers developed a mentoring club led by African-American teachers. Through this program, the school began to bring parents to volunteer in classrooms, so that "they [could] get a feel for an hour and a half what goes on instructionally at Ricki Lee."

Leadership at Ricki Lee High School
Most of the teachers we spoke with at Ricki Lee characterized Mr. Isaacs as a strong and popular principal who initiated and supported most of the

school's responses to external accountability pressures. Despite their general disagreement with district and state notions of accountability, teachers responded to Isaacs's call to improve math instruction for ninth and tenth grade students, particularly among African-American students. A few teachers extended this call and created a mentoring club for the target population of students. Ultimately, the school's recognition of its struggling subpopulation bore fruit: in 2000, 85.4 percent of African-American tenth graders passed the TAAS, an increase of one hundred percent.

Ricki Lee's schoolwide response to threats to the principal's job appeared to demonstrate a fairly strong degree of internal alignment, with directives from the principal supported and distributed among teachers. Yet Ricki Lee's response also appeared to be both reactive and defensive. African-American students had scored far below their peers on the math section of the TAAS for years before the school received a "wake-up call" from the state in the form of a low-performing designation. Additionally, administrators and counselors cited the underexemption of special education students as a reason for their designation, when in fact the school had exempted more African-American students than any other subgroup from the TAAS.

Miramar High School

Miramar High School is an urban school in a midsized Texas city. Of the school's 2,160 students, 92.8 percent are Hispanic, 4.6 percent are white, and two percent are African American. The school also has a population of over 150 students taking English for Speakers of Other Languages (ESOL) classes. About eighty percent of Miramar's students are considered economically disadvantaged, the highest proportion in Miramar's district and in our sample of six Texas schools. Three years prior to our first visit in January 1999, consistently low academic performance prompted the district superintendent to replace 59 of Miramar's 132 teachers and staff members. Since then, scores on the TAAS have increased steadily, a clear source of pride among teachers and administrators. The personnel we interviewed appeared to be much more accepting of accountability pressures from Austin than those at Ricki Lee. In fact, since so many teachers were new to Miramar, it appeared that the teachers and staff had built a new identity around accountability and its mechanisms.

Interpreting the Policy and Relating It to the Preexisting Story of the School

Due to its district's decision to reconstitute the school staff, Miramar was more profoundly affected by accountability than Ricki Lee. The departure of so many teachers, along with the arrival of a new principal who practiced a very centralized style of leadership, caused the school to quickly distance itself from its preexisting story and to forge a new identity based on the mechanisms and measures of accountability.

Prior to taking the job at Miramar, Mr. Zachary, the principal, had worked at the highest performing school in the district. Three years before our first visit, the superintendent had asked him to move to Miramar, which was then the district's lowest performing school. Several months after Zachary took the position, the district fired all of its employees and then required them to reapply for their jobs. Approximately fifty percent of the staff and teachers were rehired, along with many new teachers. According to Zachary, the reconstitution helped him to assemble a "staff that would be committed to success for all students, regardless of where they came from."

The central agent in the redesign of Miramar High was the local school district. In addition to reassigning the principal and executing the school's reconstitution, the district initiated a magnet program in health professions that attracted approximately two hundred new students from other schools and districts. At the time of our visit, the magnet program had almost three hundred students, most of whom came from outside of the school's service area.

As a result of his strong mandate from the district, Mr. Zachary exercised a strong top-down leadership role in the school's reorganization. Aside from making hiring decisions about teachers and staff, the principal redesigned the traditional schedule to what he described as a "four-by-four accelerated block" in which students took four ninety minute classes every day and completed a year's work in just one semester. He also placed strong emphasis on student achievement data, distributing test score data to teachers and setting benchmarks for improving student test scores. Initially, he focused on improving TAAS performance, but once those scores had improved, he led the school toward greater emphasis on EOC exams, the PSAT, and the SAT, which he considered to have higher academic content.

Changes on campus were accompanied by increasing test scores. Between 1995 and 1999, the percentage of Miramar students passing all sections of the TAAS increased from 22.6 to 59 percent. During the same period, pass rates increased from 54 to 77.2 percent on the reading section of the TAAS, from 69.1 percent to 87.4 percent in writing, and from 26.4 to 66.9 percent in math.

It was clear that Miramar felt a collective sense of pride about the school's success in raising test scores. This pride may account for the staff's generally positive attitude about Texas's accountability system. While teachers and administrators at Ricki Lee High School considered high-stakes accountability as a distraction, most of the personnel we interviewed at Miramar appeared to embrace the state's role in holding them accountable. For example, a technology teacher insisted, "TAAS is making us prove, yes, you are doing the job." These comments suggest that the school's identity and sense of purpose were tied up with their recent history as a new school rising from the ashes of reconstitution. Rather than distracting the school, accountability policies actually helped to define Miramar and its mission.

Interpreting/Making Sense of the Data Generated from the Policy Mr. Zachary told us that half of his battle in changing the culture of the school was simply to make teachers aware of test scores and what they represented. He told us that prior to his arrival at the school, teachers "were not aware of what was going on in the school, as far as test scores go." Consequently, Zachary considered one of his primary jobs to be providing them with information and making that information meaningful by setting targets for improvement. The principal's first step was to compile grade reports to show teachers how they compared with their colleagues in terms of grade distributions and failure rates. He also began to schedule meetings with teachers whose failure rates he believed to be too high.

Mr. Zachary also began to make use of TAAS and EOC scores to set goals and benchmarks for school progress. For the first several years after Miramar's reconstitution, the school's administration emphasized improvement of TAAS scores. All teachers did fifteen minutes of TAAS preparation a day and students who had failed were pulled out of regular classes to prepare for their next try. Following Zachary's lead, teachers developed two new programs—one in math and one in English—that attempted to teach TAAS skills in the context of more lively and student-centered instruction. Judging by test results, these efforts paid off, as Miramar's TAAS scores steadily increased, raising the school from last to third in the district in the percentage of students passing the test. During the same time, Miramar's district became the first in Texas to receive "recognized" status.

Determining What to Do about Teachers and Determining Who Is Going to Teach "This Stuff" By reconstituting Miramar and replacing nearly half of its teachers, Miramar's school district played a major role in determining what to do about teachers. As a result of this unusual opportunity to reconfigure the teaching staff, Zachary was able to ensure that those who stayed, along with the new teachers hired, would be more open to making instructional changes. Mr. Zachary considered the freedom to hire and fire teachers an important tool in assembling a high-quality teaching staff. As he explained in our interview, he believed that principals in Texas enjoyed a major advantage over those in other states: "You know, when we're talking about teachers, I think a critical part that needs to be understood is that we do not have the union for our teachers. It's totally different the way we operate, but when I talk to my colleagues in other states, they have very strong teacher unions, they are very much protected. So, a teacher doing a poor job in a classroom could be there forever."

Many of the teachers at Miramar agreed with Mr. Zachary's conclusions. The English department chair reported, "After the reconstitution, the way the faculty was made up was much easier for change to take place, because these were generally younger teachers who were more willing to receive some outside input and do things a little bit differently." A math teacher observed that after the reconstitution, "Somehow people who needed to be gone were gone," and added, "The new teachers don't have bad habits."

In the math department, several teachers adopted and received training in a new math program to teach algebra and geometry to freshmen and sophomores. The program, which emphasized group work, math applications, and technology, allowed students who participated for a whole year to earn credits for both algebra and geometry. Several teachers involved with the program told us that, because they emphasized reading and problem-solving, their students scored better on the TAAS and algebra I EOC exam than other students. In fact, one teacher argued that recent improvements on the EOC algebra I exam had vindicated teachers in the program, who had been criticized by other teachers for their unorthodox teaching. Teachers in the new math program also confirmed Mr. Zachary's assertion that he supported instructional freedom, observing that Zachary funded their training in the program and even allowed them some control over the students they accepted into the program. By hiring teachers who fit his vision of aligning the school toward state accountability policies, Mr. Zachary had also ensured that instructional leadership on the part of his teachers would also align with those policies.

Determining What to Do with Students at Risk of Not Meeting the Standard
Mr. Zachary sought to test as many students as possible, including students taking ESOL classes and special education students. Despite the possibility that such inclusive testing would result in high failure rates, Zachary also refused to create remedial classes for students who failed the TAAS the first time, arguing that such classes would short-change students in the long run. Yet the administration did establish several mechanisms to assist students who had failed or were at risk of failing the TAAS. For example, juniors and seniors who had not passed all sections of the TAAS were occasionally pulled out of regular classes to receive tutoring.

An example of two band instructors illustrates Miramar's sense of collective responsibility for student success on the TAAS. The instructors discovered that one of their senior band students had failed the math portion of the TAAS and began tutoring her to prepare for the next try. The instructors also initiated a peer tutoring program to pair top students with those struggling in their classes, and, if need be, to allow them to spend class time working on algebra or English instead of band.

Leadership at Miramar High School

From his first day at Miramar High, Mr. Zachary was on a mission from the school district to reconfigure the organization and instructional practice of the school. His strong mandate from the district, along with the district's decision to reconstitute the school, allowed Mr. Zachary to shape the composition of his teaching staff. Once he had assembled an acceptable group of teachers, he clearly communicated his vision of the administrator-teacher partnership: administrators would set test-based goals and benchmarks, and teachers would be responsible for classroom instruction. Within that framework, teachers were free to experiment with new ideas and approaches. The teachers who exhibited leadership in their departments by developing new instructional strategies did so within the framework of Zachary's goal of improving scores on the TAAS and EOC exams.

As a result of Mr. Zachary's strong leadership, all of the teachers we talked to at Miramar appeared to understand and agree with their roles in the school's post-reconstitution project. In fact, by focusing so strongly on state benchmarks such as TAAS and EOC passage rates, Zachary seemed to model the school's mission into meeting and exceeding the state's expectations at every step, thereby constructing the school's internal system around the external accountability policy.

Cityscape High School

Cityscape High School, the orthogonal school from our Texas sample, is a collection of six different magnet schools on a single campus. The six schools offer a wide range of vocational and academic areas: education and social services, business, government and law, health, science and technology, and talented and gifted. With the exception of the science and technology and talented and gifted magnets, the separate schools share a common academic center that provides core courses required for graduation, such as mathematics, English, and foreign languages. Each magnet school has its own principal, and all six principals report to a single executive principal. We conducted most of our interviews with the principal and teachers of the Education and Social Services (ESS) magnet school, which is designed to prepare students for careers as teachers, counselors, social workers, and child care workers.

Interpreting the Policy and Relating It to the Preexisting Story of the School

Accountability is a complex issue at a magnet center like Cityscape High School. Although each separate magnet school produces a school report card and is rated according to its TAAS scores and other measures, the instruction of TAAS subjects (reading, writing, and mathematics) occurs largely outside the magnet schools, in Cityscape's Academic Center. Consequently, many administrators and teachers feel distanced from the accountability mechanisms that personnel in other schools feel so keenly. At the same time, administrators at each center are held responsible for their students' scores on the TAAS.

Like many principals in Texas, Mr. Wentworth, the principal of the ESS magnet school, felt strong pressure to improve test scores and maintain an acceptable state rating. Teachers at the ESS magnet did not feel the same pressure as the principal to improve test scores. Due to the nature of the ESS magnet's classes—featuring subjects like child care, counseling, and teaching preparation—most of the teachers wrote their own curriculum, and several even wrote their own versions of the district's benchmark test. Although most of the ESS teachers reported trying to work extra math into their teaching to help prepare their students for the TAAS, they did not consider their courses as preparation for external tests. In fact, most of the teachers at the ESS magnet school reported that they had never seen the TAAS.

Interpreting/Making Sense of the Data Generated from the Policy The TAAS scores for Cityscape's ESS magnet increased steadily in the years before our visit. Between 1994 and 1998, the percentage of ESS students passing the TAAS had increased from 29.2 to 81.6 percent. In 1998, all students in the magnet passed both reading and writing components of the TAAS. On the math section of the TAAS, 81.3 percent passed in 1998, compared to 29.2 percent in 1994. As a result of its high TAAS scores, the ESS magnet earned "recognized" status from the state of Texas in 1998. The same year, three of the other magnet schools at Cityscape—which are rated separately by the state of Texas—had one hundred percent pass rates on the TAAS and earned "exemplary" status.

Mr. Wentworth recognized the need for the ESS magnet to look good relative to the other magnet schools at Cityscape, both to maintain the school's reputation and to compete in recruiting good students. Despite enjoying TAAS passage rates far above the other schools we visited in Texas, Wentworth felt pressure to raise them even higher. Consequently, he stressed the importance of "looking at the data" and working hard to become Cityscape's fourth school to receive exemplary status.

Determining What to Do about Teachers and Determining Who Is Going to Teach "This Stuff" Mr. Wentworth identified his students' math performance on the TAAS as the primary obstacle to reaching exemplary status. He also described his students' scores on the algebra I EOC exams as "terrible," and he argued that Cityscape's best teachers should teach algebra I rather than more advanced subjects. Yet the organizational structure of

Cityscape High complicated Wentworth's efforts to respond to these issues. None of the six teachers in the ESS magnet school explicitly taught math, and the math teachers in Cityscape's Academic Center answered to the school's executive principal rather than to Mr. Wentworth. As Wentworth explained, "I don't know what all the math teachers are doing."

Mr. Wentworth and his teachers responded to the challenge of preparing students for state math tests in two ways. To begin with, the principal encouraged his own teachers to integrate more math into their daily teaching. To supplement his students' math instruction, Mr. Wentworth hired a math teacher from another school to offer after-school tutoring. Yet he also recognized that tutoring programs only work if students are motivated to attend them. Discussing three students from the previous two years who had failed to graduate because they had not passed the math section of the TAAS, Wentworth observed: "There are some factors here that I don't have any control over. I mean, their math skills were just as good as other kids' math skills, and the other kids passed. But the factor I don't have any control over was they would never get themselves—despite pleas and begging and fussing and many conferences with parents—they would never get themselves to tutoring on any consistent basis. So I have no control over the effort, if you will."

Determining What to Do with Students at Risk of Not Meeting the Standard
Despite the ESS magnet's large population of minority and economically disadvantaged students, the school's ability to select its students reduced the prominence of this presenting a problem in the life of the school. The school also intervened early for struggling students, requiring all entering ninth graders who had scored below the fiftieth percentile on the reading or math sections of the TAAS to attend a three-week preparation course during the summer. After taking the TAAS in the tenth grade, the handful of students who failed the math section each year usually received tutoring and passed the test on the next try. Students had a much more difficult time passing the algebra I EOC exams, but the stakes were much lower for students and schools than with the TAAS, so low scores did not prompt widespread concern.

On the other hand, many teachers at Cityscape commented on growing pressure from the district and school administration to place more students into Advanced Placement courses. Part of the pressure came as the result of a grant from a local foundation that provided training and paid stipends to AP teachers and reimbursed exam fees for students who passed the test.

Leadership at Cityscape's Education and Social Services Magnet
Much like the principals of Ricki Lee and Miramar, Mr. Wentworth felt considerable pressure from his district and state accountability systems.

Consequently, he attempted to encourage a strong schoolwide response to improve test scores. Yet Wentworth faced several constraints in his mission to recruit good students and raise the status of his magnet school. Unable to exert a strong influence on math teachers outside of his small magnet, he turned to his own teachers, who made sporadic and half-hearted attempts to integrate math instruction into their classes. He also hired a math teacher to give after-school tutoring, but he could not require struggling students to participate.

Wentworth's teachers did not actively resist his pleas to teach more math; they simply did not see math instruction as an essential element to the school's mission of preparing students for careers in teaching, counseling, social work, and child care. Moreover, because many of them wrote their own curriculum and there were no district exams to measure how much their students learned in their classes, they did not feel accountability pressures as acutely as their principal. As a result of both Cityscape's organization and the ESS magnet's mission, Mr. Wentworth found himself unable to respond fully to the myriad pressures placed on him by the state, his district, and Cityscape itself.

Conclusions

Our two-state analysis of leadership in response to accountability pressures reveals a number of patterns regarding the nature and distribution of leadership in different contexts. To begin with, in each of the three Texas schools, as well as Byrd in Kentucky, the principal emerged as the central leadership figure, directly involved with responses to accountability policy in observable ways.

What accounts for the central role of the principal in the Texas schools? The state's notoriously high-stakes accountability policies may generate more immediate and rapid consolidation of authority in the principal's hands. While teachers at schools such as Cityscape face the threat of being reassigned if they are not deemed effective, Texas's accountability policies assign a much greater and more direct weight to principals of low-performing schools. Such a scheme can result in different scenarios, from a schoolwide effort to rally around the principal, as in the case of Ricki Lee, to a principal's district-driven mission to reorganize school staff, as at Miramar. Both cases resulted in the concentration of authority in the principal, accompanied by limited but aligned initiatives by school personnel.

Although the principal was also a central figure in our single better-positioned school (Byrd), he did not have to take the school as far to get it into alignment, allowing him to be more subtle and savvy with his mobilization of the school. As a result, he was able to spend his energy on how the school could respond coherently, not whether the school would respond. Following his cue, school personnel also took on leadership roles in a coherent fashion, generating the type of "stretched" leadership described by Spillane, et al. Indeed, perhaps as a result of a combination of greater internal alignment and lower stakes than in the Texas schools, Byrd was the only school in our sample that followed the Spillane model. This suggests that high accountability stakes may be one of the context factors that inhibit the distribution of school leadership. The four schools mentioned above also appeared to enact responses that were more aligned with external accountability policy than Binghamton or Baleford. This can be explained by the greater accountability pressure in Texas, and the greater internal alignment (meaning less distance to travel in aligning with external requirements) in Byrd. Also, at Binghamton and Baleford, the principals were less central in the leadership story. Binghamton's principal tried to respond but her actions did not emerge in a compelling way. Baleford's principal saw himself as the school's culture setter and seemed only indirectly connected to the responses of accountability.

Perhaps the most striking feature of our comparison is the dramatic difference across the states in our target schools. In Texas, where there are more immediate and observable stakes, such as reconstitution, the schools seem to act more coherently and under more coherent leadership. In Binghamton, the weaker sanctions do not inspire the school to cohere, and the school continues to be fragmented and unorganized in its leadership and response.

Finally, the orthogonal schools in our sample (Baleford and Cityscape) present a special case in which school leaders must conform to—and in some cases choose between—their unique educational missions and external accountability pressures. In the case of Baleford, the principal and other school personnel framed Kentucky's accountability system as an external reinforcement to the school's internal mission of preparing inner-city children for successful careers. At the same time, the school's leadership did not appear consistent or coherent in achieving this mission across departments. Conversely, the principal at Cityscape's ESS magnet in Texas demonstrated great concern over aligning his school's teaching to meet the state's and the school's high standards; but he met resistance from his teachers, who did not consider test preparation to be in line with the school's mission of preparing students for service careers. In this special case, the organizational structure of the school did not allow the concentration of leadership the principal required to make the changes that strong accountability policies invariably require. Nonetheless, Cityscape was able to achieve high scores on the TAAS high school exit test.

Notes

1. Apprentice is a Kentucky term. This suggests that these students are identified as at risk of not reaching the "proficient" category on the state assessments.
2. See Rhoten, et al., in this volume, for a description of changes in Texas's accountability system in 2002–2003.

References

Abelmann, C., R. F. Elmore. 1999. When accountability knocks, will anyone answer? CPRE Research Report Series: University of Pennsylvania, Consortium of Policy Research in Education.

Elmore, R. F. 2000. Building a new structure for school leadership. Washington, D.C.: The Albert Shanker Institute.

Spillane, J. P., R. Halverson, and J. B. Diamond. 2001. Investigating school leadership practice: A distributed perspective. *Educational Researcher* 30:23–28.

CHAPTER 5

Listening to Talk from and about Students on Accountability

MELISSA CHABRÁN

I showed up, I did the work, I should pass.
—Ring, twelfth grade student

In math, [you] know that "log" will come in. Classes go with tests.
—Rivera, eleventh grade student

Accountability for student performance, coupled with standards and assessments, directed at students, teachers, or schools, is a growing part of U.S. school reform. Policies outlining specific accountability plans, with clearly defined consequences tied to student assessments, are typically part of most states' educational reform strategy. Often, those consequences take the form of high stakes for students, where promotion and graduation from high school is tied directly to students passing state assessment(s). In other cases, there are no explicit stakes for students. Stakes fall on schools, as students' performances on a test determine how a school is publicly ranked, and whether it is rewarded or penalized.

Ultimately, the effects of accountability policies depend on the cooperation of the students. Our findings in this essay raise questions about test measurement and whether many state assessments are capturing what states expect students to know with reliability and validity. Our study also raises questions about student motivation and, consistent with Abelmann and Elmore (1999), questions whether the assessment itself is enough. For example, do students do their best on the test so that it truly reflects what they can do? Stakes in the form of direct sanctions for students may not be enough. Students may be disconnected from what they do in school or believe that they cannot do well on the test, thus decreasing their motivation to do well. At the same time, there are other stakes connected to tests for students that some schools are working to incorporate into their internal accountability structure. These include direct incentives and rewards for students to perform well on the test, connecting test results to the reputation of their school, and connecting test performance to a sense of school community.

How students respond to these policies is central to the issue of accountability and student performance on state assessments. Assumptions about student motivations are embedded in the logic of these high-stakes accountability systems. Test administrators assume that the incentive of graduation motivates students to do well on a state assessment. But whether students are actually motivated by state assessments is unclear. Yet, many accountability policies with high stakes attached to state assessments assume that this alone will motivate students to do well on these tests or pay significant attention to them. Indeed, research suggests that there are many potential influences on student motivations and attitudes, including their past achievement, perception of their own competence, social environment, and community context (Stodolsky, Salk, and Glaessner 1991; Hidi and Harackiewicz 2000).

In this essay, we explore how students respond to accountability policies by examining their talk about state assessments, motivation, and conceptions of accountability. We also examine some of their administrators' and teachers' talk about student responses and motivations in policy environments where high stakes exist for students and in others where stakes exist only for the school. Although our work provides insight into what researchers and policy makers might ask students, uncovering some interesting issues, it is meant to be a *preliminary* look at how students might respond to accountability systems. To gain this insight, we examine student responses to accountability systems from the point of view of teachers and administrators across the states in our study sample (Kentucky, New York, Texas, and Vermont), and from students who took part in focus groups at our three New York schools.

Finally, this analysis provides a look at where teachers and students locate each other in the accountability process. Prior research by Raviv, Raviv, and Reisel (1990) compared student and teacher perceptions of the classroom environment, finding that students and teachers were in relative agreement ". . . regarding ideal, [rather] than the actual classroom environment" (p. 155). It is useful and indeed necessary to conduct similar inquiries with regard to how students and teachers think about accountability systems and implementation.

Each of the four states discussed in this paper takes a somewhat different approach to standards-based accountability. While all four states in our project have accountability systems centered on state assessments, three of the four attach high stakes of some kind to their assessment, and only two of the three have high stakes for students. In Kentucky, there are no direct stakes for students, although some pressure is felt at the school level to produce improving annual aggregate student results on the Commonwealth Accountability Testing System (CATS), which replaced the former Kentucky Instructional Results Information System (KIRIS) assessment system in 1998. The continuous improvement of Kentucky schools and districts is measured by an accountability index, which incorporates CATS scores. Stakes in Kentucky are felt at the school level with rewards and sanctions for adults. New York has crafted a different system of accountability where students' scores on the Regents exam determine whether or not they graduate from high school. This is a shift from a state policy that formerly awarded two types of diplomas—one a "local diploma," attained after passing a battery of Regents Competency Tests (RCTs), and the other, a "Regents diploma," awarded after passing series of higher level exams. Texas's accountability system combines both Kentucky and New York's approach and goes beyond both. Texas provides for a strong district role in ensuring that schools improve on the Texas Assessment of Academic Skills (TAAS) as well as on the End-of-Course (EOC) exams, which also feed into the accountability system. Like Kentucky, there are penalties or rewards for schools for performance, and, similar to New York, students' high school graduation is contingent upon passing the TAAS. Finally, Vermont's focus on improvement, or "action planning," as a means of building capacity in the schools presents a fourth model of accountability. The state does not provide for any stakes for students as a consequence of performance on the state assessment, the New Standards Reference Examination (NSRE). Its stakes for schools consist of publication of schools' test scores.[1]

In each of these states, we selected three (or six, in Texas) metropolitan high schools[2] as part of our sample. Table 5.1 below displays how our study design characterizes each of our sample schools. We saw each of these schools as being either "better positioned" with respect to the policy or as a "target" of the policy. Finally, an "orthogonal" school has a mission different from the other schools and its standards may or may not be congruent with state standards and assessments.[3] We found variations in student responses to the policy by both state and school type.

Table 5.1 Study sample schools

State	Better-positioned schools	Target schools	Orthogonal schools
Kentucky	Byrd	Binghamton	Baleford
New York	Rivera	Robinson	Ring
Texas	Texoma	Ricki Lee, Eames, Calin, Miramar	Cityscape
Vermont	Glen Lake	Garrison	Graham

Student Responses to High-Stakes Testing Systems

Stakes for students can have a variety of meanings. What we most frequently associate with "high stakes" is graduation from high school dependent upon a statewide assessment or exit exam. In our conversations with students, this is how we referred to high stakes. In this section, our analyses of how teachers and administrators talked about students and accountability also reflects both researchers' and respondents' tendency to equate high stakes with high school graduation dependent upon student performance on a state assessment.

Anxiety-Producing Tests

Both teachers and students in our study sample saw high-stakes tests as anxiety-producing mechanisms. In Texas, where the system of high stakes has been in place for over ten years, and in New York, where the graduating class of 2000 had to pass the English Regents examination and the graduating class of 2001 had to pass both the English and math Regents examinations, teachers referred to the test as a source of strain for students. One teacher from Texoma, our better-positioned school in Texas, talks about how the TAAS is everywhere. She is concerned that the emphasis on the TAAS has an adverse effect on students: "I have a very strong personal philosophy that we don't need to holler that word so much and I stress that everywhere I go, quit talking TAAS. We don't need to TAAS, TAAS, TAAS, TAAS, TAAS to these kids, just teach and be sure you're teaching those TAAS objectives and the test will take care of itself. Our new superintendent said that very same thing when she came in. She said, don't even put the word TAAS in the Campus Improvement Plan. Just put how you're teaching those objectives and maybe that will relieve some of the stress that we've put on kids."

Students at our better-positioned school in New York—Rivera—expressed similar concerns about the increasing Regents exam requirements for students in their state. "Incoming freshmen, I feel so sorry for them" [because of increased testing requirements]. One student at Ring, the New York orthogonal school, had similar things to say about the required assessment. She said with the Regents exam, a student could pass by guessing, or fail because they were not taught material on the test. Ring students said, "We get intimidated by the tests." Another student saw this issue a bit differently, saying that she preferred exams to portfolios and exhibitions because she sometimes got nervous during presentations. In fact, many Ring students thought they could do well on the Regents exam, although they had not yet taken it, unlike at some of our other New York schools.

New York teachers agreed that the Regents made students anxious, and also speculated that the mandatory exams have different meaning for students depending on the type of school they attend. One teacher at Rivera said,

> I think it scares a lot of them, because they know that if they don't pass it, they're going to fail for the year, for the most part. In some cases, a student that just passes . . . that just misses by a few points, can move on; but in most cases, when they fail the Regents, they fail the course, and have to repeat the entire year. We give very difficult tests. So maybe the Regents is a little bit better for them; in some of the high schools that are giving very watered down exams, the Regents hits them like a wall . . . like a brick wall.

A Ring teacher discusses why the test is not good for students at her school:

> We're not a test-taking school. The kids are used to this culture and to ask particularly the kids who have been here since the beginning and this is their senior year, junior year, to ask them to totally change their culture, the way of learning, the way of assessment, the way of thinking, is very unfair. Even with all the rumors and all the talk, kids are even excited now, even though we got the waiver [from the test] this year, they're still excited about it, they're still like anxious about it, to put that kind of stress on them. And us, too, as teachers. It's definitely not a good thing.

Ring developed their own system of assessment for accountability, with portfolios and exhibitions, prior to the policy change. Learning is very individualized as a consequence of the school's mission and their existence as a small school serving immigrant students. Ninety percent of their students go on to college after graduation. The school has been working to demonstrate to the state that its alternative curriculum and assessment system do align with the New York standards. However, many teachers and administrators at this school expressed uncertainty about whether they would have to participate in the Regents (Siskin 2000). In contrast to the Ring student described previously, who prefers exams to portfolios, another Ring student would choose the portfolio process over the Regents exam. This student felt that the portfolio system allowed them to better demonstrate their skills, whereas the Regents did not allow students to show what they knew. Indeed, students contrast this type of high-stakes accountability with other types of accountability to demonstrate what they know. Finally, students at Rivera said that they would prefer a Regents exam that required that students show their work [as opposed to multiple choice].

"It Works Here" versus "Teaching to the Test"

Some students and teachers thought that high-stakes exams helped students focus on the course content in both the classroom and on the test. At the same time, some teachers and students characterized this as "teaching to the test," while others talked about the clarity the test provided on expectations and as a source of motivation for students to do well. At Rivera, both administrators and teachers talk about how the school's standards had been high prior to the shift in policy. Students, in the past, had taken the Regents as part of their coursework in their high-level classes. The school then saw the new policy as compatible with its prior role. Prior to the policy implementation of Regents for all students, a large percentage of Rivera students received Regents diplomas by passing all necessary tests. Despite this positioning or alignment with the state policy, some teachers believe that students need the focus of a required Regents exam, even at Rivera: "I think a lot of them are very motivated, but they have so many things to think about, even the smart ones, their last priority is class and especially if the summer's coming and there's so many other things they want to be doing. I think the Regents actually keeps them a little focused and if it wasn't there, then forget it, there'd be no reason for them to be here."

One student at Rivera expressed a similar sentiment, saying that without Regents exams, students would not be focused and would not put in any effort. She explained that some students just don't care. A teacher at Robinson, our New York target school, responded similarly, saying that tests, while creating pressure, also help motivate students: "Tests are always a threat in the child's mind, any human being's mind. Or the rigidity of the atmosphere of the Regents, or an RCT test is everything like, 'oh, man.' It'll have an impact. I tell them, act like you're being tested all the time, act like you're being watched or judged all the time, and that removes that pressure or limelight from being tested, 'Oh, my god, I'm here for a two- three-hour test.' It'll have an impact, if not physical, a mental, psychological impact on them."

Another student at Rivera found the Regents exams to be helpful. She felt these exams led to clearer expectations about what they were to learn. When asked how the Regents affected students' learning outside of class, she said "It works here. Because with many teachers, class has to go along with it. [It] has to go to a certain curriculum. In math, [you] know that 'log' will come in. Classes go with tests." From this student's perspective, the content on a Regents exam was inseparable from the content in their courses. Some teachers we spoke with did not necessarily see this as a positive outcome of a high-stakes accountability system. One teacher at our target Texas school, Ricki Lee, was concerned about how many teachers taught to the test and the effect that it was having on students: ". . . I know we were held accountable for a lot more things than these kids nowadays are being held accountable for. I know that we didn't always have things spoon-fed to us. These kids nowadays, what I'm noticing, is they don't want to work or anything. They want instant gratification . . . That's what's happening now, these teachers are teaching for the tests, for the TAAS, and once they get that, you know, it's like, the kids are like, okay, it's over with, blah, blah, blah. Like, all right now, now what. But you can't even carry on an intelligent conversation about anything."

Inconsistent Expectations versus Taking the Test Seriously

Students' and teachers' views differed in their discussion around how they understood the policy. Some students were concerned that this policy change was inconsistent with expectations that had been articulated to them by teachers and administrators. Rivera students told us that the use of the Regents had been an ongoing debate in their school. They explained that at their school, if you failed the Regents, you got an F. At the same time, if you got an 85 on the Regents, the teacher could still fail you. They expressed the need for consistency. They said, the Regents and school requirements "[have] to go with each other." One female student talked about getting a 64 on the Regents chemistry exam and failing the course. She said "I showed up, I did the work, I should pass." Rivera students also saw inconsistencies with external accountability structures like higher education. They expressed concern about the need to pass the Regents in order to graduate from high school but not to go to college. "I'm going to college in Virginia. Money is on the line. If I don't pass the Regents, I don't graduate, I lose everything [tuition, down payments, etc.]. When you're a senior, you've got all this riding on you. The Regents don't even count outside New York." This seemed quite important given that until 2000, the Regents did not have implications outside New York.

Many teachers, however, thought that despite the high-stakes nature of these exams in both New York and Texas, students were still not taking them seriously. In speaking about Texoma's improvement on the TAAS over the years, one teacher says,

> A lot of them get a lot better, but sometimes when they take tests, they don't take it seriously. And the first question they ask is, am I going to get a grade for

this? And if you tell them, well, no, it's whatever, they don't seem to do their best . . . now, of course, the state test, the TAAS test, they start getting more serious . . . by them having the opportunity to take it, what, five or six or seven times, some of them even in their sophomore year don't take it that seriously. They have, what, six more times to take it before their senior year. I would say it's probably better having it [the TAAS], because it just kind of breaks the big picture down into little pieces . . . If you're doing your very, very best, and if your best interests are linked to the students, you're consistently trying to motivate them and giving them materials, teaching them skills that will help them be better thinkers, then once you do those things the more, that's all you can really do, because you can lead a horse to water, but you just can't make him drink . . . And so, they have to be motivated internally, and I motivate them externally, but they have to be motivated internally . . . And you can do everything under the sun, outwardly, but at some point, it has to be inside. And a lot of students lack internal motivation.

When we asked a Rivera teacher how students were responding to the Regents, she said,

I don't think they're taking it as seriously as they probably should. As I said before, some kids will say, "Well, if I don't get a Regents diploma, you know, so what, big deal." Some seem very upset about it and say, "How dare they say that I can't go on to the next grade if I don't pass the Regents."

Perhaps this indicates that New York students may not be aware of the high-stakes nature of the Regents for them. New York students asked "why [the] school requires it when the state doesn't?" However, a teacher at Robinson, our target school in New York, thought that the new Regents requirements were making changes for the students in that school: "They're very well aware of the fact that they need to pass the Regents to graduate from high school. I'm sure they have a sense they really have to try a little harder than how they've been trying throughout their school career. But we'll see how this plays out."

In general, both students and teachers saw high-stakes exams as anxiety producing among students. Their opinions on whether or not the tests served a purpose that was helpful to student learning is mixed. Some thought high-stakes tests provided the focus and clarity of the content to be learned and tested, while others thought these high-stakes accountability systems promoted "teaching to the test" in a way that was unhealthy for student learning. Finally, students and teachers differed on how they thought students understood the policy. While many students talked about the high-stakes exam conveying inconsistent expectations either within the school or within the system of higher education, teachers talked about students not taking the test seriously.

When Stakes Are Located Elsewhere

Both Kentucky and Vermont are states where the consequences of the assessment system are focused somewhere other than on the students, if at all. In Kentucky, stakes are felt at the school level, and in Vermont, it is less clear that the effect of a school's performance on the state assessment, which is published, is felt by any particular actor. In speaking with teachers and administrators in both these states, it became clear that one of their main challenges is getting students motivated for the courses or the state assessment when these forms of accountability do not hold any meaning for them.

They Don't Take the Tests Seriously

Similar to schools in New York and Texas where there are high stakes for students, schools in Kentucky and Vermont experience frustration at getting students motivated for state assessments and interested in their performance. For instance, teachers at Binghamton, the target school in Kentucky, talk about sharing the school's scores with the students. When asked how students reacted to their school not doing well on the state assessment, one teacher said they were "Nonchalant. Just—'Oh, well.'"

Teachers at both Binghamton and Baleford talked about some of the reasons they think students are not motivated for this assessment. As one teacher at Baleford recalls, students have little ownership in taking the state assessment: ". . . I'll be honest with you, in the past, when the kids did the old KIRIS, it was basically done in either eleventh and twelfth, it's kind of moved about, it started with twelfth and kind of moved back to eleventh. The kids did not really have any ownership in it and basically they performed for us and that was it. I mean they did it out of a respect and a liking for us and so on, more than anything. And now with the testing going on [at] all levels, it's, I think, a little bit more difficult with kids. Ninth graders, they see no value in it whatsoever."

At Binghamton, motivation is a similar challenge. There, teachers say the students do not care about their CATS scores. Teachers say students think, "Why do I care what my CATS score is?" At Baleford, when asked about students' perspectives on the test, the principal said that students are not held accountable. "And because they are not held accountable, that means that they see it as a joke." These problems are further complicated because of the timing of the score release. As one Binghamton teacher said, "The fact is, the students aren't accountable for their scores. The scores come back too late to use them for or against a student. I mean if you have a student sleep through all this test, the year's over. We got individual scores for last year's test, about a month and a half ago maybe. So it's like a year behind on the reporting, so you can't use the scores for anything, be-cause it's already gone."

At Binghamton, there was also a feeling as with the New York students, that students were not aware of the accountability policy and Kentucky's reform in general. One teacher said, "I don't think most of them really understand, you know, the standards and all that. They do understand that as a school we're being evaluated based on our scores."

In examining teacher talk about this problem, it seemed that the lack of seriousness surrounding the test was widespread among students. However, one Binghamton teacher clarified how pervasive the problem really was: "I would say that maybe 20 to 25 percent of the kids really don't take it seriously. Most of the other kids do try. But I think there has to be a better way to test them, so that they can see that it is important. I mean, we can stand up here and say that it's really important that you try your best on this test, but that's not enough sometimes."

Faced with this problem of motivation, many teachers in Kentucky schools are turning toward strategies that provide incentives for students to do well on the exam (Siskin and Lemons 2000). When asked what happens in the school when testing occurs and whether students were nervous about the change in the test in Kentucky, the principal said, "Students don't really care. They don't react like us [the teachers and administration]." As a result, the school turns to a system of external rewards and recognitions to try to motivate students to take the state assessment seriously and do well on it. "And so we got to do a lot of bells and whistles and, you know, do dances for them, and all that kind of stuff, to get them excited about learning."

Incentives to get students excited about the assessment and learning in general take many forms, including tying it to what students care about and how school fits into their lives. As one Binghamton teacher recalls,

> You find out what they have to go through . . . and you can understand in a hurry why some of these kids are not that motivated to come into a classroom. They know they're coming in here and getting a meal in the morning, they're getting a meal in the afternoon. So they're getting lunch and breakfast taken care of, and other than that they just want to survive. So the academics are just something where we've got to figure out a way of making them think it's a little bit more important . . . and so they're just putting in time trying to get through high school. Some of them are not really worried about trying to get through high school, they're just trying to get till they're old enough to get out of high school. There's a lot more going on than what I even know.

Other mechanisms for motivation are more tangible and tied to the school culture, and include rewards and penalties for performance. Some rewards include free time, pep rallies, a relaxed dress code, exemption from final exams, free food, prom passes, and recognition. The principal at Byrd recounts their strategy at a rally they held to motivate students to do well on CATS: "Last year we rented these sumo wrestling things you blow up. It makes a guy. Two of my teachers came out . . . And we had last year's score and then this year's goal. That was your number on the back. Sumo wrestlers don't have numbers, but who cares. And so they did some kind of fake wrestling match and, of course, the new goal won, just anything to be funny."

Penalties for poor performance include a decreased grade in a class or on a test and a withheld driver's permit. Grades were very important to students. As one Byrd teacher said, "This is a very grade motivated school and notice I didn't say knowledge motivated, I said grade motivated. And some of these kids will do any thing to get a good grade on something."

Helping students understand what they need to know and that they were capable of performing well on the assessment was a recurring theme in most of our states. The Byrd principal noted how they let students know they have support.

> We also go around to the mayor, we go to the university's basketball coach, if there are any celebrities cutting through the city, we'll get them on a thirty second tape saying, "Look, I've heard about your school, good luck I know you can do this." And, thus, we splice it all together and we show about a fifteen minute video to let them know it's important . . . But do you know that it takes all of our energy to get these kids to do their best. We don't have to do that on the driver's permit test. We don't have to remind them to bring pencils. We don't have to do anything. They'll study. And the same thing with the ACT, we don't have to.

Indeed, most prevalent in conversations with teachers and administrators in states like Kentucky, where the stakes are located elsewhere, was the issue of motivation and the need for students to see the state assessment as meaningful to their lives. As a Baleford teacher says,

> Until it's a part of their accountability, they're not going to take it seriously. That's very distant for them. You know, if I get this on the score. Well it's very distant for them. And all their lives they've been tested, tested, tested. It doesn't mean anything. It didn't mean anything to me when I was there. It didn't mean anything to me until I went to regular college . . . I think it's good to have standards to which you're working, but I think kids need to be a part of the process and need to know, need to see it as a value to them. You can't force feed anybody anything. I know from my own experience. I taught senior English the last four or five years that I taught. And when the kids saw it as an integral part of their lives, what we were dealing with, I had no problem getting them to even read Hamlet. You know, reading Hamlet, they could see what it was all about, the connection.

In summary, teacher talk about how students respond to the state assessment system when the stakes are not located on them was somewhat similar to how they talk about students when they are the recipients of the consequences. Issues here concern student motivation about the test, which was more prevalent in states with no stakes for students, particularly with the use of incentives and the need to connect the content to what students care about. What was quite different was the absence of any discussion around testing anxiety, teaching to the test, and focus. Integrating student voices into a discussion of accountability in Kentucky or Vermont, would, no doubt, enlighten this further.

Multiple Means of Motivation

In our study, "with remarkable consistency, across the states and types of schools, teachers and administrators struggle with the short term, and immediate problem of how to motivate students to perform on the tests" (Siskin and Lemons 2000, 6). Approaches to this problem were varied, but two motivating factors that surfaced frequently and which also resonated with our conversation with students were (1) having a sense of school pride and (2) having a culture of "community," found in our orthogonal schools or in a particular subject area, such as music and band, where teachers talked about students as having real ownership of their learning.

School Pride

How their school appears to others is important to students. In Kentucky, despite the fact that the state assessment does not have direct stakes at the student level, students were concerned about the public nature of score release. In these cases, teachers and administrators talked about how students saw it as important that their school appeared favorably, and they were well aware when it did not. Some adults in the school, in fact, tried to use this as a motivating force. As the principal at Baleford, our orthogonal school in Kentucky, says, ". . . so why should they be nervous about a test? I hope they are, because they want their school to do well." In speaking about how she got students to want their school to do well, the Baleford principal notes how they recognized individual student performance publicly in the school, but tied it to the larger school: "It's climate and culture. I mean, yeah, doing the recognitions for one day, you're doing it because you know it's going to cause them to respond differently in a program. And so the pride factor, you know? 'I go to [Baleford].' Kids back in their neighborhoods, they're about what goes on. And if you're at a school that's not doing well, everybody in the world knows it. And so they don't want to be a part of that. And they avoid situations like that, just like you do."

In New York, the reputation of their school seemed to be a source of motivation for Rivera students. They talked about going to college and participating in the opportunities Rivera offered them to help in this regard. In this conversation about college, students talked about information that institutions of higher education had about them and which the students perceived as unfavorable to colleges, including (1) that they are minority, (2) that they are from New York, (3) that they attended public schools, and (4) that their income was not high. They said that the school reputation helped their prospects for college, given these factors. In Kentucky, the Baleford principal expressed something similar about students there: "What we do is try and say you're representing [Baleford], and you know what people say about [Baleford] every place. We want to be able to hold our heads up. So that works in our favor."

At Binghamton, the target school in Kentucky, school pride cuts across many activities and filters into the testing arena. One teacher at this school talked about how the success of the basketball team helps motivate students to do well generally, including performing well on the CATS: "A lot of it is, just, the kids want to look good. I mean, we've had a really good athletic year this year with our school. Our basketball team went to the state tournament, finished in the top eight or the elite eight. And the students got a lot of good press and the school got a lot of good press, and the students this year are really excited about it and they want to look good . . . And the kids have just gotten on the bandwagon with all this press and they want to look good, so that's just helping by itself." As discussed previously, Byrd uses videos and wrestling matches to motivate students by creating a sense of school pride and pride at the grade level.

Another motivating factor for students seemed to be their own learning. In New York, Rivera students talked about graduation from high school in order to move on to college and apply what they learned in high school to their collegiate studies and future professions. Ring students said that pride motivates them and that if you are learning, you feel successful. They also explained that high-stakes tests made them feel like they were not able to learn. A Binghamton teacher emphasized the need for ". . . a lot of practice and motivating to let them know that they can do it, because I think they just look at it and think they can't and they just close the book."

The Baleford principal reinforced this sentiment, tying it to the need for the school to help students feel that they are capable of doing well on these exams: "When they print school data in the newspaper, parents look at that, and they avoid the schools that do not appear to be doing well. And so there's parents looking at it, kids are looking at it. I mean, they're not crazy, they know. I guarantee you every kid in this building can name for you the schools in this district that they think are the best schools in the district. And so, sure, they're talking about it. Most people won't give them credit for really having the pride, because most schools aren't there. They aren't doing, they aren't approaching it the way we approach it. But I tell you again, climate and culture. What we better do . . . is figure out a way how to augment the self-esteem of our students systematically."

School pride seems to be a large source of motivation for most students, although it has different meanings at different schools. In our better-positioned and target schools, school pride seemed to be very concrete and clear. For instance, at our target schools, students must be motivated to uphold the reputation of the school and meet the expectations that come as a result of it. Finally, in our orthogonal schools, school pride seemed to be more of a tension and threat, where teachers and administrators are concerned that the new accountability policy will undermine students' motivation to learn. This tension may not be congruent with motivating students toward the test.

Community and Culture

The missions of the orthogonal schools seemed to be unique from other schools in our sample. In examining data from our orthogonal schools, we found that most of the teachers and administrators spoke of their students as highly motivated. Additionally, in some conversations with teachers across all of our study schools, we found that students who were meaningfully connected to the school or a program within the school were motivated. Here, teachers and administrators talked about students perceiving the school or program as integral to their lives.

In Baleford, our Kentucky orthogonal school, a teacher talked about students being highly motivated because of the nature of the school.

> [They are] very motivated, very career oriented. They're here for a purpose. Baleford is a magnet school, so we don't have a home-school district boundary. Kids don't come here because they have to. They come here because they choose to enroll. Coming to Baleford is almost like going through a college application [process] because the students have to fill out an application, they have to have two letters of recommendations, they have to write an essay on why they want to come to this school, and then they have to send a copy of their grades in.

Teachers at our New York orthogonal school, Ring, had similar things to say about their students, "We don't have any resistance like some of these schools where the kids say, 'You can't tell me nothing.'" Other teachers at Ring talked about motivating students by having them be active learners in their work, sensing a gap between the content, pedagogy, and the way it is assessed. One teacher says of the Regents,

> They don't learn anything from taking that sort of test. My philosophy is that students learn by doing something, by participating in a step-by-step process, producing something . . . So for me, it's not the actual answer, but learning how to answer it that's important. Yesterday, we were talking about cancer. Whether they remember that there's a receptor on the cell, what the name of

that receptor is, that there are these things called growth factors, I couldn't care less if they remember that five years from now. But what I do want them to remember is that in cancer cells stop functioning in a certain way. If they want to find out what that way is, they would be able to find out what that is and be able to maybe understand something about it . . . I don't expect them to remember receptors, and that's what Regents, SATs, and those sorts of achievement tests look at. Like I said, from what I understand, Regents are slowly moving away from that . . . the way the questions will be set up is that you have to do some thought beforehand, and your answers will be based on the work that you've done, which is very similar to MCATs, medical school tests, law school tests.

Participating in outside competitions, events, and activities, students who are involved in the band or a music group also seem to be highly motivated and connected to the school. As one teacher at Robinson, our New York target school says, "Some of them come here without any interest at all. Some of them come very motivated. Some get motivated because their best friend got motivated, and it's a domino effect. It builds up like that because it's the nature of music and art." The Ricki Lee band teacher echoed this sentiment, talking about how students in the band are also very connected to other parts of the school, "Well . . . they are in the band, but they're also in athletics and extra-curricular things after school. I mean, they're involved. Our kids are involved."

Overall, as is consistent with prior research, there are many factors that motivate students to do well in school and on exams. In our study sample states, common themes that emerged as motivation for students to do well on the state assessment, whether or not high stakes were attached for them, included a sense of school pride, or "wanting to look good," as well as feeling that they, as students, were connected to part of a school culture that was meaningful. Indeed, these are sources of motivation that are interrelated and which schools in our study seek to cultivate.

Conclusions and Implications for Further Study

Across all states in our study, implemented policies that outlined accountability systems elicited some type of response from students. In New York and Texas, both states with high stakes for students, there seemed to be more talk of anxiety surrounding the statewide assessment, clear or mixed expectations, and "teaching to the test" than in our states where there are no direct stakes for students. In these states, and in Kentucky, specifically, talk from teachers and administrators seemed to center more on how to motivate students to do well, incentives that might be offered, or leverage that a school had in using these assessments in their work with students.

What emerges from our analysis is that there are a *variety* of stakes for students, even with the presence of a high-stakes test. Direct stakes that tie graduation to student performance on a test may not be operating as intended to motivate students. Other stakes, or sources of motivation, that are present in all of our study states, but which are more indirect, include school pride and the community of a school or program. From our research, these seem to be just as important to students as high school graduation. Whether stakes were direct or indirect, students in our study questioned the inconsistent messages they seemed to be getting about the state assessment. We saw this in discussions about high-stakes accountability and what matters to colleges as well as in the disparity between course content and tests.

Finally, there seemed to be a degree of variation in what students and teachers focused on when they talked about how students responded to high-stakes accountability. While students talked about the need for clear and aligned expectations from their school, the state, and higher education institutions, teachers talked more about how students need to take these tests more seriously. We heard similar things from teachers in Kentucky and Vermont. At the same time, students and teachers were in relative agreement when talking about the anxiety around the test and how it provided focus.

Overall, these patterns of responses from high school students as reported by students themselves or teachers and administrators indicate that students are thinking quite meaningfully about how accountability policies in their respective states affect them. Accountability policies designed to motivate students may not be working. These preliminary insights cause us to recommend further examination into whether policies intended to affect students and their learning are on target or not. In this small sample, the overall response of students points to issues that may lead to unintended consequences for students and schools, particularly where high stakes are involved.

Notes

1. For a more detailed discussion of state policies concerning accountability for those states in our study, see Rhoten, Carnoy, Chabrán, and Elmore, "Conditions and Characteristics of Assessment and Accountability: The Case of Four States," in this volume.
2. All schools have been assigned pseudonyms and all persons are referred to as female to ensure confidentiality.
3. These terms (better positioned, target, and orthogonal) were assigned to the schools with respect to their position in responding to the policy. For instance, a "target" school was seen as not having successfully prepared their students based on prior measures, where the "better-positioned" school's prior performance on existing assessments was adequate. For a detailed discussion of project design and school positioning, see Siskin and Lemons, "Internal and External Accountability and the Challenge of the High School," presented at the American Educational Research Association, April 2000.

References

Abelmann, C., and R. Elmore. 1999. *When accountability knocks, will anyone answer?* Philadelphia, PA: University of Pennsylvania, Consortium for Policy Research in Education.

Hidi, S., and J. M. Harackiewicz. 2000. Motivating the academically unmotivated: A critical issue for the 21st century. *American Educational Research Journal* 70: 151–179.

Raviv, A., A. Raviv, and E. Reisel. 1990. Teachers and students: Two different perspectives? *Measuring social climate in the classroom. American Educational Research Journal* 27: 141–157.

Rhoten, D., M. Carnoy, M. Chabrán, and R. Elmore. 2000. The Logics and logistics of assessment and accountability: The case of four states. Paper presented at the annual meeting of the American Educational Research Association, New Orleans, Louisiana, April.

Siskin, L. 2000. *Daydreams and nightmares: Implementing the new Regents exam in New York.* Paper presented at the annual meeting of the American Educational Research Association, New Orleans, Louisiana, April.

Siskin, L. S., and R. Lemons. 2000. Internal and external accountability and the challenge of the high school. Paper presented at the annual meeting of the American Educational Research Association, New Orleans, Louisiana, April.

Stodolsky, S. S., S. Salk, and B. Glaessner. 1991. Student views about learning math and social studies. *American Educational Research Journal* 28: 89–116.

CHAPTER **6**

The Impact of Accountability
Policies in Texas High Schools

MARTIN CARNOY, SUSANNA LOEB, AND TIFFANY L. SMITH

Making schools accountable through state testing was the preeminent educational reform of the 1990s. Thirty-nine states now administer some form of performance-based assessment; twenty-four states attach stakes to their tests; and forty states use tests scores for school accountability purposes (Stecher and Barron 1999). Proponents argue that using student scores on curriculum-based tests as a measure of school effectiveness encourages teachers to teach the curriculum. It sets a minimum standard against which schools can be judged; and it quantifies school "quality" in a way that parents and politicians can easily understand. By setting student improvement goals for schools, the state can motivate school personnel to reach continuously higher, while also identifying those schools unwilling or unable to meet the prescribed goals.

Critics argue that such testing does not promote "real" improvements in student learning. Rather, teachers and principals are motivated to meet "standards" by teaching to the test. Instead of creating an improved learning environment, these crude forms of assessment may reduce opportunities to learn higher-order skills, particularly for low-income students (McNeil and Valenzuela 1999). Critics also claim that state testing increases disadvantaged students' probability of dropping out by forcing students to repeat grades (Haney 1999, 2000; Shrag 2000).

The most visible state-testing program is in Texas. The Texas Assessment of Academic Skills (TAAS) is a battery of state tests given every spring to all students in public schools in grades three to eight and again in grade ten, where passing it serves as a requirement for high school graduation. Schools are evaluated both on the percentage of all of their students passing the TAAS and on the percentage of their low-income and minority students passing. Rewards for doing well and sanctions for doing poorly are both implicit and explicit. Schools that perform well relative to state norms are given an "exemplary" designation and financial bonuses to spend on pet projects. Schools that do poorly are given an "inadequate" designation. "Inadequate" schools get new management if they do not improve by the following year. Designations are widely publicized, so parents know how their children's school rates. Since designations take into account the proportion of disadvantaged students and the proportion of African-American and Latino students in a school, being exemplary in a poor or largely minority school may mean a lower pass rate than in an all-white or high-income school.

The reason so many educational policymakers and politicians nationwide are looking to Texas is simple: the state has apparently achieved great success in raising average test scores and in closing the gap between disadvantaged and advantaged students, at least in the lower grades. Students in Texas have made substantial gains on the TAAS in all grades. In addition, they have made gains on an independent measure of achievement gains, the National Assessment of Educational Progress (NAEP). The NAEP results show Texas and North Carolina making the largest average gains among all states from 1990 to 1997 (Grissmer and Flanagan 1998). When states' fourth grade students are ranked by their 1996 NAEP mathematics scores, only five states come out ahead of Texas. Significantly, all five have much lower minority populations than Texas. The gains have been smaller on the fourth grade NAEP reading test but are still higher than gains nationally.

Because of Texas's large Latino and African-American student population, educational gains in the state depend heavily on how well these minority groups do in school. The 1996 NAEP results for Texas's eighth graders and high school seniors are not as positive as those for fourth grade, mainly because the gap between minorities and whites in eighth grade did not decrease (and may have widened) in the higher grades (Fisher 2000; Haney 1999). In 1996–2000, Texas's mathematics scores in fourth grade continued to climb mainly because of large gains for black and especially Latino students. A higher proportion of Texas's white, black, and Latino students exceeded the basic skills level in the NAEP math test than their racial/ethnic counterparts in other states. Texas's Latino students scored higher by far in fourth grade math than Latino students in other states (see NAEP, 2001). Part of the difference in scores may have been caused by a greater percentage of minority students in Texas excluded from the test. Texas excluded about the same percentage of minority students from the NAEP because of learning disabilities and language proficiency as many other higher scoring states, but increases in the percent of African Americans and Latinos excluded between 1996 and 2000 in states such as Texas and North Carolina did reduce their gains relative to other states, especially on the fourth grade test (Carnoy and Loeb 2003). Even so, Texas student gains in basic math skills at this level in the 1990s are impressive.

The 2000 NAEP math gains in Texas on the eighth grade test are much smaller, and Texas remains in the middle of the pack among states (Carnoy and Loeb 2003). However, the gains for Latino eighth graders in Texas in 1996–2000 were much higher than the national average Latino gains. Although Texas's accountability system seems to have been much better at raising minority students' *elementary* school NAEP math scores than scores in middle school and high school, Texas's Latino students appear to have made major gains on the eighth grade test as well.

The effect of TAAS-type accountability on student performance in the higher grades is important. It does not make much sense to claim that student outcomes are improving if the criterion used to measure academic achievement does not result in "outcomes that count" for students' life success, such as increased school attainment or increased achievement sustained over time. In today's world, we measure better education by problem-solving competencies, high school completion and college attendance and completion. These are the "signals" that society values.

Even if the implementation of the TAAS has not led to higher achievement or attainment for students, it may be beneficial in providing parents with information about their children's achievement and about the relative performance of the schools in their neighborhoods. However, if the TAAS leads to poorer student outcomes, then critics would have a strong case for seeking alternatives to state testing. Haney (2000) argues just that. He finds that high school completion rates have faltered as a result of the TAAS, especially among Latino and African-American students.

The objective of this essay is to review Haney's findings and examine, to the extent the data allows, the impact that TAAS has had on students' educational attainment. We do this in two ways. First, we assess trends over time in statewide measures of test scores, progression through high school, high school completion, and high school seniors' college plans. Second, we analyze data on high schools to estimate whether rising test scores are coincident with rising dropout rates. We find strikingly high retention in the ninth grade that has increased over time. However, this trend began well before the implementation of the TAAS. If there is a link between retention and state policies it is likely to date back to the 1984 reform. Across high schools, we find little relationship between the TAAS and dropout rates. To the extent that this relationship does exist, it appears that higher TAAS scores in schools are associated with reduced, and not increased, dropout behavior.

Background

Texas's current educational reform has its roots in two distinct conflicts. The first was the challenge to the unequal distribution of resources among Texas school districts, a result of the need to supplement state funding of education with local property taxes. These additional taxes created large differences among districts, differences that were highly correlated with the ethnic composition of the district. Texas's largest minorities—Latinos and African Americans—went to schools that received considerably fewer resources than schools that were predominantly Anglo. The second conflict arose in the 1970s from a new group of businesses based on high technology and services that challenged the hegemony of Texas's traditional agricultural and oil interests.

The present educational reform began in 1984 with a push by a group of businessmen, headed by H. Ross Perot, to bring Texas into the high-tech age and to resolve pressures by low-income minority groups for equalized school funding.[1] By 1991, the reform had gone through two rounds (1984 and 1987) and was institutionalized into Texas politics. Aside from increasing funds to low spending districts, it included a strategic plan that recommended "new learning standards for each grade, measuring learning by linking statewide assessments to those standards, holding schools accountable for results, but not dictating to teachers and principals how to achieve the results" (Grissmer and Flanagan 1998, 28). Ann Richards, the newly-elected governor, implemented this "decentralization" reform that gave control to the state over standards and testing, but to schools for choosing how to meet state goals. The reform was continued after 1995 by Richards's successor, George W. Bush.

In 1990–91, the TAAS was used for the first time in the tenth grade as a requirement for high school graduation. It was applied to the present complement of grades in 1994. The TAAS was still a basic skills test but was somewhat more difficult and more comprehensive than the earlier TEAMS test used in the 1980s and early 1990s.

The Texas Education Agency sets state curriculum standards (requiring three math courses, including algebra I in ninth grade, for high school graduation), administers the TAAS, and determines the levels of test performance considered unacceptable, acceptable, recognized, and exemplary. Local school districts can set higher standards and are responsible for implementing improvements to bring students in their schools to satisfactory performance levels on the TAAS.

With the increased publicity given to school-by-school success, adequacy, or failure on the TAAS, and the increased national attention given to Texas's success in increasing test scores, the TAAS began to take on a life of its own. Local school districts, responsible for the testing standards, saw that the simplest route to getting higher pass rates was to focus on the test itself. From our observations and interviews, it appears that teachers and principals in schools with a higher percentage of lower income, African-American and Latino pupils are more likely to focus on teaching the test than those in schools with higher income pupils. [2]

Achieving exemplary status is also important for high-income schools. Even in high-income schools, however, it is the lower-income, lower-achieving pupils who appear to get more test preparation. This is logical. High- or even middle-achieving pupils are likely to find the test relatively easy and have a high probability of passing. Allocating much time to teaching these students test material is unlikely to increase school ranking as measured by pass rates.

Since the test is geared toward assessing student performance on a pre-scribed curriculum, it can be convincingly argued that teaching the test to lower-achieving students is not such a bad thing. Not only that, but because of the way the test results are measured, minority scores carry their own weight, forcing schools to focus on these students. All of this has had the effect, testing advocates claim, of improving the reading and math of lowest-income and minority groups the most. Thus, the original goals in the 1984 Act of pushing the system up from the bottom have been maintained. Joe Johnson of the University of Texas's Dana Center claims that:

> . . . teachers were expected to get students to demonstrate proficiency on those objectives, and so, in essence, schools are doing what they have been asked to do. They are teaching students these objectives. So, when you look at those objectives, many of them are central to what we would want anybody's children to learn about reading, mathematics, and writing. What's absolutely clear, when you visit many of the schools and look at instruction in those schools, you see that students are in fact getting opportunities to learn challenging content. They're learning the objectives that are being presented, and they're able to demonstrate their learning on the TAAS test, as well as on other measures (Interview, June 4, 1999).

Critics, however, are not convinced. Linda McNeil and Angela Valenzuela argue that,

> The pressure to raise TAAS scores leads teachers to substitute commercial TAAS-prep materials for the substance of the curriculum . . . Subjects tested by TAAS (reading, writing, and mathematics) are reduced, in the test and test-prep materials, to isolated facts and fragments of facts. This artificial treatment of these isolated components may enable children to recognize those components on a multiple-choice test, but does not necessarily enable them to use these components in other contexts (McNeil and Valenzuela, 1999, p. 5)

Overview of Academic Outcomes

Test Scores

Passing rates on the math TAAS have improved substantially in every grade, particularly for disadvantaged students. Table 6.1 presents the results for all students who took the test. When special education students who took the test are omitted, the results are slightly higher. It should be noted that these figures represent the percentage of students who "passed" the TAAS, not the percentage score on the TAAS. Gains on the reading test are as large or larger.

The state-level NAEP scores show similar improvements during this time period. For example, gains in scores on the fourth grade math NAEP in Texas outpaced math NAEP gains nationally from 1992 to 2000. The NAEP reading scores in Texas also improved and kept pace with national gains between 1994 and 1998 (Fisher 2000). Texas eighth grade math scores on the NAEP went up about one-third of a standard deviation between 1990 and 1996, and continued to rise significantly in 1996–2000 (Carnoy and Loeb 2003). In 1998, 76 percent of Texas eighth graders read at basic levels or better compared with 74 percent nationally (Fisher 2000). On the whole, the test scores of Texas students have improved over the 1990s, as reflected by TAAS scores and other measures.

An important issue, however, is whether these much higher passing rates on the TAAS (and higher NAEP scores) are reflected in other measures of academic success. Although the TAAS is more difficult than the TEAMS was, it is still a test of very basic skills. Indeed, one analysis argues that the minimum competency test given in the tenth grade is essentially an eighth grade test, and maybe not even that (see Sandra Stosky, www.taxresearch.org, 1999). For example, 57 percent of blacks, 67 percent of Hispanics, and 83 percent of whites passed the 1996 fourth grade math TAAS test. On the fourth grade math NAEP test, 47 percent of blacks, 55 percent of Hispanics, and 85 percent of whites passed at a minimum competency level.

In addition, it is not clear that the convergence in scores across racial/ethnic groups seen with the TAAS, carries through to other outcomes. Fisher (2000) argues that the TAAS scores show the black-white and Latino-white gap declining on the fourth grade math and reading tests, while the NAEP results suggest that the gap is staying constant or increasing. Although the results for eighth grade math are less clear because the NAEP gains are measured for 1990–1996 and the TAAS for 1994–1999, Fisher claims that these suggest that the TAAS may sharply overstate minority gains.

Enrollment Trends

Two other academic outcomes worth considering are the dropout rate and the "finishing rate," (i.e. the proportion of ninth or tenth graders who get

Table 6.1 Percent Meeting Minimum Expectations on Mathematics TAAS, by Grade, 1994–2002

	1994	1995	1996	1997	1998	1999	2000	2001	2002
Grade 3									
Whites	72	81	82	86	86	90	93	93	94
African Americans	41	53	57	64	62	65	79	77	80
Latinos	49	62	65	72	71	79	83	82	83
Disadvantaged	47	60	63	70	68	75	81	80	81
Grade 6									
Whites	70	75	84	87	89	93	94	96	97
African Americans	37	40	57	62	70	75	79	84	88
Latinos	46	47	63	69	75	81	83	87	91
Disadvantaged	43	46	61	67	73	80	82	86	90
Grade 8									
Whites	70	70	78	83	88	92	95	96	96
African Americans	32	30	44	55	66	74	81	85	86
Latinos	40	37	51	61	71	80	85	89	90
Disadvantaged	37	35	49	59	69	78	84	87	88
Grade 10									
Whites	68	71	75	81	85	89	93	94	96
African Americans	32	35	43	51	58	66	74	79	85
Latinos	40	42	51	57	65	73	80	83	88
Disadvantaged	39	40	49	55	63	71	79	82	87

Source: TEA (www.tea.state.tx.us/student.assessment/results)

to twelfth grade or to graduation). Dropout rates in middle and high school (seventh to twelfth grade) as reported by the Texas Education Agency (TEA) declined for all groups from 1994 to 1999, a continued decline from even higher dropout rates in the 1980s. The average reported dropout rate for all groups went from 6.1 percent in 1989–90 (Shrag, 1999) to 2.8 percent in 1994 to 1.6 percent in 1999.[3] Latinos had the highest dropout rate in both years, but that declined as well, from 4.2 percent to 2.3 percent. In our population of Texas high schools (ninth to twelfth grade) dropout rates followed a similar pattern, declining from 2.6 percent in 1993–94 to 1.3 percent in 1998–99. Rates in low-income high schools fell even further, from almost six percent in 1993–94 to 1.8 percent in 1998–99 (see Table 6.2).

Critics have expressed serious doubts about the meaning of the dropout rate figures (Haney 2000; Shrag 1999). Many students disappear in the accounting process. Haney (2000) argues that the reported dropout rate is not consistent with the high school finishing rate. He finds that the ratio of high school graduates to enrollment in the ninth grade three years earlier declined suddenly for white and black and Latino students simultaneously with the introduction of the tenth grade TAAS in 1990–91. He argues that the finishing rate then recovered for white students the following year, 1991–92, and rose slowly and steadily for the rest of the decade. For blacks and Latinos, Haney argues, the finishing rate also rebounded but less (Haney 2000, Figures 5.1 and 5.2). "This indicates that the TAAS exit test has been associated with a 50 percent increase in the gap in progression from grade nine to high school graduation for nonwhite students as compared to white students" (Haney 2000, 68).

Haney is not the only one who finds a disparity between the official dropout rate and student progression through high school. Colvin (1999) writes, "Statewide, one out of three white students and one out of two African-American and Latino students did not graduate on time with their class in 1998. In addition, of those who graduated, only about a third of the African-American and Latino students had taken a full complement of college prep courses."

Ninth to Twelfth Grade Progression   We plot the three year rolling average of the ratio of high school graduates to ninth grade enrollment three years earlier in Figure 6.1a and the ratio of twelfth grade enrollment to ninth grade enrollment three years earlier in Figure 6.1b. The ratios clearly fell between the early 1980s and the early 1990s. However, our estimates suggest that the downward trend ended shortly after the implementation of the tenth grade TAAS in the early 1990s. Tenth graders in the first year of the test would not have been in twelfth grade until 1992. By 1992, almost

Table 6.2 Sample Statistics for Key Analysis Variables

	Overall	Urban	Suburban	Nonmetro	Rural	Urban <40% Free Lunch	Urban >40% Free Lunch
TAAS 10th grade pass rate 1998–99	78.89	70.12	78.45	80.38	81.90	76.96	64.08
	(12.02)	(12.84)	(9.82)	(10.26)	(12.70)	(10.69)	(11.52)
	1134	*175*	*208*	*416*	*335*	*82*	*93*
TAAS 10th grade pass rate 1993–94	55.57	44.26	57.43	56.90	58.66	56.42	33.53
	(16.37)	(16.95)	(14.66)	(13.76)	(17.60)	(14.53)	(10.45)
	1134	*175*	*208*	*416*	*335*	*82*	*93*
Dropout rate 1998–99	1.33	1.66	1.40	1.39	1.03	1.50	1.80
	(1.32)	(1.03)	(0.95)	(1.52)	(1.32)	(0.89)	(1.12)
	1134	*175*	*208*	*416*	*335*	*82*	*93*
Dropout rate 1993–94	2.55	4.61	2.84	2.53	1.34	3.25	5.82
	(2.32)	(3.28)	(1.83)	(1.88)	(1.57)	(2.51)	(3.42)
	1132	*174*	*207*	*416*	*335*	*82*	*92*
Ratio 12th grade enrollment 98–99 to 10th grade 96–97	0.83	0.74	0.80	0.84	0.88	0.78	0.70
	(0.12)	(0.11)	(0.10)	(0.09)	(0.14)	(0.09)	(0.11)
	1134	*175*	*208*	*416*	*335*	*82*	*93*
Ratio 12th grade enrollment 95–96 to 10th grade 93–94	0.83	0.72	0.81	0.83	0.89	0.77	0.68
	(0.13)	(0.10)	(0.11)	(0.10)	(0.16)	(0.10)	(0.09)
	1129	*174*	*208*	*416*	*331*	*81*	*93*
% black enrollment 1998–99	10.68	22.49	11.46	8.79	6.39	18.44	26.06
	(16.50)	(26.51)	(16.14)	(11.90)	(11.12)	(21.00)	(30.23)
	1134	*175*	*208*	*416*	*335*	*82*	*93*
% Hispanic enrollment 1998–99	28.75	47.61	28.37	24.52	24.40	29.40	63.66
	(28.15)	(31.31)	(30.44)	(25.79)	(23.45)	(19.32)	(31.13)
	1134	*175*	*208*	*416*	*335*	*82*	*93*
% lunch program enrollment 1998–99	37.46	44.39	29.03	33.09	44.49	24.76	61.69
	(20.78)	(22.17)	(24.52)	(17.49)	(17.70)	(9.85)	(14.07)
	1134	*175*	*208*	*416*	*335*	*82*	*93*

Note: Standard deviations are in parentheses and sample sizes are in italics.

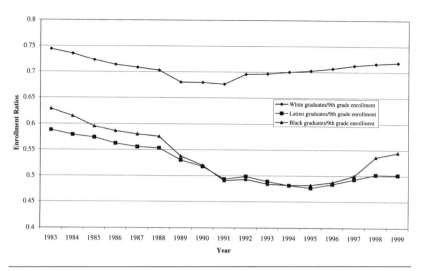

Figure 6.1a Texas: High School Graduation Compared to 9th Grade Enrollment Three Years Earlier, Three-Year Rolling Averages, 1983–1999

all of the decrease in high school finishing had already occurred. The introduction of the TAAS clearly did not cause these declines. Furthermore, it appears that the ratio of graduates to ninth grade enrollment increased substantially for whites and blacks in the second half of the nineties, even as twelfth grade enrollment compared to ninth grade enrollment was generally declining (except for blacks) in the same period.

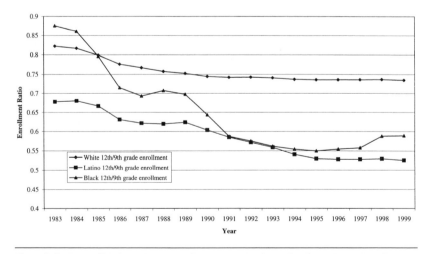

Figure 6.1b Texas: 12th Grade Enrollment Compared to 9th Grade Enrollment Three Years Earlier, Three-Year Rolling Averages, 1983–1999

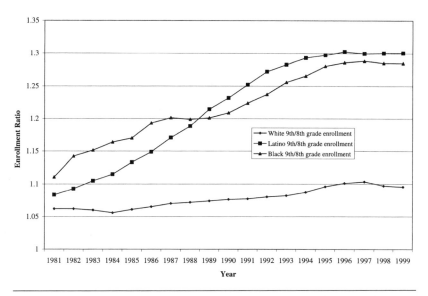

Figure 6.2 Texas: 9th Grade Enrollment Compared to 8th Grade Enrollment One Year Earlier, Three-Year Rolling Averages, 1981–1999

Ninth Grade Retention The decreases that we see in high school finishing were caused either by a decrease in the relative size of the twelfth grade or an increase in the relative size of the ninth grade. Haney points to the increased retention of Texas ninth graders—especially black and Latino ninth graders—after 1985 (Haney 2000, figure). He estimates that the ratio of ninth to eighth graders one year earlier rose steadily for minority groups from 1985–1988 and then again from 1990–1995. The total increase in retention between 1985 and 1995, as measured by this ratio, was about 20 percent, from 1.10 to 1.30. The rise for whites in the same period was much slower but positive, from 1.05 to 1.10.

We plot three year rolling averages of the ratio of ninth grade enrollment to eighth grade enrollment one year earlier (Figure 6.2). Our results confirm that retention of black and Latino students has been rising rapidly since the early 1980s. Retention rates for whites have also increased, but at a much slower pace. The rise in the retention rate stabilized and even slightly declined at the end of the 1990s, however, and this may reflect in part, rising TAAS and NAEP scores in the lower and middle grades.

Haney, Shrag, and others postulate that higher ninth grade retention rates are closely tied to the tenth grade TAAS and result in higher high school dropout rates and lower graduation rates. There is no doubt that retention rates for minority students have risen greatly during the reform period and have only tailed off in the past four to five years. However, there is no compelling evidence that the implementation of the tenth grade TAAS in 1990–91 was responsible for rising retention rates. Increasing standards and assessment, which began in 1984 in Texas, are associated with increased retention, particularly for blacks and Latinos, but this increase does not appear to be linked specifically with the introduction of the tenth grade TAAS.

Rising retention rates should be associated with declining finishing rates if students, retained in ninth grade, then drop out of school. This was the case in the late 1980s, for both whites and minorities, suggesting that dropout rates increased during this time. However, increased retention does not necessarily result in decreased finishing. Haney implies that the reported decline in dropout rates in the 1990s is inconsistent with rising retention rates in the early 1990s. But, except for the sudden drop in finishing rates in 1990–91, there appears to be little relation between Haney's estimates of changes in ninth to eighth grade ratios and his estimates of twelfth to ninth grade ratios during this period. Retention rates for black, Latino, and whites students increased but finishing rates did not fall.

Other High School Finishing Measures A third measure of attrition, twelfth grade enrollment compared to eighth grade enrollment four years earlier, avoids much of the problem of rising enrollment in the ninth grade year. The rolling average ratio remains virtually constant for whites at 0.8 from 1987–1998, and for Latinos at 0.7. Attrition only increases substantially for African Americans, and that occurred in the 1980s, not in the 1990s. As significant is the rapid increase in survival rate of African-American students (twelfth to eighth grade enrollment ratio) in the 1990s and the large increase in graduation rate (graduates to eighth grade enrollment ratio) in the 1990s. High school graduation ratios—as measured by graduates/eighth grade enrollment four years earlier—at the end of the 1990s were at historically high levels for all three racial/ethnic groups (Figures 6.3a and 6.3b).[4] In Figure 6.4, a plot of the ratio of twelfth grade enrollment to tenth grade enrollment two years earlier, shows a decline for all groups, but especially for blacks and Latinos, in the 1980s. For blacks this ratio has increased since 1993.

The bottom line is that about 30 percent of black and Latino eighth graders and about 20 percent of white eighth graders statewide do not finish with their cohort. About 15 percent of white tenth graders, about 20 percent of black tenth graders, and about 25 percent of Latino tenth graders do not reach the twelfth grade with their cohort. However, it is difficult to argue that the tenth grade TAAS, in and of itself, is to blame for either higher retention rates in ninth grade or for higher attrition rates for eighth and tenth graders. Indeed, to some extent, an opposite case can be

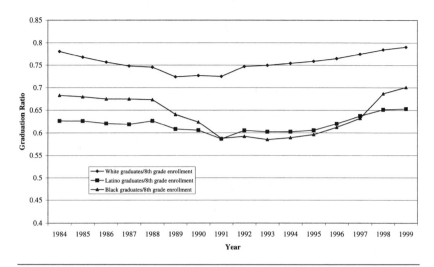

Figure 6.3a Texas: High School Graduation Compared to 8th Grade Enrollment Four Years Earlier, Three-Year Rolling Averages, 1984–1999

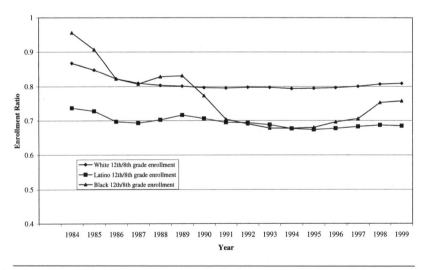

Figure 6.3b Texas: 12th Grade Enrollment Compared to 8th Grade Enrollment Four Years Earlier, Three-Year Rolling Averages, 1984–1999

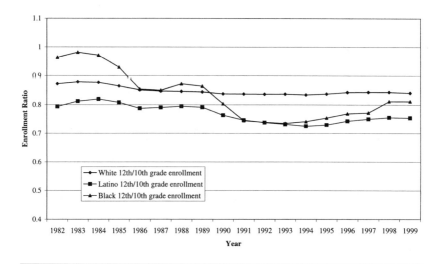

Figure 6.4 Texas: 12th Grade Enrollment Compared to 10th Grade Enrollment Two Years Earlier, Three-Year Rolling Averages, 1982–1999

made that in the 1990s the continued pressure to raise academic achievement may have increased high school survival rates to twelfth grade for African Americans and kept survival rates from falling for Latinos despite massive immigration in the 1990s. Rising graduation rates may also have been partially the result of accountability pressures, although it is risky to ascribe a direct connection.

College Plans The intention to go to college is another important measure of student success. The proportion of high school seniors who take the SAT or ACT, their scores on the SAT/ACT, and the rates at which Texas high school graduates go to college all rose sharply in the 1980s, but have slowed down in recent years. Figure 6.5 shows the proportion of Texas high school graduates with college plans. This percentage fell for whites and Latinos in the 1990s, but rose slightly for African Americans. For high school graduates the gap between black/Latino and white college plans has been halved, from seventeen percent in 1985 to about eight percent in 1997. Overall enrollment in Texas colleges rose six percent in 1990–1996. White enrollment fell in these years, so the entire increase was due to black and Latino college enrollment increases (NCES, 1999).

Progression through High School We summarize the enrollment, graduation, and college plans trends for white, black, and Latino students in Fig-

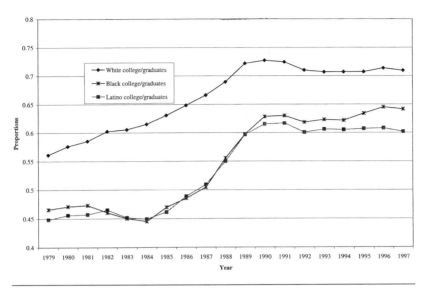

Figure 6.5 Texas: Proportion of High School Graduates with College Plans, by Race/Ethnicity, 1979–1998

ures 6.6a, 6.6b, and 6.6c. For whites, the difference between eighth and ninth grade enrollment increased in the 1990s, but this did not seem to result in a greater gap between eighth and tenth grade enrollment during this time, nor in an increase in the difference between tenth and eleventh grade enrollment. The difference between twelfth grade enrollment and graduation actually decreased in the 1990s, and this explains much of the increase in graduation rates for whites and Latinos.

For African Americans, we observe some important anomalies in the data. For example, the twelfth grade numbers appear to be wrong for 1988 and 1989. However, the data do show a clear increase in the number of black students being retained in the ninth grade throughout the time period. The mid-to late-80s and the mid-to late-90s saw the steepest increase in the retention rate. The gap between eighth and tenth grade enrollment widened in the early-to mid-90s, indicating that many of these retained students may be dropping out of school. The difference between tenth and eleventh grade enrollment also increased. But the difference between eighth grade and graduation has remained fairly constant, in part because the gap between the graduation rate and eleventh grade enrollment decreased in the 1990s. This suggests that retained students who dropped out would have been the ones most likely to drop out in the later grades if they had not been retained.

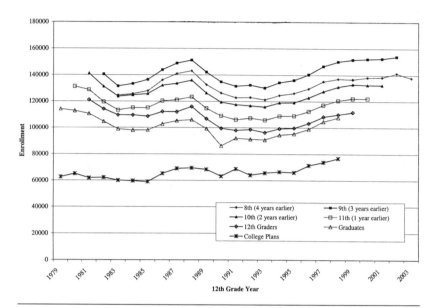

Figure 6.6a Texas White Enrollment Trends by Grade

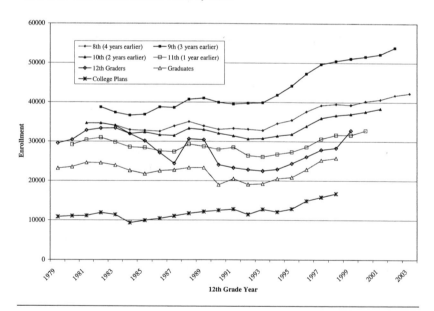

Figure 6.6b Texas Black Enrollment Trends by Grade

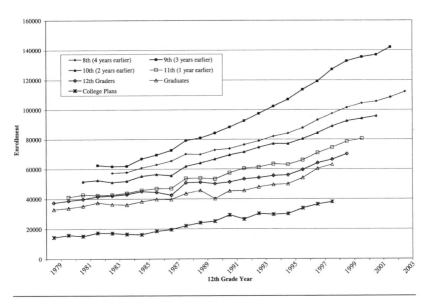

Figure 6.6c Texas Latino Enrollment Trends by Grade

For Latinos the trends are very similar to those for blacks, except that for Latinos there is an increase in the gap between eighth grade enrollment and graduation, occurring between 1988 and 1994. The percent of high school graduates who have college plans has increased substantially for both blacks and Latinos.[5]

Summary of Enrollment Trends   The statewide enrollment data shows large changes in enrollment patterns over the past fifteen years. In particular, ninth grade retention has increased dramatically. In addition, the proportion of eighth graders who make it to twelfth grade four years later decreased until the early 1990s and appears to have increased in recent years, especially for African Americans. However, there is no obvious connection between the implementation of the high stakes TAAS and these statewide enrollment trends, except possibly for sharply increased twelfth grade survival rates for blacks in the second half of the 1990s. Thus, if anything, despite increased retention rates in ninth grade, high school finishing rates may, on net, have been *positively* affected by the TAAS in recent years, although we have no evidence of such a causal relationship.

Overall, then, we could conclude that Texas's strong accountability system may have contributed to greater retention in the 1980s, hence to lower high school survival rates, but that since the mid-1990s, it may be contributing to higher high school finishing rates. Hence, the TAAS exit test may ultimately have had a *positive* effect on improving high school attainment, contrary to the claims of its critics. There is certainly no evidence that the exit test increased dropouts (reduced survival rates) of minority groups, since, to the contrary, they seem to be improving their graduation rates relative to eighth grade enrollment four years earlier. Although that increase is much more attenuated for Latinos than for blacks (and whites), immigration rates for Latinos have been high in Texas for the past twenty years, and language proficiency issues in the Latino population have surely had a dampening effect on Latino high school survival rates, independent of efforts to improve achievement in primary and middle school.

In addition to its aggregate statewide effects, the TAAS may have had differential effects across schools. To explore this further we use school level data to test whether there is a relationship across schools between gains in the TAAS passing rate and other student outcomes. We now turn to these estimates.

Model and Data for School-Level Analysis

At the individual level, educational achievement has a strong positive effect on educational attainment (Carnoy and DeAngelis 2000). However, at the high school level, when compulsory education laws do not compel students to complete, the relationship is more complicated. Increasing average achievement in high school (as measured by TAAS passing rates) can produce increased average student attainment. But, at the same time, increased average achievement can be the result of higher dropout rates among lower achieving students. So rising average achievement in high school may result in higher completion rates, or it may be the result of lower completion rates. In the first case, rising achievement is positively related to rising completion rates; in the second, it is negatively related. In the case where neither effect dominates, they may offset each other.[6]

We are interested in the relationship between TAAS scores and other student outcomes. Imagine two possible scenarios. In the first, an emphasis on increasing TAAS scores increases the overall quality of schooling, leading to gains in student learning on multiple levels and decreases the dropout rate. In an alternative scenario, however, increased emphasis on TAAS comes at the expense of other learning or leads to efforts to screen students *before* they take the TAAS. This may lead to increases in the dropout rate, either as low performing students are forced out of schools in order to increase school average TAAS scores or as students choose to leave. Students may choose to leave because they fear that they will do poorly on TAAS, because they are retained in earlier grades, or because the learning environment has deteriorated.

We would like to assess whether and to what extent the TAAS has affected students' educational attainment. We are particularly interested in whether schools that have been able to increase their TAAS score have done so in conjunction with increased student attainment or have paid the price of decreased student attainment. In keeping with this goal, we will look across schools to see the relationship between the change in the TAAS score and the change in student attainment. Have schools that have experienced an increase in average score seen an increase in student attainment as well?

Unfortunately, a good measure of student attainment is not available so we have to use proxies. We considered three measures: the school reported dropout rate, the tenth to twelfth grade survival rate, and the ninth to twelfth grade survival rate. We define the tenth to twelfth grade survival rate as the number of students in the twelfth grade in one year divided by the number of students in the tenth grade two years earlier. The ninth to twelfth grade survival rate is defined similarly. In order to determine which measure to use, we ran some simple correlations. The correlation between dropout rate and tenth to twelfth grade survival is -0.23 for 1998–99 indicating that the two measures may be picking up similar trends but that at least one of these measures has large errors. Consistent with measurement problems, differencing makes the correlations even lower (likely a result of substantial measurement error) so that the correlation between the change in tenth to twelfth grade survival and the change in the dropout rate is -0.065. However, the ninth to twelfth grade measure appears to have even greater flaws. Surprisingly, the tenth to twelfth grade survival rate is not correlated with the ninth to twelfth grade survival rate ($r=-0.033$ for 1998–99) and the dropout rate is, in fact, positively correlated with ninth to twelfth grade survival ($r=0.18$).

One check of the usefulness of our attainment measures is to look at the correlation between the measures and the socioeconomic status of the school. In general we would expect a positive correlation between attainment and status. We find that the percentage of students who are enrolled in the free lunch program is essentially equally correlated with both the dropout rate and the tenth to twelfth grade survival rate (0.16 and -0.17, respectively) while it is uncorrelated with the ninth to twelfth grade survival rate (-0.014).[7] This is further indication that the ninth to twelfth grade measure may not be a good measure, and so we eliminated it from our choice of attainment measures. While we look at both remaining measures, we concentrate on the dropout rate because we have it for the longest time period, 1994 to 1999. We can construct the tenth to twelfth grade survival rate only from 1996 to 1999.

Table 6.2 describes our sample, providing means, standard deviations, and sample sizes for the main variables that we use. It presents these descriptives for the full sample of high schools, as well as for urban, suburban, nonmetro, and rural schools. In addition, we separate urban schools into those in which less than forty percent of students enroll in free lunch programs and those in which greater than or equal to forty percent of students enroll in free lunch programs. We see that urban schools perform considerably lower on the TAAS than other schools and that poor urban schools have the lowest average performance.

In keeping with the state trend, average TAAS scores have improved over time in all groups. We see that dropout rates are particularly high in poor urban districts though they have improved dramatically over this time period. As a comparison, the survival rates are lower in poor urban schools and have improved the most in this set of schools. However, the extent of improvement is small and much less than the decline in dropout rate.

Regression Results

Table 6.3 presents bivariate regression results for the relationship between the change in the TAAS score from 1994 to 1999 and the change in the dropout rate from 1994 to 1999. The coefficient measures the percentage change in the dropout rate associated with a one percent increase in the TAAS score. We find that, on average, schools in which TAAS scores increased by ten percent, dropout rates fell by 0.24 percent. This relationship is driven by poor urban schools. In urban schools in which greater than forty percent of the students are eligible for the free or reduced price lunch program, a ten percent increase in the TAAS is associated with an almost twelve percent decrease in the dropout rate. These results suggest that schools that saw increases in the TAAS also saw increases in student attainment.

There are a number of possible explanations for these findings. It may be the case that schools with increasing TAAS scores have actually improved and thus the dropout rate has fallen. However, there are a number

Table 6.3 Bivariate Regression Results of the Change in Log Dropout Rates on the Change in Log TAAS Score.

	Overall	Urban	Suburban	Nonmetro	Rural	Urban <40% Lunch	Urban >40% Lunch
Coefficient	−0.024	−0.104	−0.030	−0.014	−0.010	0.437	−1.178
Standard Error	0.005	0.019	0.011	0.008	0.005	0.565	0.275
R-Square	0.024	0.151	0.035	0.008	0.011	0.009	0.162

Table 6.4 Specification Checks

4a. Controls for Change in Free Lunch (Campus and District), in % Black and % Hispanic

	Overall	Urban	Suburban	Nonmetro	Rural	Urban < 40% Lunch	Urban > 40% Lunch
Coefficient	−0.398	−0.890	−0.423	−0.208	−0.237	0.699	−1.145
Standard Error	0.119	0.232	0.310	0.221	0.217	0.560	0.306
R-Square	0.026	0.164	0.037	0.009	0.058	0.117	0.183

4b. Controls for Change in Free Lunch (Campus and District), in % Black, and in % Hispanic plus Change in the Retention Rate between ninth and tenth grade.

	Overall	Urban	Suburban	Nonmetro	Rural	Urban < 40% Lunch	Urban > 40% Lunch
Coefficient	−0.406	−0.930	−0.449	−0.188	−0.248	0.783	−1.153
Standard Error	0.120	0.234	0.324	0.223	0.217	0.538	0.307
R-Square	0.030	0.194	0.038	0.009	0.081	0.188	0.197

4c. Controls for Change in Free Lunch (Campus and District), in % Black, and in % Hispanic plus instrument for 1994–99 changes in TAAS with 1995–98 changes in TAAS

	Overall	Urban	Suburban	Nonmetro	Rural	Urban < 40% Lunch	Urban > 40% Lunch
Coefficient	−0.714	−0.804	−0.312	0.041	−0.062	0.302	−0.677
Standard Error	0.243	0.338	0.606	0.467	0.761	0.737	0.569
R-Square	0.022	0.193	0.037	0.005	0.077	0.176	0.175

of other hypotheses worth checking. First, it is possible that schools that see a rise in the economic situation of their students may see a gain in both TAAS scores and other outcomes, even if an effort to increase the TAAS score hurt student attainment. In other words, the fact that changing economic situations would tend to have a similar effect on both test scores and attainment may overshadow a possible negative effect that increased emphasis on the TAAS may have on student attainment. In order to take this possibility into account, we reran the above analysis but this time included controls for changes in the percentage of students in the free lunch program both at the campus and district level, as well as controls for changes in the percentage of black students and in the percentage of Hispanic students. These results are given in Table 6.4, section 4a. The same trends are evident. Increases in the TAAS score are associated with decreases in the dropout rate and this is particularly true for poor urban schools. In poor urban schools a ten percent increase in the TAAS is associated with an eleven percent decrease in the dropout rate.

Second, it may be the case that students drop out before the tenth grade because they know they will need to pass the TAAS in order to graduate. In order to check whether this phenomenon is driving our results, we added a control for the change in the ninth to tenth grade retention rate. This measure is calculated as the ratio of tenth graders in 1998–99 to ninth graders in 1997–98 minus the ratio of tenth graders in 1994–95 to ninth graders in 1993–94. Table 6.4, section 4b gives these results. This addition makes little difference. In poor urban schools a ten percent increase in the TAAS again is associated with an eleven percent decrease in the dropout rate.

There are two more factors worth considering. The first is effects of "regression to the mean." If we have a school that just happened to have a high performing class in 1993–94, they would have a low dropout rate and a high score on TAAS in that year. If we compare this with a normal class in 1998–99, then we would see that the TAAS scores and the dropout rate have moved together. That is, in this school the TAAS has gone down and the dropout rate has increased. Usually we count on regression to get rid of this problem because some school is likely to have had a particularly low performing class in 1993–94. However, in this case, this low-performing class in another school only worsens the bias. In this second school, we would see a gain over time in TAAS and a decrease in the dropout rate. The TAAS and student attainment would again be moving together and we would overestimate the relationship between attainment and test score. Regression to the mean, then, leads to an upward bias in our estimates. Luckily, it is not difficult to adjust for this problem. We instrument for the change in the TAAS score from 1993–94 to 1998–99 with the change in the TAAS score from 1994–95 to 1997–98. This process essentially uses only the variation across schools in the change in test score that is consistent between the two periods, and thus gets rid of the change due to particularly good or bad cohorts.

The same technique also helps alleviate our second concern. This second concern is measurement error. The test score is likely to be an imperfect measure of any class's ability on the test. This imperfection will lead to a bias toward zero in the estimated relationship between the dropout rate and the test score. Instrumenting reduces this bias by using variation in the test score change that is consistent over the two time periods. Table 6.4, section 4c presents the instrumented results that adjust for regression to the mean and measurement error. We find a slightly smaller effect in poor urban areas, but still, a ten percent increase in TAAS is associated with a seven percent decrease in the dropout rate, both overall and in poor urban schools.

While we believe these results are informative, it is also useful to look at alternative outcome measures. Tables 6.5 and 6.6 give the results using changes in the tenth to twelfth grade retention rate, changes in the ninth to tenth grade retention rate, changes in the percent of students taking the SATs, and changes in mean SAT scores (controlling for changes in the per-

Table 6.5 Bivariate Regression Results for Alternative Outcome Measures

Full Sample

	Tenth to twelfth retention	Ninth to tenth retention	Percent taking SAT*	Mean SAT*
Coefficient	0.00078	−0.0056	0.029	−0.213
Standard Error	0.00036	0.0215	0.036	0.165
R-Square	0.0042	0.0001	0.0054	0.0064

Urban Schools with > 40% of Students Enrolled in Free Lunch Program

	Tenth to twelfth retention	Ninth to tenth retention	Percent taking SAT*	Mean SAT
Coefficient	0.00171	0.00087	−0.00141	−0.1126
Standard Error	0.00161	0.00233	0.1464	0.3043
R-Square	0.0112	0.0014	0.0222	0.0310

Percent taking the SAT includes additional control for the change in the dropout rate and mean SAT includes additional controls for percent change in the dropout rate and change in percent taking the SAT.

cent taking). The results for the alternative outcomes do not show a consistent relationship between TAAS scores and other student outcome measures. We do find a positive and statistically significant relationship between change in TAAS score and change in the tenth to twelfth grade retention rate for the full sample in the bivariate regression. The point estimate for poor urban schools indicates a stronger effect, consistent with the trends for the dropout rate observed above; however, this result is not statistically significant at conventional levels. We found no other statistically significant effects in the simple regressions. We also ran full regressions which instrumented for the change in TAAS score from 1994 to 1999 with the change from 1995 to 1998 and included controls for changes in district free lunch enrollment, campus free lunch enrollment, percentage of Hispanic students, and percentage of black students. These results are summarized in Table 6.6. None of the estimates are significant at conventional levels.

Discussion

The explicit objective of Texas's school accountability system is to improve educational outcomes among the state's four million public elementary

Table 6.6 Full Regression Results for Alternative Outcome Measures

Full Sample

	Tenth to twelfth retention	Ninth to tenth retention	Percent taking SAT*	Mean SAT*
Coefficient	.0010535	.0127075	.0501501	−.2442977
Standard Error	.0010098	.0607834	.0975375	.164205
R-Square	0.0100	0.0038	0.0059	0.0289

Urban Schools with > 40% of Students enrolled in Free Lunch Program

	Tenth to twelfth retention	Ninth to tenth retention	Percent taking SAT*	Mean SAT
Coefficient	0.00096	−0.0060	−0.0143	−0.178
Standard Error	0.00191	0.0045	.3091	0.912
R-Square	0.018	0.137	0.084	0.115

Percent taking the SAT includes additional control for the change in the dropout rate and mean SAT includes additional controls for both percent change in the dropout rate and change in percent taking the SAT. Mean SAT analysis for the first sample and tenth to twelfth retention for the urban sample include controls but are not IV, because of convergence difficulties.

and secondary students. Rising pass rates on the TAAS suggest that this objective is being met. Texas's students have also made substantial gains on some of the NAEP tests, specifically in fourth and eighth grade math. This would appear to validate claims that rising pass rates on the TAAS may, indeed, indicate real learning gains, or at least learning gains as they can be measured by such tests.

As we have shown, other important indicators of educational success, namely high school progression rates, began to rise in the late 1990s. High school graduation rates in the second half of the 1990s rose substantially, especially for African Americans, and, indeed, seem to be reaching higher levels than in the past. Whether this is due to increased testing and school accountability is hard to say. So it appears that rising TAAS scores on the tenth grade high-stakes test have not had a negative impact on educational outcomes that count, namely high school completion and the likelihood of attending college, and may have had a small positive impact. Even so, high school graduation rates are still not high in Texas. Only about seventy percent of African-American eighth graders, sixty-five percent of Latino eighth graders, and about eighty percent of white eighth graders graduate four years later.

Our results suggest that claims of rapidly increased retention of blacks and Latinos in the ninth grade since the implementation of the Texas education reform in 1984 are absolutely true. However, claims that increasing retention is directly attributable to the new tenth grade TAAS exam that students must pass in order to graduate is not supported by the data. Neither does statewide enrollment grade-by-grade support claims that statewide dropout rates increased after 1990.

We have shown, using school-level data, that there is a positive relation between lower dropout rates and higher TAAS scores on the tenth grade TAAS in the 1990s. That is, those high schools that have had larger increases in their students' pass rates on the tenth grade TAAS have also had larger declines in dropout rates. The relationship is largest among urban high schools serving low-income students, and continues to be significant and large even when we correct for possible sources of bias in the coefficient of test score increase on dropout rate. However, our results also show that there is a much weaker relationship between increases in the tenth grade TAAS pass rate and the proportion of tenth graders reaching twelfth grade two years later. The corresponding relationship for urban high schools serving low-income students is positive but not significant. We also do not find a relationship between increasing TAAS score on the tenth grade test and either the proportion of SAT/ACT test takers or the high school's average SAT score.

There are a number of possible explanations for the weakness of the relationship we find between TAAS scores and other outcomes. First, the data simply may be too inaccurate to capture any effects that exist. The low correlation among our various high school progression and completion measures raises serious concern about the estimation of dropout rates by high schools. Much of our analysis depends on the reliability of our outcome measures. The data on high school enrollment comes directly from the Texas Education Agency, but there are evident anomalies in both the aggregate data and the data on individual schools.

Yet, let us assume that these data anomalies are such that our results remain valid: rising TAAS pass rates have not had a major impact on educational attainment. The difficulty of the tenth grade TAAS may simply have been set at a level that would not substantially impact the prevailing dropout rate. The proportion of students statewide who cannot pass it (after repeated tries) may be synonymous with the proportion that would have dropped out anyway. This is not an unlikely scenario, given the political sensitivity of high school completion rates. Another possibility is that not enough time has passed to observe the consequences of the TAAS. If we are currently viewing the full effect of the test, however, it appears that it has not been particularly successful at improving educational outcomes with high social value, such as high school completion or college attendance.

Enrollment data for recent years hint at a possible turning point in high school progression trends. Ninth grade retention has leveled off in the past three years and graduation rates relative to ninth and eighth grade enrollment have increased. That could mean that high retention rates in ninth grade and high attrition rates from eighth to twelfth grade are relatively "short term" investments in raising the "quality" of Texas's high school graduates. However, retention and attrition are still high, particularly for minority groups. Unless graduation rates continue to rise steadily and college attendance increases more rapidly, especially among disadvantaged minorities, critics may be right that Texas's accountability system is not the most effective way to improve minority students' opportunities to learn and to increase their social mobility.

Notes

1. The state legislature had already passed the Equal Opportunities Act in 1979 to begin to address financial inequities, but the Reform Act of 1984 was the major educational reform of the period.
2. These schools teach both the elements of the curriculum that will appear on the test and techniques for taking the test. Our observations suggest that the majority of the time is spent on the material and not on test-taking skills.
3. See www.tea.state.tx.us/perfreport/aeis/hist/state/html.
4. The rapid decline in twelfth grade enrollment relative to eighth and ninth grade enrollment four and three years earlier for African Americans is probably an artifact of errors in enrollment statistics for that group in the 1980s. Considering the data on graduates relative to ninth and eighth grade enrollment, where the ratio is only somewhat higher for blacks than for Latinos in the 1980s, the error is probably in the twelfth grade enrollment for blacks.
5. The irony, then, is that when blacks and Latinos graduate high school, they are much more likely than in the past to go to college, either two- or four-year, yet their likelihood of graduating high school with their eighth grade class or even getting a regular high school degree remains about 15 percent less than for whites—at a low 0.65, compared with almost 0.8 for whites.
6. The same complexity pervades the relationship between rising achievement and the proportion of students taking the SAT/ACT.
7. The results are similar, though slightly stronger, if we look only at urban schools: the tenth to twelfth grade retention rate is not correlated with the ninth to twelfth grade retention rate ($r = -0.016$ for 1998–99); the correlation between dropout rate and tenth to twelfth grade retention is -0.28; the percent of students who are enrolled in the lunch program is essentially equally correlated with both the dropout rate and the tenth to twelfth grade retention rate (0.28 and -0.35, respectively) and uncorrelated with the ninth to twelfth grade retention rate (0.06).

References

Carnoy, M., and K. DeAngelis. 2000. Does Ability Influence Individual Earnings, and If So, by How Much? Stanford, CA: Stanford University School of Education.

Carnoy, M., and S. Loeb. 2003. Does external accountability affect student outcomes: A cross-state analysis. Educational Evaluation and Policy Analysis, 24(4): 305–332.

Colvin, R. L. 1999. Texas schools gain notice and skepticism. Los Angeles Times, 6 July.

Fisher, F. 2000. Tall tales? Texas testing moves from the pecos to wobegon. See Bracey, G. 2000. The 10th Bracey report on the condition of education. Phi Delta Kappan, 82(2):133–144.

Grissmer, D., and A. Flanagan. 1998. Exploring rapid achievement gains in North Carolina and Texas. Washington, D.C.: National Education Goals Panel.

Haney, W. 2000. The myth of the Texas miracle in education. *Education Policy Analysis Archives,* 8(41), [http://epaa.asu].

McNeil, L., and A. Valenzuela. 2001. The harmful impact of the TAAS system of testing in Texas: Beneath the accountability rhetoric. Houston, Texas: Rice University, Department of Education. [http://www.ruf.rice.edu/~ctreduc/research.html].

National Center for Educational Statistics (NCES). 1999. *Digest of educational statistics.* Washington, D.C.: NCES.

Shrag, P. 2000. Too Good to Be True. *The American Prospect* 11(4): 46–49.

Stecher, B., and S. Barron. 1999. Test-based accountability: The perverse consequences of milepost testing. CRESST and RAND Education. Paper presented at the annual meeting of the American Educational Research Association, Montreal, Canada, April 21.

CHAPTER 7

When an Irresistible Force Meets an Immovable Object
Core Lessons about High Schools and Accountability

LESLIE SANTEE SISKIN

Introduction

What happens when an irresistible force meets an immovable object? When a movement with the force and fervor of standards-based accountability reform hits the massive, highly stable, and reputedly reform-resistant form of the American high school? Something, the song lyrics tell us, has to give. But after more than a decade of focused and forceful reform effort, it is not at all clear what that something will be. Do high school structures give way before the mounting pressure of high stakes tests? Or do standards-based accountability advocates need to throw in the towel, and see this attempt, like so many before it, relegated to the long list of faded reform efforts?

My purpose in this chapter is to examine that challenge, to map the intersection of accountability and the high school by marshalling what we know—and what we still need to know—about the organizational particularities of those schools and the pressures of these policies.

To do so, I draw heavily on data from the three year CPRE study on accountability and high schools. In this project, we selected four states (Kentucky, New York, Texas, and Vermont) that were all active in the testing movement, but had taken quite different strategic approaches to standards-based accountability (see Rhoten et al. in this volume). Within each state, we worked with at least three high schools within an urban—or at least metropolitan—region. In two states, these schools are all within a single district: "Tate County" in Kentucky and "River City" in New York. In Texas, we interviewed in six schools in two districts, "West City" and "Central City" (all district and school names are pseudonyms). The schools were "positioned" somewhat differently with respect to accountability policies: at least one we selected as the "target" of the reform (a school that had not been performing well by traditional measures, but that had not been declared failing or selected for reconstitution); one was somewhat "better-positioned" (not a highly selective exam school, but one that has traditionally performed well on standardized achievement tests); and another fell into a category we called "orthogonal" (a school, sometimes a small school, with an articulated and distinctive mission, whose standards might not be congruent with state standards or assessments). Finally, while we interviewed administrators and teachers across the schools, we focused most intensively on four subjects—two that commonly are tested (math and English), and two that are not (music and technology).

From these data, the challenge of the high school—for both policymakers and practitioners—emerges in terms of:

- The magnitude of change;
- The difficulty of setting standards;
- The higher stakes for schools (and students) associated with accountability;
- The problem of timing;
- The differences among high schools;
- The contexts of teachers, and finally, and most importantly,
- The high school students themselves.

The magnitude of change demanded from high schools—
as organizations—is dramatically different from
what is demanded of elementary schools.

The demands of standards-based reform call for a clarification and articulation of goals in elementary schools, for focused attention on instruction, for improvement and intensification of effort at what they were already designed to do—to prepare third graders to enter fourth grade, and fourth graders to enter fifth. High schools, on the other hand, are being asked to take on a new task—something they were not designed to do—to prepare students for a defined minimum academic standard, and to get all students to graduate by achieving that standard. We have certainly not organized high schools so that all students would take the same content, or meet the same standards to graduate. In fact, comprehensive high schools were historically designed to do precisely the opposite; since the highly influential midcentury Conant report, their design imperative has been to serve democratic purposes and accommodate diverse student populations by creating a wide range of programs, and a differentiated curriculum.

That idea of differentiation, of the "bell curve" of abilities in high schools, has been central to the organizational design of the comprehensive high school, from the tracks that accommodate the large bulk of students in the general courses to the small number of students along the right tail in Advanced Placement classes. It remains powerful even when challenged by the concept of (minimum) standards that *all* students should meet. So, just as it resurfaces in the state comparisons of school scores, it surfaces in a teacher's explanation of how the school has changed to meet the new standards, how all students now encounter the same content and take the same test: "Then we compare them, and it would make sense to us that the honors kids should have a lot of high grades, and then accelerated have some high grades; they should spread themselves out. If we are assessing them correctly, that's the way it should be. That shouldn't reflect badly on the [lower level] teacher."

At worst, that strong differentiation devolved to large scale tracking, with differential access to resources that was less the result of careful diagnosis of students' individual interests than of placements tied to the color of their skin, the accent of their speech, or the appearances of social class (Anyon 1995; Lee, Bryk, and Smith 1993; Metz 1991; Oakes 1985).

Teachers across our schools, like educators in national opinion polls, embraced the ideal of high standards for all students as means of reducing those inequities, both within and across schools, as "the right thing to do," as "mak[ing] the system more fair" (Siskin 2000a). Many "applauded" the state for stepping in not only to set common standards, but also to establish common assessments and accountability that would force the issue of equity across schools.

Though teachers might applaud the ideal of common denominators and equal access, they did not equate this with narrowing the curriculum to provide one common experience, or to achieve a common outcome for all students. Instead, many worried that too much emphasis on the common core of academic subjects would betray the ideals of the comprehensive high school and the values of the school community: individual choices for students, preparation for diverse career paths, accommodation for different talents, opportunities for extracurricular activities, and room for social growth. In particular, educators frequently expressed concern that the emphasis on academic tests is undermining the value of vocational skills.

Teachers, students, and communities have developed a number of different, and sometimes competing, expectations of what is important for a high school to provide and be accountable for: safety, vocational counseling and training, extracurricular activities as well as academic programs.

And they have come to expect that students will, and should, participate in different activities suited to their own individual needs and interests (Little 1999; Lee 2001; Lucas 1999; Wasley, Hampel, and Clark 1997; Wilson and Corbett 2001). Holding all students, within and across schools, to the same high academic standards without sacrificing the advantages of that diversity would be a radical reform indeed; a formidable challenge for both policymakers and high schools.

High school is a fundamentally different arena for deciding what standards to set—what knowledge counts and how to count it.

In the first efforts toward standards-based education, policy makers, educators, national subject associations, and public panels engaged in long and often heated debates about what high school graduates should know and be able to do. Over time, they produced long lists of valued content in each traditional subject area, and new skills seen as suited to the needs of the twenty-first century (see Murnane and Levy 1996). While this effort is generally framed as a shift from inputs to outcomes, from counting seat time or Carnegie units to rewarding achievement, the shift from a comprehensive curriculum to a more narrowly academic one is profound. The reflex response has been remarkably similar across states: the reassertion of the traditional categories of "core" academic subjects. Math and English always appear, science and social studies quite often, the arts, woodworking, or problem-solving are increasingly rare. Yet agreement on the specifics of what will be on the short list, the essential knowledge and skills without which no high school student can graduate, still poses tremendous difficulties for policymakers and practitioners.

There is wide agreement, for example, that all students need literacy and numeracy, and relative agreement on the content and skill levels that all *elementary* school students should achieve. But at the high school level, where curriculum and faculty are officially and organizationally divided along subject lines, the questions are far more complicated, and states are struggling with the question of which subjects will count in their accountability systems. Does *every* student need to appreciate music, or to be able to play an instrument? Should they be required to demonstrate mastery of world history, or U.S. government, or both? How well does *every* student actually need to perform on a chemistry test?

The question of "what subjects count?" highlights perhaps the most farreaching, and largely unanticipated consequences of the turn to highstakes testing. It does not just measure knowledge; it changes the nature of knowledge itself by specifying its proper subjects. This effect is most evident and problematic in the organization of the high school, in its subject-specific departments and interdisciplinary teams. Accountability reforms heighten the stakes for both in unprecedented fashion, as states reassert the traditional subject disciplines, but reconfigure the resources and status they command. Subjects not tested risk becoming "not real," losing staff and time in the schedule, and thus their very footholds in the schools (see Siskin, in this volume). Those that are tested assume greater importance: if passing all tested subjects is the requirement for a diploma, then passing *each* one of those subjects becomes a single measure that determines whether or not students will graduate.

The "real" standards and test pressures affect what happens within subjects as well: evolution disappeared from the science standards in three states; within our own sample, several English teachers lamented the demise of literature as they shifted their focus to the five-paragraph essay on which students will be assessed. In the most extreme example, music teachers in Kentucky, who worried that under that state's new accountability system "music teachers are not real teachers," put pressure on the state to include theirs among the tested subjects. What they won instead was a compromise that "backfired." The state created a new composite subject that *would* count: visual/performing arts and humanities, that no teacher had ever taught and no student had taken. At the same time the policy brought about a change in how it would be counted—from actual performance assessments to paper and pencil tests. For our target schools, this requires new knowledge, new textbooks, new curricula, and new teaching assignments—and student schedules that preclude electives such as band. At schools like our better-positioned, more middle-class one, however, the new content can be added on the side, downloaded from a CD the students have created, or simply brought in from home . . . while the band course plays on.

The possibility that schools, particularly low-performing schools, will be pressed to narrow curricula in order to match what is asked on high-stakes tests raises concern among critics of standards-based accountability at all grade levels (McNeil 2000; Haycock and Huang 2001). The concern at the high school level, however, is particularly pointed, for it calls into question the very purpose of the comprehensive high school: to bring and keep large numbers of students by offering a broad range of curricular offerings suited to their tastes and talents. To some degree this is precisely what reformers had in mind. "Gut" courses that had become holding tanks with little substance would be eliminated, and all students would have access to the more advanced and rigorous academic core. Recent studies suggest that, to some degree, high school course options are narrowing as prescribed, at least on paper. More algebra classes, more AP courses, and, as Chicago observers attest, a more general shift "from warehousing and managing student behavior to focusing on serious student learning" (Hess and Cytrnbaum 2001, 4; see also Gutierrez and Morales 2001; Lee 2001; Lucas 1999; Miller and Allensworth 2001; Porter 2001).

What happens inside schools, however, may not be what reformers envisioned. In some cases, teachers take on the challenge, finding new materials or devising new approaches to reach students who would not have had access before (see DeBray et al. 2001; Gutierrez and Morales 2001). In other schools, students who had been remanded to "basic" math are now assigned to classes *called* algebra; but since those classes have the same teachers, the same students, and the same textbooks, it's not clear what has actually changed. In still others where curricular offerings have not changed, the schedule and the experiences of students have. In one Texas school, for example, the pressure of the math test is high, but so is the number of low-scoring students. In response, the school has provided intensive intervention. Selected students take one period of math, one of remedial math, and another of test prep math. There is little time for other subjects, none for electives, and it is difficult to imagine a more perverse incentive for preparing well-educated high school graduates.

Under such pressures, what happens to untested subjects and to the students who found intellectual and social homes there? In which subjects, and in how many subjects, and for what ends can high schools reasonably prepare students? Questions about what knowledge high schools do and should offer to all students, and what kinds of knowledge might be locally, socially, or culturally situated take on new importance in this climate.

Some states are returning to the idea of a two- or even three-tiered system, in which all students must pass a set of tests to earn a high school diploma, but a subset who pass more subjects, or at higher levels, will qualify for an Honors diploma or special endorsement. Few states have given serious consideration to the question of whether all students actually need to—or, if given the chance, would choose to—perform to the same high level in all subjects, or whether they might achieve at high standards in different subjects— selecting the exam areas as they do with SAT II tests and AP exams, or as students traditionally have done with the A levels and O levels in the U.K.. The issues of selectivity and what counts do not disappear even when there is general agreement about the need to test a particular subject. Testing math, for example, opens up the question of what kinds of math deserve attention. So far the tests have moved fairly quickly toward demanding higher-level skills of algebra and geometry; the states, however, have been slower to require that all students are actually taught those subjects before they take the tests (Grimes 2001).

While the standards movement intended, at least partly, to ensure that students would be equipped for the economy of the twenty-first century, accountability systems have had to rely on the measurement tools and the knowledge base of the twentieth century. States are still working to develop consensus and precision around standards, and to devise adequate and reliable assessments of those standards. If the subject matter we want *all* high school students to know is not clearly linked to assessment, imposing high-stakes tests seems both inappropriate and counterproductive.

The stakes are higher in high schools.

In high-stakes accountability at the elementary and middle school level, schools are the principal objects of sanctions. But in high school, high stakes are also aimed at students. State accountability policies are moving to make diplomas contingent on externally set exams, or on demonstrated competencies in externally set performance reviews (Goertz and Duffy 2001). As an English teacher in New York reminded us, when scoring a high stakes test, "You're looking at a paper; that's a human being. That's a kid reading or trying his best to get through state requirements." Ironically, in a system theoretically designed to benefit students, high school students may be the only people held directly accountable *as individuals* for achievement scores.

That also makes the stakes higher for accountability systems. Whereas states and districts may be willing to embrace the idea of ending social promotion, or of remanding students to summer schools, the actual denial of a diploma is a consequence of a different kind, with political and legal implications, as well as financial and logistical ones (see Heubert 2003; Fuhrman, Goertz, and Duffy 2003).

Teachers we interviewed in our study made a sharp distinction between standards, which they applaud, and the standardized high-stakes tests they deplore. Positive statements about raising standards were often followed with a pause, or a "but"—and a prediction of negative consequences, of rising failure rates, and increasing numbers of dropouts. Here practitioners depart from the sentiments and expectations of the policymakers, for they are much more worried that there will be what one calls "a lost generation"—students who have not been prepared to meet the standards but will not be able to graduate without passing the tests. That pessimism, reported one New York teacher in the first year of the test, was widespread: "The general feeling among teachers is, this is going to be our last graduating class of any sizeable proportion, that next year it's going to be really bad."

State policymakers are caught in a dilemma around how high to set the bar for high school standards: if too many students fail, they risk a "lost generation" and a loss of public support; if too many pass, they risk not being taken seriously. The risk of high stakes and bars set too high seems more likely as many states introduced their new tests to low passing rates. In state after state, despite variation in policy particulars and in particular tests, results consistently pointed to high schools, especially urban high schools, as an ongoing site of crisis—the weakest link. More than half of California's high school students failed in their first round of testing; in Arizona, only twelve percent passed the 1999 math test. When Massachusetts first administered its new MCAS exams, only twenty-seven percent of Boston's tenth graders passed the English section, and sixteen percent the math.

Such numbers are numbing for any level of schooling, but when nearly insurmountable bars are set at the endpoint of the high school, violence enters the vocabulary of policy. New York's Commissioner for Education, for example, acknowledged that under the newly reformed Regents policy, which he proudly proclaimed one of the hardest tests of any state, there would be "casualties." Lorrie Shepard, an authority on assessment, compared high-stakes testing to "Darth Vader and the Death Star" (Jehlen 2001). Across these state policies, where graduation becomes dependent on meeting the standard, and meeting the standard becomes equated with passing a particular test, high casualty counts indeed seemed likely.

Faced with low scores, and with stakes so high for students and for the system, high school exit testing seems to have retreated somewhat in the past two years. Federal legislation continued to press for increasing accountability and more tests—but in 2001 specified annual testing only from third to eighth grade. Several states, while not quite silenced on high school accountability, moved to soften the pressure, to delay deadlines, or to narrow the scope of their testing systems. While twenty-four states had made passing a test a graduation requirement, many had created what were, in effect, time-release systems—where students would take the tests now, but not feel the full effects till later. (see Fuhrman, Goertz, and Duffy 2003, for more on states' responses).

A likely scenario for high school exit exams may be what we observe in Texas. As Carnoy, Loeb, and Smith report in their essay in this volume, the TAAS tenth grade high school exit exam has not had a significant negative effect on graduation rates since its introduction in the early 1990s. The state seems to have set the difficulty of the test or, alternatively, graded the test, in a way that satisfies the demands of those who want greater accountability, but that does not create political problems by pushing even more low-income whites, blacks, and Latinos out of high school. Indeed, more recently, graduation rates have been rising, especially for black students, but also more gradually for whites and Latinos. Although the exit test may not have been the cause of this increase, Texas officials could claim that, contrary what critics claimed and what teachers and the public feared, a "moderate-level" test eventually contributed positively to high school survival and graduation rates.

If the Texas model prevails, it is likely that "standards," at least as reflected in that high-stakes high school test, will not compromise the expectations of parents that almost all students who do their work regularly should pass their courses and graduate with their class.

Timing is a different problem for high schools.

For many teachers and administrators, buying time is the only action that makes sense for high schools. Unless the standards are phased in, grade-by-grade, reaching them seems impossible. They talk frequently, and intensely, about what we came to call "behindedness"—the huge gap between what the standards demand and the skills their students have (see Lemons, Luschei, and Siskin in this volume). While elementary schools may have students scoring two or three years below grade level, high schools have students who may be as many as five or six years behind.

In New York, where high-stakes testing hit the high schools very rapidly, a teacher complained that "they really hit kids over the head very hard with it. I think it was not phased in." Another explained it as a problem of social promotion, of underpreparation, the problem that the standards movement is actually intended to fix: "That's why they're changing the standards. And they *should* be making them higher, but they've got to start at the very bottom, with kids in kindergarten, and they are now. But then, they're going and giving us the tests in high school . . . the kids haven't been prepared."

Teachers describe the problem as the long-term absence of standards and accountability in the system—a system that has historically promoted students to high school without providing them with the education they need to succeed in academic work. In the most optimistic view, gradually phasing in standards-based education would create a self-correcting system: students taught to standards at "the very bottom," in kindergarten or third grade, would carry the reform with them, raising skills as they rise through the grades.

But the hope of teachers in new systems like New York's are challenged by the more skeptical comments of teachers in Kentucky and Texas, for in those states the high school students of today *are* the students who have been participating in standards-based accountability systems since they were in kindergarten (see also Haycock and Huang 2001; Marks 2000). At our target school in Kentucky, the principal reminded us several times of the challenge of teaching in a high school where "seventy-five percent of our ninth graders are scoring in the first, second, or third stanines." A math teacher told us of helping his sixth grade niece with her math, and realizing that most of his tenth grade students were not performing at that level. Another estimated that several of his students are working at a second-grade level.

That problem is compounded by the question of just what grade level means in high school, and *when* an accountability system should assess whether students have reached it. If the purpose is to measure what students are expected to learn in high school, should an exit exam be given at the end of high school—when they have had the full opportunity to learn it? What would schools do with twelfth or fourteenth graders who have not passed? Would high school seniors remember what they had learned in ninth grade biology to take a high school science test? Alternatively, should they instead choose, as most states have, to test in tenth grade—so students have more opportunities to retake the test (even if they haven't yet taken the geometry class)? The risk of two, or even three years of "senioritis" in students who had officially met graduation standards as sophomores may seem like a relatively small problem, but for some schools it seems risky indeed. High schools need to address the challenges of timing. Doing so means rethinking high schools as organizations.

High schools are different from each other; they receive and respond to the policies in different ways, but context is important.

Some high schools confront large numbers of sophomores who have passed the state tests; others are more worried about large numbers of juniors and seniors who have not. While high schools differ in substantial ways from elementary schools, they also differ significantly from each other. They range from small schools of two hundred, to large and even huge schools of five thousand students, from comprehensives to career academies, magnets for science, and schools for the performing arts. Some responded to the early rounds of reform by restructuring, creating interdisciplinary houses, even breaking up large schools into small ones. Some hold on to their traditional ways with pride, others in despair. The amount of variation in the high school system is tremendous—in terms of size, purpose, organizational structure, culture, and capacity, as well as achievement level. Although state policy may require the same standards for all schools and students, the specific contexts are quite different, and context matters (McLaughlin and Talbert 2001).

Within our study, we observe dramatic differences in how the schools are positioned relative to the policy, particularly in states where the sanctions associated with accountability are weak (Vermont), moderate (Kentucky—no exit test), or strong but just being implemented (New York). There, the contrasts between different types of schools were more evident than the differences between states, although the states were selected for their diverse approaches to accountability. But in Texas, where sanctions are stronger than in Vermont or Kentucky and have been in place much longer than in New York, there are much smaller contrasts among school types—all three types of schools align with state testing sooner or later (see DeBray, Parson, and Avila in this volume). All of our sampled schools were actively responding to the policy and working hard to meet the challenge, but in many ways they (including those in Texas) were trying to solve different problems. In the challenge of standards-based accountability, the problems that each school has to confront, and the capacity it can draw on to confront them are largely a matter of how the school was positioned in the first place.

The primary challenge in what we called "better-positioned" schools was to extend—to provide the academic programs they were offering *most* students to *all* students. In our large districts, each of which offered some choice at the high school level, these "better-positioned" schools were not the most selective exam schools, but were considered "pretty good" to start with and were often chosen by academically-oriented students. They were organized to prepare students for college, with a traditional core academic curriculum, and subject departments, with certified teachers, most of whom had taught high-level courses. So for an English teacher here, neither the content nor the testing were really new: "I think that if you had been teaching English the way you should have been teaching English, there is no reason why this exam should be difficult or you should be bent out of shape." But teachers had been able to forget, or ignore, that not everyone had been teaching "the way you should have been" and not all students had been reaching the standards. Although the starting point may be easier to find in these schools, their challenge is not small: ensuring that the last ten percent or twenty percent are prepared to pass the new exams is a difficult task. At the River City school "a third of the students had failures" in one or more courses, but with the pressures of the new policy, these failures now lead to redeployment of their most qualified faculty, to tutoring and after-school programs, and sometimes—though they say not often—counseling students and their families to try another school.

For the "target" schools, which the schools' low-achieving students are often counseled into, the problem they have to solve is more how to *invent*: they don't have the academic structures and strategies in place to prepare their students for these new standards. That may mean creating new classes or taking on new teaching assignments; but these schools find less in the way of internal resources to help them with this. As one principal laments, looking at her school's report card, "How do you even know where to begin?" These are not the lowest-scoring schools in their states—in our Vermont target, they celebrated when the newspaper published the list of the very bottom-ranking schools and they weren't on it. But in three of the states the majority of their students are typically not reaching the standards; and though teachers speak of "working hard" and "overload," they see little reason to expect that will improve and turnover is high. Qualified math teachers are hard to find, so teachers have been conscripted from Title 1 and business programs; in one year four teachers were hired for, but then left, the physics class. Many attribute that to "a lot of extenuating circumstances, things that are beyond our control within the building that affect our test scores. And we feel like those concerns fall on deaf ears." In Tate County, an English teacher described hers as "a school for the disenfranchised parent and student. Parents who weren't successful in school themselves don't know how to play this system, and so, therefore, their kids aren't successful. And I think that's what's happened here." To some degree, this may be a problem of low, or self-fulfilling expectations, but the contrast between two schools in the same district is striking: at the target school, seventy percent of the students qualify for the free lunch program, at its better-positioned neighbor, the figure is twelve percent. In the target, twenty percent qualify for special education services, and another twenty percent for ESL; at the better-positioned school, they "don't offer any remedial classes," so students with special needs are discouraged from applying.

Our target school in River City is a comprehensive high school, where for many years students have performed poorly on standardized tests; before it was a graduation requirement, fewer than ten percent of their students had qualified for Regents diplomas. Like the Tate County target, they've organized around improving safety and order, around interdisciplinary programs devised to attract students to school and attach them to a faculty team. They can point to substantial improvement: applications to the school are up, as is attendance; suspension and violent incidents are down. Those may be necessary first steps, but they are not enough to improve test scores. So, for these schools, the problem is a broad one, and they worry that many, or even most, of their students will be unable to pass the new test: "I think we're going to graduate fewer kids . . . we're supposed to have four or five hundred kids graduating; we're probably going to find ourselves with 150 or possibly 200." While the task of preparing students seems generally daunting, the challenge of preparing those students they see as most at risk seems almost impossible. The lack of adequate safety nets or additional resources seems, to some teachers, almost unconscionable: "There's no safety net for immigrant students; there's no safety net for special ed students."

Nevertheless, of the four target schools we studied in Texas, in the mid-1990s two responded to the threat of tough sanctions from the state by re-organizing under new administrations around longstanding Texas test-based standards. A third went through a crisis during the two years we interviewed in the school. The low math test scores of African-American students on the Texas exit test put that school's principal in jeopardy. Faculty intensified their efforts to raise scores by providing more remedial classes and focusing even more on the test itself. They succeeded in recording a series of substantial gains over the next two years. Our Texas experience suggests that high schools with weak internal alignment can align with external standards when the pressure is strong enough and sustained. Although all the target schools in Texas faced the same barriers and lack of resources as those in other states, under intense pressure they did align on the exit test to get the passing rates up. Indeed, by 2001, two years after our last interviews, all four target schools had acceptable ratings.

For the schools we have called "orthogonal," the policy presents a different problem: how to survive, to maintain a specialized mission under the pressure of high-stakes, standardized testing. One orthogonal school, for example, had traditionally provided special focus on African-American studies, community service, and career preparation—but has dramatically shifted its programs to center the standardized academic core demanded in its new policy context, while struggling to hold on to its historical pride and sense of providing something "special" and especially valuable to its constituents.

The concern takes on special intensity in the case of our River City orthogonal school, a small school where an administrator called the new policy "threatening . . . Not to my job, but to our philosophy. And philosophy is everything." This is a school that by design operates outside the "mainstream" of district high schools, and by choice serves only immigrant students. They, like the better-positioned school, have some capacity to select students, but they have chosen students whose scores on the English language battery lie in the lowest quartile. The students, in turn, have chosen this particular school instead of a more comprehensive one; their incoming tests scores may be low, but teachers describe them as "motivated," as "oriented" toward their particular focus, and as filled with "a lot of school pride." This school is not organized around traditional department lines, but around an innovative—and nationally renowned—program for teaching English and subject-based content at the same time. The ideal of high standards is not seen as a problem: they expect students to attend regularly, work hard, and graduate, and well over ninety percent of their students do. They have developed a demanding performance-based assessment system, and annually send more than ninety percent of their graduates on to college. But standardizing course content and standardized tests leads many here to a profoundly pessimistic view about the potential failure rate of their students, and about the future survival of their school.

The idea of "no exceptions" and no excuses has been a central element of standards-based reform since its inception. But in cases like New York, the potential conflict between *high* standards for all students and the *same* standards, as measured by standardized assessment of all schools and students, has come into sharp focus and into an ongoing court case. When the standards and the stakes are so high, and the schools are starting—or aiming to continue—in such different positions, policies that don't take account of the differences between high schools risk unintended and undesired consequences.

When standards-based accountability is relatively weak, it may actually exacerbate the very inequities they were designed to alleviate. Our sample of schools is small, yet it suggests that when the external accountability message is less than forceful, schools that start out "better-positioned" relative to the new standards extend what they are doing, making adaptive improvements. They are able to employ their own internal accountability systems, to draw on staff capacity, to reduce the "general" tracks of nonacademic courses, and to provide additional time and a focused curriculum to students at risk. At the same time they are able to reduce the numbers of at-risk students they admit and retain, and to attract more academic students and teachers as their "higher scoring school" status becomes more public. The "targets" of the reform, on the other hand, are much less likely to respond in these "weak" situations, or are likely to take much longer to respond. The Texas sample suggests that it takes a loud, clear, and long-term set of standards with sanctions to push schools with low internal alignment to take systematic action to improve. When they do, they generally go the "low" road of teaching to the test. At the edges of the system, the small schools, the special mission schools, the "orthogonal" outliers that had provided some of the few existence-proofs that high schools could be successfully transformed and in urban contexts, may be pulled back from what made them distinctive. However, as the Texas case suggests, such orthogonal schools are still generally better positioned to respond to external standards than targeted schools.

In the high schools, engaging, or even reaching, teachers entails different strategies and different structures.

High bars and looming graduations create a daunting set of unfamiliar demands for secondary school staffs, since accountability reform demands not only that all students should be expected to meet high standards, but that *teachers* will be expected to adequately prepare them to do that. Many teachers argue that policymakers are out of touch with local realities, particularly the harsh realities of underfunded and underperforming urban schools. At a hearing where state policymakers talked of "raising the standards for all students," a teacher asked incredulously, "Do you not understand that there are some schools where not one student will be able to graduate?" For reformers to reach an understanding with those who must implement reforms in the classroom, they need to recognize the demands that standards-based accountability imposes, not just on teachers in general, but on those who teach in the high school in particular. Teachers are very aware of this call to change; unlike many previous reform efforts, they generally agree with its ideals, but, as noted earlier, their agreement insists on the distinction between the standards they support and the tests they deplore.

Teachers' agreement and engagement are essential elements of the reform, particularly since they are quite forthcoming about the fact that they themselves will not be held directly accountable for the academic achievement of their students. As one teacher said, "What I'm not accountable for, I think sometimes—facetiously I say it—if every kid failed math in this school, I would still have a job." If anything is going to happen, then, it will be because teachers look at the new demands, see them as possible to achieve and as worth their support and effort.

To capitalize on that support and allay the fears, reformers must work through the specific barriers posed by the particular organizational structure of high schools. The lever they must pull is long, extending from the state through many layers of bureaucracy into the classroom, where, finally, the change has to take place. To communicate even straightforward information is difficult from that distance; at River City, for example, teachers who applauded the standards movement could not always tell what the policy actually required, when it would take effect, or what the consequences would really be.

Reaching teachers with professional development support for changes in instruction is even more complicated; in high schools, instruction is subject-specific, so teachers need to be addressed, not just as teachers, but as math teachers or English teachers or music teachers (see Siskin, in this volume). In many cases, high school teachers are being asked to teach what they have not taught before, what they are not certified to teach, or, quite simply, what they do not have the capacity to provide. The 1998 Department of Education figures show that twenty-eight percent of math teachers and fifty-five percent of physics teachers have neither a major nor minor in their subject; another analysis estimates the figures at one in three math teachers, and one in four English teachers, who are teaching "out-of-field" (Ingersoll 2001). Those shortages are more critical factors in the schools that are the very target of the reform, where an administrator asks "who is going to teach this stuff?" Each high school teacher who either cannot or does not provide sufficient "opportunities to learn" the new standards translates into approximately 150 students who don't receive them. Not only are teachers faced with new courses (like the humanities), but many teachers, after years of teaching general classes, suddenly find themselves teaching what had been the honors track.

Where we did find teachers engaged in substantive and sustained conversations about teaching to the new standards was in their own departments, but few departments were organized to facilitate these conversations. Without the time to engage in these conversations on a regular basis, teachers had little opportunity to work on the standards, to learn what the standards entailed, or even to become knowledgeable about the new policies. This is not, I would argue, because these are unmotivated or resistant teachers; it is more a result of the relative absence of departmental mechanisms around information sharing, standards-work, and talk about teaching and learning.

The professional development and capacity-building endeavors of many districts and states, however, seem to assume that principals are the key agents of instructional leadership and support. As one principal explained: "In terms of assisting us, and that's what it is, it's a support and assist to the schools, providing us with expertise in the areas, doing staff development with [the principals] so we can then turnkey it with our staff. We meet monthly ... Last month's principals meeting was focusing all on social studies, and we had some people come in and do presentations, and then we as principals worked together on stuff that's going to be on the new exam for social studies." The concept of having principals get together and work on the "stuff" that's going to be on the tests is probably quite valuable—but the probability of high school principals going back to "turnkey" meaningful changes, given the size of their faculties and the complexity of the changes entailed in standards-based work, seems quite low.

In the absence of serious investments of time and support to change what is taught and how, the impact of standards-based accountability on student achievement in high schools is likely to be disappointing. In high schools, that investment has to take place subject-by-subject, addressing the level of particular content materials, expectations for students, and teaching strategies—which generally means it has to take place in subject departments (Aguirre 2000; Gutierrez and Morales 2001; Siskin and Little 1995; Stodolsky and Grossman 2001; Wetterstein 1993). Otherwise, schools that are better positioned to start with, and whose internal structures correspond to the external demands of the subject-specific standards, may be even further advantaged in the educational marketplace. There is a growing body of research, for example, that links subject expertise to student performance (especially if students have consecutive years)—but finds that, as in our sample, shortages of academically prepared teachers are higher in poorer schools, and that high-stakes testing encourages teachers with higher qualifications to move to higher scoring schools (Hanushek, Kain, and Rifkin 2001; Haycock and Huang 2001; Ingersoll 2001). So as the curriculum narrows (or rises, depending on your point of view), the questions of who will teach these courses, and how they themselves will be prepared to prepare students take on new salience.

In high schools, students play a central and active role in the reform.

Finally, but foremost in teachers' minds, students themselves are a central element in the particular challenge of the high schools. They play multiple roles in the process and products of standards-based accountability: they are the bottom line and the intended beneficiaries, a resource and a result (see Chabrán in this volume).

High schools differ in critical ways from elementary schools, not simply in the early hour at which the school day begins, or the larger size of physical and organizational structures; they are full of adolescents, and the interactions between teachers and teenagers are quite different from those with younger children. High school students are not like younger students who "can be compelled to perform," explained a music teacher, who splits his time between teaching elementary and high school classes. Instead, as young adults they see a teacher as "more like a peer," so that "[teachers] have to earn their respect," and students have to be "convinced" that there is a reason to engage in schoolwork. Nor, a principal observed, are high school students quite like adults: "they don't react like us."

Yet high school students are making—and see themselves as old enough to make—important choices about what they need to know, and what they are willing to do: they decide which schools to attend, which days to come (or cut), whether to stay in school or drop out, what courses they will take, and how much effort to put into an exhausting battery of state tests. Some, perhaps aspiring lawyers, elect to study English and social studies, but plan to hire accountants to deal with the math problems in their lives. Others know, or think they know, that they will be musicians or mechanics and that they do not need academic courses at all. Some even organize boycotts, or create websites in opposition to high-stakes tests. They are old enough to ask why, and to demand and deserve a meaningful answer.

With remarkable consistency across the states and types of schools, whether or not the stakes are high, teachers and administrators struggle with ways to convince and connect to adolescents, with what we have called the "mystery of motivation" (Siskin and Lemons 2000). How to motivate high school students to engage in academic work has always been difficult to some degree, but it poses a particular challenge under the demands of standards-based accountability, when all students are expected to achieve high standards in all tested subjects—and teachers search for convincing answers to why everyone needs to know the quadratic formula, or how to write a five-paragraph essay.

At its core, the design of an effective accountability system depends heavily on the answers it can provide, on the motivation of students and the meaning they attach to what they are expected to achieve. The assessments rely on a set of critical conditions: that students actively engage in the effort, attend their classes, show up to take the exams, and take the tests seriously. Achieving those conditions, in turn, depends on convincing students they have reason to participate and a reasonable chance of success—which entails schools organized to prepare them, qualified and committed teachers to educate them, community consensus on what the next generation needs to know, and the political will to provide the particular resources to make that possible in every school. As standards-based accountability reform enters the era of second generation revisions, those conditions remain a challenge for high schools, and the high school remains a challenge to the reform movement.

References

Abelman, C., and R. F. Elmore. 1999. When accountability knocks, will anyone answer? Philadelphia: Consortium for Policy Research in Education.

Adams, J. E., and M. W. Kirst. 1999. New demands and concepts for educational accountability: Striving for results in an era of excellence. In *Handbook of Research on Educational Administration*, ed. J. Murphy and K. S. Louis, 463–489. San Francisco, CA: Jossey-Bass.

Aguirre, J. M. 2000. Examining teacher beliefs related to algebra competency in the context of "Algebra for all" mathematics reform debate. Tucson, AZ: Paper presented at the Psychology of Mathematics Education—North American Conference XXII.

Angus, D. L., and J. E. Mirel. 1999. *The failed promise of the American high school.* New York: Teachers College Press.

Anyon, J. 1995. Inner city school reform: Toward useful theory. *Urban Education* 30(1): 56–70.

Ball, S. J., and R. Bowe. 1992. Subject departments and the "implementation" of national curriculum policy: An overview of the issues. *Curriculum Studies* 24(2): 97–115.

Boyer, E. 1983. *High school: A report on secondary education in America.* New York: Harper & Row.

Conant, J. B. 1959. *The American high school today: A first report to interested citizens.* New York: McGraw Hill.

Cross, C. T. 1998. The standards wars: Some lessons learned. *Education Week on the Web.* Available at http://www.edweek.org/October 21, 1998.

DeBray, E., G. Parson, and K. Woodworth. 2001. Patterns of response in four high schools under state accountability policies in Vermont and New York. In *From the Capitol to the Classroom: Standards-based Reform in the States*, ed. S. Fuhrman, 170–192. Chicago: National Society for the Study of Education, University of Chicago Press.

Doyle, D. P. 1999. De Facto National Standards. *Education Week on the Web*, July 14. Available at http://www.edweek.org/July 14, 1999.

Education Commission of the States. 2000. *The progress of education reform 1999–2001: Assessment.* Denver, CO: Education Commission of the States.

Education Commission of the States. 2000. *The progress of education reform 1999–2001: Standards.* Denver, CO: Education Commission of the States.

Fine, M. 1991. *Framing dropouts: Notes on the politics of an urban public high school.* Albany: State University of New York Press.

Firestone, W. A., and R. E. Herriott. 1982. Prescriptions for effective elementary schools don't fit secondary schools. *Educational Leadership* 40(3): 51–53.

Firestone, W., D. Mayrewitz, and J. Fairman. 1998. Performance-based assessment and instructional change: The effects of testing in Maine and Maryland. *Educational Evaluation and Policy Analysis* 20: 95–113.

Fuhrman, S. H. 1999. *The new accountability.* Policy Brief RB-27. Philadelphia: CPRE.

Goertz, M. E., and M. Duffy, with K. LeFloch. 2001. *Assessment and accountability systems in the 50 states.* Philadelphia: CPRE.

Grimes, M. 2001. California confronts algebra anxiety. *Boston Globe/Los Angeles Times,* 24 June.

Hanushek, E., J. F. Kain, and S. G. Rifkin. 2001. *Why public schools lose teachers.* National Bureau of Economic Research. Available at http://www.nber.org 2001.

Haycock, K., and S. Huang. 2001. Are today's high school graduates ready? *Thinking K-16: Publication of the Education Trust* 5(1): 3–17.

Hess, G. A., and S. Cytrnbaum. 2001. The effort to redesign Chicago high schools: Effects on schools and achievement. In *Research on High School Reform Efforts in Chicago.* Chicago: Consortium on Chicago School Research.

Heubert, J. P., and R. M. Hauser, eds. 1999. *High stakes: Testing for tracking, promotion, and graduation.* Washington D.C.: National Academy Press.

Ingersoll, R. M. 2001. The realities of out-of-field teaching. *Educational Leadership* May: 42–45.

Jehren, A. 2001. Interview with Lorrie Shepard: How to fight a "death star." *NEA Today online.* Available at http://www.nea.org/neatoday/0101/intrvw.html.

Kahne, J., C. A. Bridge, and J. O'Brien. 2001. *Teacher learning counts: Improving instruction in one urban high school through comprehensive staff development.* Research on High School Reform Efforts in Chicago. Chicago: Consortium on Chicago School Research.

Kirst, M. 2001. *Overcoming the high school senior slump: New education policies.* Washington, D.C.: National Center for Public Policy and Higher Education.

Lee, V. 2001. *Restructuring high schools for equity and excellence: What works.* New York: Teachers College Press.

Lee, V., A. S. Bryk, and J. B. Smith. 1993. The organization of effective secondary schools. *Review of Research in Education* 19: 171–267. Washington, D.C.: American Educational Research Association.

Little, J. W. 1999. Teachers' professional development in the context of high school reform: Findings from a three-year study of restructuring schools. Unpublished manuscript.

Little, J. W. 1993. Teachers' professional development in a climate of educational reform. *Educational Evaluation and Policy Analysis* 15(2): 129–151.

Lucas, S. R. 1999. *Tracking inequality: Stratification and mobility in American high schools.* New York: Teachers College Press.

Marks, H. M. 2000. Student engagement in instructional activity: Patterns in the elementary, middle, and high school years. *American Educational Reseach Journal* 37(1): 153–184.

McLaughlin, M. W., and J. E. Talbert. 2001. *Professional communities and the work of high school teaching.* Chicago, IL: University of Chicago Press.

McNeil, L. 2000. *Contradictions of school reform: Educational costs of standardized testing.* New York: Routledge.

Meier, D. 2000. *Will standards save public education?* Boston: Beacon Press.

Metz, M. H. 1990. How social class differences shape teachers' work. In *The Contexts of teaching in secondary schools,* ed. M. McLaughlin, J. Talbert, and N. Bascia, 40–107. New York: Teachers College Press.

Murnane, R., and F. Levy. 1996. *Teaching the new basic skills: Principles for educating children to thrive in a changing economy.* New York: The Free Press.

National Commission on Excellence in Education. 1983. *A nation at risk: The imperative for educational reform.* Washington, D.C.: National Commission on Excellence in Education.

Oakes, J. 1985. *Keeping track: How schools structure inequality.* New Haven: Yale University Press.

Olson, L. 2001a. *States adjust high-stakes testing plans. Education Week on the Web.* Available at http://www.edweek.org/January 24, 2001.

Olson, L. 2001b. *A quiet crisis: Unprepared for high stakes. Education Week on the Web.* Available at http://www.edweek.org/April 18, 2001.

Porter, A. C. 2000. The effects of upgrading policies on high school mathematics and science. *Brookings Papers on Education Policy 2000.* Washington D.C., Brookings Institute: 123–164.

Powell, A., E. Farrar, and D. Cohen. 1985. *The shopping mall high school: Winners and losers in the academic marketplace.* Boston: Houghton Mifflin.

Schwartz, R. B., and M. Robinson. 2000. Goals 2000 and the standards movement. *Brookings Papers on Education Policy 2000.* Washington, D.C.: Brookings Institute.

Siskin, L. S. 1994. *Realms of knowledge: Academic departments in secondary schools.* London and New York: Falmer Press.

Siskin, L. S., and J. W. Little. 1995. *The subjects in question: Departmental organization and the high school.* New York: Teachers College Press.

Siskin, L. S., and R. Lemons. 2000. *Internal and external accountability: The challenge of the high school.* Paper presented at the annual meeting of the American Educational Research Association, New Orleans, LA.

Sizer, T. R. 1984. *Horace's compromise: The dilemma of the American high school.* Boston: Houghton Mifflin.

Smith, M., and J. O'Day. 1991. Systemic school reform. In *The Politics of Curriculum and Testing,* ed. S. Fuhrman and B. Malen, 233–267. New York: Falmer Press.

Stodolsky, S., and P. Grossman. 2001. Changing students, changing teaching. *Teachers College Record* 102(1): 125–172.

Uriarte, M. 2001. The high stakes of high stakes testing. In *The Poweer of Culture: Teaching Across Language Differences,* ed. Z. Beykont. Cambridge: Harvard Education Publishing Group.

Wasley, P. A., R. L. Hampel, and R. C. Clark. 1997. *Kids and school reform.* San Francisco: Jossey-Bass.

Wetterstein, J. A. 1993. Leadership strategies of exemplary high school department chairs: Four cases of successful 'middle managers.' Paper presented at the annual meeting of the American Educational Research Association, Atlanta, GA, April.

Wilson, B., and H. D. Corbett. 2001. *Listening to urban kids: School reform and the teachers they want.* Albany: SUNY Press.

CHAPTER **8**

Accountability and Capacity

RICHARD ELMORE

Q: How many psychiatrists does it take to change a lightbulb?
A: Only one, but the lightbulb has to really want to change.

The central message of this book is that educational accountability systems work—when they work—by calling forth the energy, motivation, commitment, knowledge, and skill of the people who work in schools and the systems that are supposed to support them. Accountability systems themselves do not directly "cause" schools to increase the quality of student learning and academic performance. At best, they set in motion a complex chain of events that may ultimately result in improved learning and performance. Our work suggests some ways that policymakers and school professionals might think more powerfully and systematically about the relationship between accountability systems and the results they produce in schools.

From the beginning of our research, it was clear to us that schools construct their own conceptions of accountability—to whom they are accountable, for what, and how. A common misconception of policymakers is the belief that policies determine how individuals and organizations think and act—what problems they regard as important, how they organize themselves to work on those problems, what results they regard as evidence of their success. One version of this misconception is the belief that schools were "not accountable" before the current wave of accountability policies, and now they are. Our research suggests that all schools, consciously or unconsciously, have well-worked-out ideas of accountability, and, most importantly, that they respond to new accountability policies by adjusting their existing ideas of accountability to the external influences introduced by the new policies. Accountability policies, in other words, work on the margins of existing organizational norms, structures, and processes in schools.

We came to this view of accountability by asking people in a variety of schools—public, private, religious, large, small, elementary, middle, and high—how they solved the problem of to whom they were accountable, for what, and how (Ablemann, Elmore, 1999; Benveniste, Carnoy, and Rothstein, 2003). What we learned is that *all* schools have deep-seated norms and predispositions that determine their conceptions of accountability. It is not the case that some schools are accountable and others are not. All schools are accountable, but different schools solve the accountability problem in very different ways. Many schools have very diffuse notions of being accountable "to the children," which often ends up meaning that individual teachers enact their own views of what their students need, unmediated by collective views within the school about what the organization believes, or what parents demand, or what public policy requires. A few schools have strong collective views of what they stand for, and well-developed organizational processes that bring those beliefs into action. We characterize the former schools as having weak, and the latter as having strong, *internal accountability*. It became clear to us that the strength and focus of internal accountability in schools was a key determinant in how they would respond to any external accountability system.

For this reason, our research has focused on schools' *responses* to accountability policies, not primarily on how schools implement these policies. This may seem a subtle distinction—after all, aren't schools supposed to respond to policies by implementing them?—but it is a distinction essential to understanding the import of our research. In our framework, a school's response to external accountability policies is determined primarily by its prior status on a number of dimensions that we group together under the general heading of *capacity*. External accountability systems work not by exerting direction and control over schools, but by mobilizing and focusing the capacity of schools in particular ways. The people who work in schools, and the systems that surround them, are not just active agents in determining the effects of accountability systems. Their knowledge, skill, values, and commitments, as well as the nature of the organizations in which they work, *determine* how their schools will respond.

Schools have a variety of initial conceptions of accountability, and they vary considerably in their organizational capacity. So, not surprisingly, accountability policies provoke a range of responses that reflect the range of variability in these initial conditions. Our research was designed to study this range of responses, and to try to understand how policies might be more thoughtfully designed to take account of it.

As we began to focus more explicitly on high schools, it became clear to us that internal accountability was only one dimension of a school's capacity to respond to external accountability systems. How much teachers know about their subjects and the pedagogical knowledge required to bring students to a level of understanding in those subjects is a key element of capacity. How leadership is defined and distributed in the school is another. How the school is organized and how people in the organization solve problems related to instructional practice is another. The resources available to the school—time, money, information, materials, and external support—are still another. Capacity, as we shall see, inheres in the relationships among these factors. Variations in capacity determine how schools respond to external pressure for accountability. And "making schools more accountable for student performance" means understanding these complex relationships, and ultimately how to enhance schools' capacity to respond to the messages they receive from accountability systems.

The American comprehensive high school provides a rich, and daunting, terrain in which to study these issues. High schools are, in many ways, the acid test of accountability policies. They are typically large, complex, and loosely-coupled organizations. They are usually balkanized into subject-based departments, each with its own distinctive culture. They deal not just with the problem of how to teach the content for which they are responsible, but they must also cope with the accumulated successes and failures of all prior years of schooling. Finally, high schools are the place where major life decisions are made about students in their transition to adulthood and further education. High school is where the impact of accountability systems is most apparent. It is also difficult to imagine a less promising institutional structure for being responsive to external pressure for change and improvement. (See Siskin, chapter seven, in this volume)

The purpose of this essay is to consolidate and focus the major themes of the book around the relationship between accountability and capacity. I will first summarize our major findings around the dimensions of capacity and how they work in determining the way schools respond to accountability policies. I will then explore some of the implications of these findings for the design and implementation of accountability policies in the future.

The Elements of Capacity and How They Work

Internal Accountability   At the center of our conception of capacity, as noted above, is the idea of *internal accountability*—the shared norms, values, expectations, structures, and processes that determine the relationship between individual actions and collective results in schools. Internal accountability answers the question of to whom people in schools think they are accountable, for what, and how. We use the terms internal accountability and level of coherence synonymously. Schools with high internal accountability tend to have more coherent, shared views of what they are trying to accomplish with students, and these views translate into visible evidence in the classroom and in the way students, teachers, and administrators relate to each other in the school. Schools with high internal accountability have high agreement on what they expect students to know and be able to do and they develop internal mechanisms that translate that agreement into concrete actions—instructional practice, supervision and oversight processes, mechanisms that focus resources on content and students that need the most work. Our research suggests that schools can construct internal accountability in variety of ways; there is no single model that seems to work for all schools. Our research also suggests that internal accountability is a matter of degree not of kind; it is not something you have or don't have, it is something you tend toward with increasing clarity.

It is also important to note that schools can have high levels of agreement around relatively low expectations for students. So high internal accountability doesn't always results in high student performance. In fact, our case studies suggest that schools often construct their initial conceptions of internal accountability around relatively low expectations for students—performance goals that are achievable in the short term. Some schools push beyond these short-term goals, others don't. The important point here, however, is that high internal accountability doesn't necessarily imply agreement on ambitious goals for student learning, although it may be correlated with that. It simply implies agreement or coherence.

Our research does suggest, however, that high internal accountability is a *necessary condition* for schools to be successful in responding to the pressures of external accountability systems. That is, schools with low internal accountability are at a significant disadvantage because it is difficult to make an essentially incoherent organization act in unison around external pressure. Schools with relatively high internal accountability, or schools that use external pressure as the occasion for developing a higher degree of internal accountability, are likely to be more successful in meeting the demands of accountability systems.

As Rhoten, et al. conclude in chapter one, as well as others (Goertz, Duffy, and Carlson, 2001), a common element of state accountability policies is that they generally treat *the school* as the basic unit of accountability. This feature is the least appreciated and most profound shift in educational politics and governance brought about by the new educational accountability. While states and localities are, to a degree, still responsible for oversight and governance of schools, the main weight of accountability falls on the school as an administrative unit. Data on student performance are collected and reported at the school level, often disaggregated by specific student populations within schools. Sanctions are focused either on individual students, who attend specific schools, or on the schools themselves. Assistance strategies, insofar as they exist, apply to schools. In effect, the states, and now increasingly, the federal government, have chosen to by-pass traditional local governance structures and focus on schools as the primary unit of accountability. Hence, the organizational capacity of the school is the chief determinant of the success of accountability policies. States and localities are successful under these policies only insofar as they operate to improve the work of schools; ultimately, it is impossible to be a "good" district or a "good" state unless those jurisdictions in some way contribute to the coherence and effectiveness of individual schools.

The problem with this strategy, of course, is that there is vast variation in organizational coherence, or internal accountability, among schools—especially high schools. The American high school, in its most common form, could be called an organizational fiction. As Siskin (1994) and others have argued, people who work in high schools, if they have any conception of organization at all, typically don't identify with the school, at least on matters of instructional practice and student learning, but with their department. School structures typically operate to reinforce, rather than to moderate, departmental differences. To assume that high schools are the primary unit of accountability, then, is to base policy on an extremely problematical assumption.

Hence, to say that internal accountability is a necessary condition for external accountability is to ask high schools to do something they are essentially not designed to do, or at least something they have little or no prior experience doing. This problem is likely to be less acute in elementary schools, where there is less structural complexity, and where the organizational culture is much less subject-matter-focused. Middle schools are likely to vary considerably in the way they look, depending on how much importance they attach to subject matter and the degree to which they are structurally differentiated.

The case studies in this volume reveal both the range of solutions to the problem of internal accountability that high schools develop and the way these solutions affect schools' organizational responses to accountability requirements. As the Debray, et al. paper in this volume illustrates, it is possible for a school to comply with the basic requirements of accountability policies without shifting significantly from lower to higher internal accountability. The authors call this "compliance without capacity." Indeed, some of the target schools in our sample—schools that were poorly situated in relation to the new performance requirements at the beginning of new accountability policies—were characterized by low internal accountability at the beginning of the study and did not change materially as a consequence of complying with the new requirements. These schools essentially did what they thought the law required, with a minimum of alteration in their basic way of organizing and delivering instruction—and, not surprisingly, produced little in the way of improved performance.

The target schools in Texas, however, present a more mixed pattern. Two of the schools (Miramar and Calin) used the Texas testing and accountability requirements to stimulate organizational and curricular improvements that in turn created a higher degree of internal accountability and resulted in significantly improved performance. Two other Texas schools (Eames and Ricki Lee) had great difficulty creating and sustaining coherent internal environments and their performance was more erratic. Still, the target schools in Texas did significantly better in performance than the target schools in our other states, in part because the Texas accountability system seems to allow for some degree of success with compliance-oriented solutions than the other systems. This possibility may account, in part, for the general pattern of closing the gap between low and high-performing students that appears in the Carnoy, Loeb, and Smith analysis (chapter six).

An important cautionary finding from these cases, however, is that compliance with accountability requirements usually seems not, in itself, to create greater internal accountability. Accountability requirements create the occasion for schools to generate higher levels of agreement on goals, expectations, and practices, but they do not make schools more coherent. External accountability in the strongest accountability states, such as Texas, may be successful in generating focus on particular school responses, such as focusing on tested content, across departments, but this does not necessarily imply increased capacity for broader academic improvement. Creating higher levels of internal accountability requires knowledge and skill on the part of the people who work in the organization and a willingness to focus that knowledge and skill on common purposes.

Nowhere is this pattern clearer than in the schools and some of the orthogonal schools in our sample. The better-positioned schools, without exception, began the process of responding to accountability policies with significant advantages in terms of their prior performance and demographics and managed to use state accountability policies to improve significantly their internal coherence and focus around content, instructional practice, and student performance. Orthogonal schools present a more mixed picture, but they too seemed to regard the accountability policies, in general, as a challenge to be met, without substantially reducing the coherence of mission that was at the basis of their philosophy, and were successful at adapting to the challenge. (Debray, et al. in this volume)

Structure Logically, the next element of capacity is *structure*. High schools are, as noted above, large organizations, and large organizations typically have more complex structures for dividing up and allocating responsibilities. High schools also have more complex tasks to perform, since high school students and their parents are beginning to make consequential life choices that lead to different outcomes. Even smaller, less complex, high schools often have more complex structures than elementary schools because of the level of differentiation required to offer students choices and to cope with diversity among students in prior knowledge.

A common pattern of response to the press of external accountability policies in the high schools in our study is to rely heavily on existing structures, at least initially, to solve the problems, rather than simplifying existing structures or inventing new ones. This pattern accords with a fundamental principle of organizational theory that the best predictor of what an organization will do at Time 2 is what is was doing at Time 1. Stability and incrementalism are fundamental properties of organizational life. Hence, the schools in our study tended to focus their main efforts on tested subjects— usually, English and mathematics. They tended to factor their responses first into departmental work in tested subjects, and then further into tested grades within tested subjects, and then still further into work with specific groups of students within tested subjects. One effect of his kind of response is that attention becomes disproportionately focused on specific courses, at specific grade levels, staffed by specific teachers and populated by specific students. Left to their own devices, then, high schools will tend to pursue responses that further fragment and specialize their structures, rather than using structures to create greater organizational coherence.

It is not difficult to see how this response might work against internal accountability. Factoring external pressure into specific subjects, courses, and groups of students puts the pressure to change only on certain teachers and department heads, and essentially sends a message to the rest of the school that accountability is not their problem. It also distorts the internal incentive structure of schools, creating strong incentives for teachers to avoid teaching certain subjects at certain grade-levels, and creating difficult problems of internal management for administrators trying to staff those courses. In the absence of strong counter-measures, designed to make the structure of the school serve the purposes of greater school-wide coherence and internal accountability, what seems to be a rational response to external pressure can actually aggravate problems of internal incoherence.

There is, in our sample, a noticeable difference between schools that treat structures as instruments for making things happen and those that treat structures as more or less fixed attributes of the work environment. Our well-situated schools, in general, and the more successful target and orthogonal schools, viewed external accountability pressures as a challenge to be met, and they tended both to rely heavily on existing structures to accomplish the work of adapting instruction to new demands, and to press for more integrative structures and process to bring the whole school into alignment around a more focused version of its mission. At Glen Lake, for example, our better-positioned school in Vermont, every department in the school—not just those in tested subject matter areas—mobilized around a process of setting specific curricular and performance objectives in annual planning cycles. This process was overseen by a school-wide committee that was composed of faculty, administrators, and students, and its decisions had considerable influence within the school, resulting in major changes in curriculum and instruction not just in English and mathematics, the two tested subjects in Vermont, but across the entire school. The point here is that the structure of high schools is not necessarily conducive to producing a coherent response to external accountability pressure. It takes conscious effort and considerable knowledge and skill to make the transition from treating structures as fixed attributes of the organization to treating them as instruments for improving curriculum, instruction, and performance. Clearly, schools with a higher degree of internal accountability were better at using structure in this way than schools with a lower degree.

One interesting, unexpected finding from our study was the way in which the balkanized structure of high schools prevented them from making use of resources and talents that lay within their own building. Performance-based accountability systems place a premium on creating common conceptions of what students should and should not be able to do with what they know. There are subject matter areas in high schools—including technology and music, the two untested subjects we studied—that have well-developed traditions and practices of performance assessment that ante-date the current period of performance-based accountability. As Siskin points out in her study of untested subjects (in this volume), most of the schools in our sample responded to external pressure for accountability by marginalizing untested subjects and by ignoring their knowledge and practice. In addition, the incentive structure created by the politics of accountability at the state level rewards subject matter specialists for having their content included in the state testing system. This resulted, in Kentucky, in the peculiar outcome of music and art—two disciplines with deep traditions of performance assessment—being collapsed and subsumed into a state-wide standards and assessment area called humanities, which turned out to be an entirely new subject in which none of the existing teachers had expertise.

There is a powerful mutually reinforcing relationship between established content and disciplinary structures in high schools and the structure of state accountability standards and assessments. As Siskin notes, the pressure on schools is to teach what the tests measure, and the tests generally measure what high schools have traditionally taught. There appears to be a remarkable lack of consciousness at the state and the school level to the distorting and narrowing effect that this relationship can have. Standards and tests reify and institutionalize existing departmental structures in high schools, making it more difficult for them to experiment with more powerful and effective ways to organize instruction. Likewise, schools and the people in them tend to use external policies as the rationale for *not* bringing more powerful and creative thinking to the way high schools are organized. School people often view simplified structures as risky in the face of subject-based accountability systems. As high schools deal increasingly with the problems educating all students to high levels of mastery the constraints of existing structures will become increasingly obvious, as will the limits on innovation created by existing standards, tests, and disciplinary boundaries.

Leadership   There is a tendency in American society, and especially in American education, to look for a leader behind every example of organizational success. And there is certainly abundant evidence for this view in our case studies. In general, the schools with stronger, more inventive, more knowledgeable, more active leaders were the schools that managed their responses to external accountability systems more effectively. But there is also evidence in our work for a more cautious, modulated, and somewhat broader view of leadership than is usually the case. The view of leadership that emerges from the analysis in this volume is first one of individual principals connecting what the authors call the pre-existing story of the school to the new story embodied in the requirements of the external accountability system. In this sense, leadership is a very traditional American construct—the individual leader providing a vision by which to lead the pack out of the wilderness into the new world. The importance of this view should not be understated. People in schools pay attention to what their designated leaders say about the crises and problems they face, and the ways leaders talk about the challenges schools face have an impact on the way people in schools think and act.

It is also true that designated leaders, especially high school principals, exercise limited leverage over teachers' hearts, minds, and practices. People in schools look continuously for daylight between what policy says and what their leaders espouse, because every shard of daylight produces a reason to question the policy and modulate their response to it. Accountability policies also create problems of an unprecedented sort for high schools, thus creating opportunities for teachers and department heads to push back against their leaders and the requirements of policy, arguing that the work simply can't be done. In schools with low internal accountability, teachers tended to stress the great difficulty, of impossibility, of their work, and to criticize leaders who tried to push them in the direction of greater focus and coherence.

For this reason Lemons, Luschei and Siskin (chapter four) favor a view of leadership that is more collective in its nature than individual. That is, leadership inheres not in the individual characteristics and traits of people in positions of authority, but in the way authority and responsibility are focused, defined, and distributed in organizations. (Spillane, et al. 2001; Elmore 2000) This view of leadership is particularly important in high schools because the scale and complexity of the organization requires a complex response. Principals, no matter how talented or charismatic, simply can't manage all the detailed work required to bring the pieces of the organization into a coherent response.

There is a relatively clear distinction in our case studies between leaders who are products of their environment and those who see themselves as active agents in changing that environment; between leaders who take the existing structure and processes of the organization as given, and adapt their leadership to them, and those who treat external pressure as an invitation to open up existing structures and to redistribute responsibility within them. In Binghampton, our Kentucky target school, for example, the principal seems to assume, as Rhoten, et al. suggest is a premise of accountability policy generally, that the existing structure and culture of the school are sound, and that the problem is how to make it work more effectively and efficiently. Binghampton, however, is characterized by weak internal accountability, abetted by a complex structure. Working within that environment, as Lemons, Leuschi, and Siskin suggest, produces a result in which only one department is actually mobilized to do the work and the school's overall response is "sporadic, fragmented and minimally distributed" throughout the organization.

By contrast, the principal of Byrd, our better-positioned school in Kentucky, takes the existing structure and culture of the school as a point of departure and constructs his task as using the pressure of external accountability to leverage improvements in the school's structure and culture. He actively manages the mandate of the accountability system, by reframing, simplifying, and focusing the state accountability requirements. He creates a new language and culture for the school around "classic standards" and "vital content" to claim ownership over the external requirements of the accountability structure. He focuses attention at the departmental level on student performance data. And he actively manages the curriculum, assignment of teachers and students, and resources from within and outside the school. The result was that departments assumed major responsibility for changes in curriculum and teaching, and leadership in the organization became stretched, or distributed, across teachers, department chairs, as well as the principal.

This kind of leadership requires people to push against the assumption that their job is to make the existing structure and culture work more effectively and efficiently. It also requires strong collective norms for determining what the most important work is to do and how it is going to get done. In other words, it requires relatively high levels of internal accountability, which is either mobilized and focused if it already exists or created if it doesn't.

These two examples set the extremes of leadership approaches in our case studies: passive, reactive, adaptive versus active, assertive, and creative. The entailments of the latter view of leadership are that the principal plays an active role in positioning the school in relation the external requirements, in creating a culture that connects the school to the new requirements, and in designing the work so as to distribute leadership and develop internal accountability structures that reinforce common purposes.

It is worth noting that none of the principals in our sample received any special managerial attention or professional development designed to help them develop a new conception of how to lead in a new accountability environment. Nor did the systems in which they worked make any explicit acknowledgement that principals were being asked to do work that might not, for perfectly understandable reasons, know how to do. Those principals who developed this knowledge and skill did so essentially on their own in a survival of the fittest mode. Those principals who did not develop this new knowledge and skill, likewise, did not seem to be aware that there was any other way to think about their work, even when they were fully aware that what they were doing was not successful. Nor is there much evidence that systems within which these principals work have a system-wide view of the requirements of strong leadership and a strategy for getting it. All the systems seemed to approach the problem of school leadership by moving people around rather than by trying to influence the knowledge and skill set that principals brought to their work. Accountability policies reinforce this view of expendable leadership by assuming that the knowledge and skill required to respond to the policies already exists somewhere in the system and that it simply needs to be mobilized and focused. The evidence from our case studies suggests that it doesn't exist in anything like the quantity, quality, and frequency required to make schools successful.

Knowledge, Skill, and Resources   So it matters a great deal what people know about how to do the work, in addition to what sort of environment they work in and how they are led. As noted in the beginning, accountability systems work by mobilizing the energy, motivation, commitment, knowledge and skill of the people who work in schools and the systems that are supposed to support them. In a sense, everything else that goes on in schools—the way the school day is structured, who teaches what, how people collect and understand data about student performance, who is responsible for what, and so on—is instrumental to improving the capacity of teachers and students to engage more effectively and powerfully in academic work. The evidence from our case studies is that schools are unlikely to get anything more than marginal results from their work by doing a better version of what they're already doing. In fact, schools that try this approach end up typically in compliance mode, which means that they reduce the policy to its minimum requirements and try to meet those requirements with as little additional burden as possible. This approach, as we've seen, leads to low performance.

Given the centrality of knowledge and skill to the success of schools' responses to accountability systems, one would expect to see major attention to and investments in human capacity in schools and school systems confronting new accountability requirements. In fact, there isn't much evidence from our case studies of major external investments in new knowledge and skill in schools. As Rhoten et al. suggest, all state accountability policies make some gesture of support and assistance to schools, usually focused on the lowest performing schools. At the ground level, from the perspective of the target schools in our sample, however, this support looks weak, sporadic, and largely ineffectual. The interventions, for the most part, don't systematically move them toward higher levels of internal accountability, or bring resources that augment curriculum and instruction in ways that have an obvious connection to the quality of academic work in schools.

Better-positioned schools, and schools with relatively high internal accountability, on the other hand, seem to recognize that increased coherence around instructional practice often requires new curriculum content and new knowledge and skill for teachers and administrators. All of the better-positioned schools in our sample engaged in some kind of deliberate process designed to improve the knowledge and skill of people in the organization: examining data on student performance and learning how to translate it into curriculum and instructional practice, changing course structure and content, changing the way individual students' work is monitored and structured. All of these changes require not just shifts in the structure of the work but changes in the knowledge and skill required to do the work.

This said, we did not see evidence in any of our schools of major infusions of professional development for teachers or principals orchestrated from the school system or the state level. In all instances, the external support was weak and sporadic. External influences tended to take the form of increased sanctions and monitoring, coupled with changes in leadership, for lower-performing schools, and benign neglect for higher-performing schools. Insofar as the schools in our sample captured resources that enhanced the knowledge and skill of their members, they did so largely on their own initiative. Again, the working theory of accountability policy as it was actually enacted in schools—regardless of the way it was written at the state level—seemed to be that the purpose of accountability policy was to mobilize and focus *existing* knowledge, skill, and resources, rather than to systematically augment and improve schools' capacity to respond.

How the Pieces Fit Together

The view of accountability that emerges from our research is that schools vary in their responses to external pressure depending on their level of internal accountability, the way they manage their internal structures, the ways in which they define and distribute leadership, and the ways in which they address the knowledge and skill requirements of the new demands of policy. Capacity inheres not in the presence or absence of these factors, but in the relationships among them. Accountability policies produce variable responses among schools based both on the initial capacities of schools and on whether schools increase or improve their capacities as they are responding to the requirements of new policies.

An important finding of our work, as noted by Debray, et al. is that school capacity seems to dominate policy in determining effects on student performance. While, as Carnoy, Loeb, and Smith indicate, the aggregate effect of accountability policies on individual students seems to be generally positive, in terms of student performance and retention in school, there is considerable variability among schools in their capacity to produce good outcomes.

This view of the relationship of capacity and accountability raises one troubling issue about existing accountability policies. If it is true, as our case studies seem to indicate, that state accountability policies are based on the working theory that external pressure for performance is designed to mobilize *existing* capacity, rather than to create new capacity, then it is possible that the long-term effect of accountability policies, other things being equal, could be to increase the gap in performance between high and low capacity schools. The relative absence in our case studies of evidence of deliberate, systematic efforts to influence capacity by states and localities makes this a troubling issue.

How one would intervene to increase and equalize capacity in schools is a complex issue. The answer depends on how the pieces of capacity fit together.

Our research suggests that internal accountability is a necessary condition that precedes any effective response to external accountability policies. Variation in internal accountability is likely to be the main variable explaining variability in schools' performance against external accountability measures. But internal accountability is not a static or stable characteristic of schools, it is a continuous variable, and it is the creation of active problem solving inside schools. Schools that have high internal accountability are likely to have it because they have worked hard as organizations to create it. This in turn means that these schools are more likely to have the capacity to manage the various structural problems posed by external accountability policies, and that they are more likely to treat structures instrumentally than to try to adapt their responses to fit into existing—often dysfunctional—structural arrangements. But working out these solutions requires a particular bias on the part of school leaders toward the creation of internal accountability and toward the use of structures. And working through these solutions requires a particular view of how leadership might be defined and distributed in the organization. In doing this work, people in schools are likely to run up against the limits of their own knowledge and skill, creating the need for access to new sources of information, curriculum, and instructional practices. To the degree that the school is successful in mobilizing and focusing the existing knowledge, skill, and commitments of it members, and augmenting it, one would expect to see systematic improvements in performance.

One thing that stands out in our case studies is that schools that try to respond to external pressure by doing what they are already doing at a higher level of efficiency and effectiveness typically don't produce substantial improvements in either practice or performance. The fact that the schools that seem to fit this pattern are disproportionately—but not entirely—target schools is troublesome. This finding suggests that the work that would be most productive in improving the responsiveness of schools to external accountability measures is work that focuses on increasing *school-wide* coherence and agreement on expectations for student performance and instructional practice, rather than focusing exclusively on focused, incremental work in tested subjects. This is daunting, difficult work in schools that are often cautious, intimidated, risk-averse because of their poor performance in the past. And it requires school leaders with a different understanding of their work than one typically finds in low-capacity, low-performing schools. Nor is it possible to think of this kind of work happening without substantial external support and resources at the local and state level designed to build the pool of people with the knowledge and skill to carry out this work in schools—not just principals but subject matter specialists, lead teachers, coaches, and so on.

It is also possible that what we observed in the target and low-capacity schools that were attempting to comply with external accountability systems without fundamentally changing their internal accountability systems was, in fact, the early stages of a longer-term improvement path. External accountability systems may force attention to issues of internal accountability and capacity in general by holding schools to external standards and scrutiny. In general, aggregate data on student performance of the kind in the Carnoy, Loeb, and Smith study seem to indicate that external pressure does produce significant effects on student academic performance. All of the target schools in our Texas case studies were able successfully to increase test scores. The issue that needs further scrutiny is the degree to which schools can manage the improvement process, from compliance-oriented decisions to major changes in their capacity, by themselves without major support.

The basic point for accountability policy, however, is that powerful responses to accountability policies require school-wide capacities that, at the moment, are highly variably distributed in the population of existing schools. To the degree that policies continue to operate on the assumption that they call forth existing capacities, rather than that they create and distribute new capacities, the effect of these policies is likely to be considerable variation in school performance.

References

Abelmann, C., R. F. Elmore, 1999. *When Accountability Knocks, Will Anyone Answer?* Philadelphia, PA: Consortium for Policy Research in Education.

Benveniste, L., M. Carnoy, and R. Rothstein. 2003. *All Else Equal: Are Public and Private Schools Different?* New York: Routledge.

Goertz, M., Duffy, Mark, and Carlson Le Floch, Kerstin. 2001. *Accountability Systems Across the Fifty States.* Philadelphia, PA: Consortium for Policy Research in Education. Policy Brief #33.

Elmore, R. F. 2000. *Building a new structure for school leadership.* Washington, D.C.: The Albert Shanker Institute.

Siskin, L. S. 1994. *Realms of knowledge: Academic departments in secondary schools.* London and New York: Falmer Press.

Spillane, J.P., Halverson, R & Diamond, J.B. 2001. "Investigating school leadership practice: A distributed perspective." *Educational Researcher,* 30 (3):23–28.

Index